ROADMAP
to Success

AMERICA'S TOP INTELLECTUAL
MINDS MAP OUT SUCCESSFUL
BUSINESS STRATEGIES

Tony

Thanks for being a "high-value relationship"
and your encouragement and support

Gratefully

Rudy

Copyright © 2012

Published in the United States by
Insight Publishing Company
707 West Main Street, Suite 5 • Sevierville, Tennessee • 37862

Disclaimer: This book is a compilation of ideas from numerous experts
who have each contributed a chapter. As such, the views expressed in
each chapter are of those who were interviewed and not necessarily of
the interviewer or Insight Publishing.

ISBN   978-1-60013-799-0

10   9   8   7   6   5   4   3   2   1

MESSAGE FROM THE PUBLISHER

The interviews in this book were conducted by David E. Wright, the President and founder of Insight Publishing and ISN Works

I'VE DONE A LOT OF DRIVING IN MY LIFE and one thing I have been smart enough to have is a dependable road map. If you don't have a good plan to get from where you are to where you want to go, you will get lost.

I've known many people who have started out in business and thought they had a good plan, but did not achieve the success they wanted. A major problem for many of these people was that they had not sought good advice from people who had achieved success. If you don't learn from the experience of others, you might achieve success but you will probably get there the hard way. You might get lost down many side roads before you find the right one.

Roadmap to Success, is a mini-seminar on how to plan for your success. The successful people in this book have the experience that will help you find what you need to create your Roadmap to Success. These perceptive businesspeople were fascinating as they unfolded their own personal road maps and told me about their various success journeys.

I invite you to set aside some quiet time and learn from these exceptional authors. I assure you that your time won't be wasted. It's not often that you can access such a large quantity of quality information that will either get you started or help you get further along on your road to success. This book is an investment in your future—your successful future!

—*David E. Wright*

TABLE OF CONTENTS

TABLE OF CONTENTS

Chapter One

COACHING THE ROAD LESS TRAVELED

TOM OLIVO

The affect that coaches and mentors have on making "fork-in-the-road decisions" and taking the road less traveled

DAVID WRIGHT (WRIGHT)

Today I'm talking with Tom Olivo, a founding partner in Healthcare Performance Solutions and President of Success Profiles Inc., a consulting firm that specializes in business performance, measurement, and marketplace research. Established in 1990, Success Profiles designs and provides organizational performance measurements, instruments, and database management services to clients, management consulting firms, and accounting firms. The focus of their service is creating business intelligence.

In his professional career, Tom has more than twenty-five years of experience in identifying, measuring, and comparing the commonalities of highly successful athletes, business leaders, and organizations. He has worked in a multitude of industries with thousands of senior executives and managers, emphasizing the importance of high performance standards consistent with best business practices. Success Profiles has measured the performance of more than a thousand organizations and developed a database of business practices that includes more than twenty-five thousand individual business units.

He is the co-author of *Impending Crisis: Too Many Jobs, Too Few People*, a business best-seller for 2003. He is considered by business leaders to be an expert in workforce optimization and is one of the most requested speakers on the topic of practical and applied performance measurement. Success Profiles has also compiled one of the largest performance management databases in the healthcare industry, which establishes baseline percentile rankings for leadership performance, job satisfaction, organizational loyalty, and professional engagement.

Tom, welcome to Roadmap to Success.

You have an extensive coaching background, first with athletes and then with executives. Will you give us some insight on the title you have chosen for this chapter, and what you mean by taking the road less traveled?

TOM OLIVO (OLIVO)

We all arrive where we are in life based upon decisions we make. Beginning in our teens, our decisions may include a field of academic interest, sports, music, art, or activities we choose to participate in. By age seventeen to eighteen, if we were fortunate enough to continue our education, it is the college we choose. If we enter the armed services, it's the branch we will serve (Army, Navy, Marines, Coast Guard). If we enter the workplace, it's the company we work for.

Most of these major decisions in our life are influenced directly or indirectly by someone we respect, trust, admire, and generally listen to; often this is a parent, relative, teacher, coach, or mentor.

Those interactions with the people who influenced our decisions usually began with just one compelling conversation. I refer to this as a C^3, which stands for a Compelling Coaching Conversation.

I believe that if everyone takes the time to examine the decision-making process for most of the major decisions in his or her life, one person will emerge as most influential in that process. That person was in the unique position to influence us toward the road less traveled or the fork in the road that was less certain and more challenging.

WRIGHT

Tom, when did one of your coaches first have a major influence on your life and what was the nature of the conversation?

OLIVO

It was July, 1973. I remember the exact moment when I decided I wanted to be exceptional at something. I was sixteen years old and had just completed my sophomore year of high school. I was attending a gymnastics training camp with one of my coaches, Bobby Lombardo. I had just completed an outstanding competitive season where I moved up the team depth chart from number five to number one and I was now considered one of the top gymnasts in New York State. It seems as though my physical maturation as a teenager occurred overnight and for the first time, I was beginning to believe in myself. I actually approached competitions expecting to win.

Bobby and I had just finished an evening workout and we were taking a moment to reflect on a beautiful summer sunset outside of the gym. He "hit me over the head" when he asked me the mother of all questions: *"Tom, do you know what separates the average athlete from the best?"*

After pausing for a moment, I answered with uncertainty, "Skill? Ability? Talent?"

"No," he said. "It's desire—the intense desire to kick ass, and unfortunately, you don't have it!"

I was stunned—speechless. I thought I worked hard (compared to others), but evidently one of the most respected people in my life didn't think so.

After a very long and uncomfortable moment of silence I said, "Do you think I can develop it?"

"I'm not sure," he replied. "It may be something that you're either born with or you're not."

I don't even remember the drive home. I didn't eat dinner and went right to bed. My mom came into my room and asked if there was anything wrong. Did I injure myself at practice? Was I sick?

I just gave the classic teenage response, "No, Mom, I'm just really tired."

She bought it and left me to pack it in for the night. Except for one problem—I was awake all night thinking about what Bobby had said.

Only now do I realize that while lying awake that night, I experienced the classic five stages of grief:

Denial: What does Bobby know anyway? That's just his opinion!

Anger: Why would he say that to me? I work as hard as anyone on the team!

Depression: If having the intense desire to "kick ass" was something I wasn't born with, maybe I'll never have it and fall short of achieving my goals. Also, would people not like me if I was that intense or acted like a jerk?

Bargaining: If I show up and work harder, maybe that will be enough? And finally,

Acceptance: Bobby was right!

I decided then that beginning tomorrow, I would approach everything I did with a level of intensity greater than ever before. If desire is indeed a major contributing factor to success, I would do whatever it took to demonstrate the desire to kick ass! I would develop drive.

Little did I know that the coaching conversation with Bobby Lombardo that summer evening would contribute more to my success in life than any other single factor.

The next day, I looked at life through a new lens. I became a student of the sport and did everything with purpose. With that, my confidence soared, my grades improved during my junior year, I improved as an athlete, and I became a better person, someone others admired. I decided that while it took courage to be driven, it was a good thing to strive for goals, to stand for something. And it was a good thing to be considered a role model, even if some people didn't like you.

July 2010, thirty-seven years later: On the surface, it would appear that the mother of all messages with this story simply involved the powerful amplifying effect that intensity and effort (drive) can have on talent and success. However, the most valuable lesson learned in this experience has little to do with developing "the desire to kick ass." For me, the lesson was the incredible power and life-altering influence of a "compelling coaching conversation."

Reflecting back on the conversation with Bobby Lombardo, I am reminded *daily* in my role as a parent and in my vocation as a business advisor how important and influential a single coaching conversation can be. The true benefits are realized only when the recipient is open to feedback and the coach delivers the right message the right way with genuine intent.

The right message, at the right time, from the right person when the recipient is coachable, has the potential to change the course of a person's life—forever.

WRIGHT

Tom, that's a powerful message. Did Bobby Lombardo realize the effect that conversation would have on you?

OLIVO

I'm sure he did, for the immediate effect of trying to motivate me to be a more intense competitor. But I don't believe that he had any idea of the influence the specific coaching conversation would have throughout the course of my life. In fact, I didn't realize the importance of the conversation until just a few years ago at my thirty-year high school reunion. I was having a conversation during dinner with my wife, Katie. We were reflecting on major events in our lives and how we ended up living in Bozeman, Montana.

We each took inventory with our major "life forks in the road" where we took the less beaten path and then thought through the decision-making process to identify who contributed the most to the process, how the decisions were made, and ultimately the end result.

For each of us, there was one person who most influenced the decision and there was one compelling conversation we could recall that seemed to tip the final decision one way or another.

In the fall of 2005, I looked up Bobby Lombardo, who is living and teaching just outside of Philadelphia; I called him to arrange a meeting over dinner. When we met, I proceeded to tell him the story of the compelling coaching conversation we'd had and the effect it had had on my life. Bobby was shocked. In tears he told me that he had no idea I had accomplished so much and that he was in any way a major contributing factor.

What began that summer evening as a simple observation on his part, followed by some coaching feedback, somehow morphed into what I now refer to as a C^3.

It was at that point when I realized that maybe somewhere along the line, I had similar "innocent" coaching conversations that I completely underestimated. I also then realized that for the right person at the right time, anyone seeking feedback about a career decision may have the same experience I had with Bobby.

WRIGHT

Many teenagers I know would have discounted Bobby's feedback and not been very coachable. What was it about him that contributed to you taking this feedback so seriously?

OLIVO

My sense is that if a person is not respected and trusted, he or she cannot effectively serve in a coaching capacity. If these attributes are not present, all feedback will be "discounted' in some way.

As teenagers, we are at a unique age when we are very impressionable. For better or worse, people can emerge in this window of time who can imprint values upon us for life. Accomplished people I've interviewed have confirmed that during this window of time, there was someone for them who most influenced their career path.

Bobby's credibility with me was rooted in the role-model behaviors he consistently demonstrated—the way he treated others, his work ethic, his optimism, and the genuine way he could reduce frustration with just a smile. He was reserved, not someone who tried to motivate people by amplifying his voice or getting overly animated. In all the years I have known Bobby, I've never seen him lose his temper. Most important was his natural ability to teach and willingness to lend a hand spotting other gymnasts on difficult skills. Through his caring actions, he became credible as a coach and therefore, it was next to impossible to discount his feedback. When Bobby spoke, people listened.

That summer evening when Bobby had the C^3 with me, he wasn't overly emotional. He looked me in the eye and was very serious. What he said was obviously something he had thought through and he was waiting for the right time to have the conversation.

WRIGHT

Many people in a management position have a real aversion to having difficult conversations (what you call C^3s). What advice do you have to help them be more effective as a coach?

OLIVO

I think it is important for them to reflect back in their career to a time when someone they respected had a similar conversation with them. Think about the challenging fork in the road they faced and the effect the C^3 had on them:

- What if the person you respected had never initiated the conversation?
- What if you had never made the compelling changes?

These reflections will help people realize they are far better off having the uncomfortable conversation than not having it. Also, avoiding the conversation and tolerating low-performing or under-achieving people only makes things worse.

It is important to frame the conversation correctly to better develop self-awareness and set the stage for self-regulation.

The coaching conversation is best set up with the "ABC" and "DEF" contrast in performance and frame of reference.

A *good coaching conversation* with an employee about some problem, D, E, and F, goes something like this:

"Bob, I've had a chance to observe you for several years in many, many leadership situations and interactions with your people. What's easy for me to say is that when it comes to 'A, B, and C,' you are exceptional. It is something you are both naturally talented at *and* you've managed to develop and improve these traits to a very high level over time.

"What is more difficult for me to say is that when it comes to 'D, E, and F,' your style and behavior actually takes away from your leadership effectiveness. This happens often and to a degree that when people see you do 'D, E, and F,' they forget about how talented you are with 'A, B and C' and all they remember is 'D, E, and F.'

"Bob, my role as your coach is to do everything I can to help you become a more consistent and effective leader in all types of situations. I will do everything I can to help you but you're going to have to take inventory with this feedback, develop better self-awareness, and work hard on the areas where you are deficient. This also means being coachable without becoming defensive.

"Bob, it's important for you to recognize that if you are successful in making the changes we outline and openly discuss, then you are going to have a lot of upside in your management career.

"It's also important for you to recognize that if you're not successful in making these changes, it can harm your chances of remaining in your current role and this deficiency could even hurt you in your career.

"Bob, I would like you to take some time to think about the feedback I've just given you and also do a little homework." Assign an article for Bob to read, speak to other people for additional honest feedback, take a behavioral assessment, and so on. The end of the initial conversation should end with:

"After you've had time for a little reflection, let's meet Thursday morning for breakfast to outline a road map and game plan for both of us. I also look forward to your input and feedback about how I can serve as your coach in this process."

Avoid being more concerned with what you say (the transmitter) than what is heard and experienced (by the receiver). The art and science of how the message is delivered is vital to how the feedback will ultimately be received. This includes the words you choose, your body language, your emotion or expression, the setting, and the timing.

Make sure that you think through what the desired outcome is ahead of time. Be very specific with your ABC and DEF examples.

Show genuine interest and that you care. The more difficult the conversation, the more you have to show through your delivery that you care.

My simple guideline for a C^3 is that you should disturb someone just enough to get them to take action but fall short of pissing them off. If you don't disturb them, there will be no perceived need to change. If you piss them off they will become defensive, not listen, and not follow through.

Recognize the five stages of grief that people will go through. Some people move through the stages quickly (as I did with Bobby Lombardo) and some will take much longer. The feedback will need to incubate and I recommend that there be another time to meet and discuss after a reasonable amount of incubation time has elapsed.

WRIGHT

Have there been other times in your life when you had someone give you a C^3 that had a significant influence on you or changed the direction of your career or your life?

OLIVO

Yes. There are eight additional C^3 conversations that each contributed to a major "fork in the road" decision resulting in taking the road less traveled to do something out of the ordinary:

The first was at age seventeen and it was about which college to attend. The conversation was with my high school coach Rod Mergardt.

The second was at age eighteen when I changed my major in college on the very first day during orientation! This C^3 was with my college coach, Pete Cahill.

The third was at age twenty-two when I decided to go to graduate school at the University of Vermont instead of entering the workforce. This C^3 was with one of my undergraduate professors, Robert Hay.

The fourth, at age twenty-five, was about a decision to move from Vermont to California. The conversation was with a business mentor Tony Thompson.

The fifth was at age thirty about a career change—to leave coaching amateur athletes and go into business. The conversation was with U.S. Diving Coach Hobie Billingsley and close friend Lloyd Kaplan.

The sixth was at age thirty-five with my wife, Katie, about deciding to leave California and move to Montana.

The seventh was at age forty about being more comfortable with major change. The conversation was with a business mentor Rick Culley.

The eighth was at age fifty when I decided to buy out my existing partners in our consulting business and focus on leadership alignment and talent management in healthcare. This C^3 was once again with my close friend and business mentor Lloyd Kaplan.

In fact, virtually every important "fork in the road" decision I have made throughout my life were executed following a C^3 conversation with someone important in my life.

I believe that everyone reading this can relate to the milestone "less beaten path" decisions that they have faced at similar times in their lives. It's important for them to realize that every day presents the opportunity to have a C^3 with someone—your children, a colleague, a person who reports to you in your role as a leader, or a friend.

WRIGHT

As a coach to high-performing athletes and to executives, what are the most challenging issues to you when you're trying to have a C^3?

OLIVO

It's choosing exactly how I will frame the conversation (as I have mentioned, the specific ABC and DEF examples). This is the art and science of the dialogue combined with the compelling element to disturb them just enough to take action and fall short of pissing them off.

Another is the specific timing—the best time when they will be receptive, not just when is convenient.

The most important challenge is their degree of ability to be coached. The "coachability" is the critical part because you can have all the other elements right and still not reach the person because he or she is uncoachable. Given that people's degree of coachability becomes the largest rate-limiting factor in their ultimate improvement, I've developed a model that illustrates the upside benefit to coaching based upon a person's degree of motivation and coachability.

How to interpret the coaching motivation model: The upside benefit of coaching is directly proportional to the degree of motivation to achieve a desired goal or outcome. In the diagram below, there are two extremes that define a person's level of intensity, desire, or commitment to achieve a goal.

On the left-hand side of the diagram, we illustrate the frame of reference where people feel they *have to improve* to achieve a goal. This is most often the case with people who sustain a major accident or injury, or recover from a debilitating illness such as a stroke, and may have limited use of their body movements or recreational functionality.

In this scenario, people may genuinely feel that there is really only one option to pursue. If they are ever going to be able to walk, hike, or possibly run again, they need the intense commitment to do whatever it's going to take to get back to full functionality. It doesn't matter what their health insurance will reimburse for the rehab costs, it doesn't matter how much work or business travel time they may lose. It also doesn't matter that they are going to sacrifice eating normal food. They *have to* do whatever it takes to get back to normal. Therefore, their degree of commitment is probably at level ten!

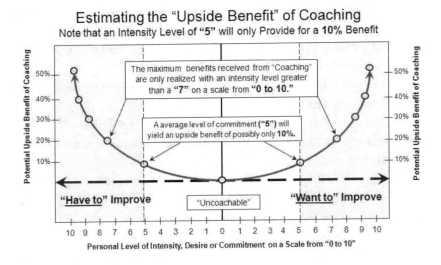

Estimating the "Upside Benefit" of Coaching
Note that an Intensity Level of "5" will only Provide for a **10%** Benefit

The maximum benefits received from "Coaching" are only realized with an intensity level greater than a "**7**" on a scale from "**0 to 10**."

A average level of commitment ("**5**") will yield an upside benefit of possibly only **10%**.

"Have to" Improve   "Uncoachable"   "Want to" Improve

Personal Level of Intensity, Desire or Commitment on a Scale from "0 to 10"

On the right-hand side of the diagram, we illustrate the frame of reference where someone *"wants to improve"* to achieve a goal. From a scale of zero to ten (zero representing virtually no interest in achievement and ten representing the ultimate level of commitment), we see that an average level of commitment will allow coaching assistance to add approximately *10 percent* upside benefit or value. As the level of commitment rises (from five to ten), we see that the benefit from coaching can possibly increase its value fivefold to a maximum upside of approximately *50 percent*. Therefore, can we conclude that virtually everyone who is interested in improving his or her performance benefits from coaching? *Yes*. Does the increase in benefit rise linearly? Probably not. It's my belief that a person's level of intensity, desire, or commitment can amplify the ultimate benefit that coaching has on overall performance.

To take inventory in your degree of coachability, take the following test and calculate your potential upside benefit to coaching.

On a scale from one to ten, with one being "not at all" and ten being "extremely," to what extent:

1. Do you respect the person providing the coaching and feedback?
2. Have you completely bought into the coach's assessment of your performance and agree with his or her feedback?
3. Do you agree with your coach's assessment of the upside benefits of improving and the downside consequences of not improving?

4. Are you willing to prioritize the improvement initiatives at the top of your to-do list rather than making the items an add-on thing to do?

5. Are you willing to devote significant time every day to the improvement initiatives?

6. Are you willing to create a written plan with a specific timeline and hard target milestones?

7. Are you willing to consistently measure your performance?

8. Are you willing to meet often with your coach for ongoing coaching and progress reports?

9. Are you willing to go public and announce to others that you are working on your specific challenges?

10. Are you willing to seek additional feedback and/or coaching from others regarding your improvement initiatives?

Add up your individual score for each item and then divide the total number by ten. This number is your personal desire level to improve score. You can now plot your score on the chart to estimate your potential upside benefit to coaching. For example, if your total score was fifty, then your desire level would be a five. This puts you in the mid-range of coachability where the upside benefit to coaching is approximately 10 percent. Note that meaningful upside benefit to coaching is only achieved with a motivation or desire score above a seven.

WRIGHT

Are there any other common examples of a C^3 that our readers may be able to relate to?

OLIVO

One of our core service offerings is to quantify the effect that leadership has on overall performance. Our leadership alignment and talent management suite of measurement tools help identify and differentiate the high-performing leaders who are "underleveraged" (those who could handle increased responsibility) from the lower-performing leaders who are "Overleveraged" (those who may be in over their head, struggling, or failing).

This process will inevitably reveal leaders who are ineffective because of their disruptive behaviors. Those leaders are usually very talented (technically) but they seem to lack the critical skill of emotional intelligence (people skills) to be successful. We have found this situation to exist in virtually every organization where we have been retained.

Occasionally (less than 20 percent of the time), these disruptive leaders develop better self-awareness, are then able to self-regulate their behaviors, improve team work with their peers, and improve as leaders. More often (about 80 percent of the time), they cannot and their disruptive behavior is tolerated by the leaders above them until the organization's senior executives' credibility as leaders is questioned and disrespected.

One of the most common C^3 sessions I have goes like this:

"Bob, your track record as CEO of this hospital is outstanding. My dashboard indicators reflect that you are respected by your board, the physicians, the managers, and by the organization's employees as a whole. And, for us, you have been coachable and a pleasure to work with.

"However, I must tell you that your executive vice president, Dan, has been consistently negative and unprofessional. This disruptive and inappropriate behavior has taken a toll of the credibility of the leadership team. We've tried to work with him and at best, he is uncoachable. In group settings, he goes through the motions to do the minimum but at critical times, he reverts to his hardwired behaviors and is unwilling to demonstrate the values that this organization aspires to.

"Bob, until recently, Dan's behavior has been seen as a negative reflection on him, and his ability to recover with people at this point is questionable. But now, unfortunately, your tolerating his behavior is seen as a negative reflection on your leadership. When you tolerate his ineffective behavior, it's as if his behavior becomes acceptable to you personally. If this is not addressed, your legacy as a leader here is likely to be tainted. If you do not act on Dan immediately, your credibility as a leader is at risk."

In the past five years, I have had this specific C^3 conversation with at least ten CEOs. In every case, it was the only way to get the executive's attention to finally act on a problem that was being tolerated. It is the classic example of how a coach should see his or her role in providing feedback that can be game-changing. Quite simply, this example fits my motto as a coach: "Ideally, you need to disturb people enough to take action but fall short of pissing them off."

About the Author

Tom Olivo is the President of Success Profiles, Inc. and a founding partner in Healthcare Performance Solutions (HPS). He has more than twenty-five years of experience in identifying, measuring, and comparing the commonalities of highly successful athletes, business leaders, and organizations. Tom has worked in a variety of industries with thousands of senior executives and managers, emphasizing the importance of high performance standards consistent with the ethic of leadership and best business practices.

Tom's work with Olympic athletes, coaches, and successful business leaders led to the development of several unique diagnostic instruments that differentiate performance. The Success Profiles methodology, combined with a measurement framework and supporting research data, proves that consistent success in business today rarely occurs by accident. Identifying and measuring the characteristics that lead to success in leaders and businesses, then using them as benchmarks for improving performance, is the basis for the Success Profiles method.

Tom is the co-author of *Impending Crisis: Too Many Jobs, Too Few People* (a business best seller for 2003). He is considered by business leaders to be an expert in workforce optimization and is one of the most requested speakers on the topic of practical and applied performance measurement.

Tom lives in Bozeman, Montana, with his wife, Katie, and daughters, Sarah and Christine. His favorite hobbies include all forms of outdoor recreation, especially fly-fishing.

Tom Olivo

Success Profiles and Healthcare Performance Solutions (HPS)
200 Longhorn Rd.
Bozeman, MT 59715
406-582-8884
tolivo@successprofiles.com
www.successprofiles.com

DISCOVER YOUR INNER RESOURCE

DR. DEEPAK CHOPRA

DAVID WRIGHT (WRIGHT)

Today we are talking to Dr. Deepak Chopra, founder of the Chopra Center for Well Being in Carlsbad, California. More than a decade ago, Dr. Chopra became the foremost pioneer in integrated medicine. His insights have redefined our definition of health to embrace body, mind and spirit. His books, which include, *Quantum Healing, Perfect Health, Ageless Body Timeless Mind*, and *The Seven Spiritual Laws of Success,* have become international bestsellers and are established classics.

Dr. Chopra, welcome to *Roadmap to Success.*

DR. DEEPAK CHOPRA (CHOPRA)

Thank you. How are you?

WRIGHT

I am doing just fine. It's great weather here in Tennessee.

CHOPRA

Great.

WRIGHT

Dr. Chopra, you stated in your book, *Grow Younger, Live Longer: 10 Steps to Reverse Aging,* that it is possible to reset your biostats up to fifteen years younger than your chronological age. Is that really possible?

CHOPRA

Yes. There are several examples of this. The literature on aging really began to become interesting in the 1980s when people showed that it was possible to reverse the biological marks of aging. This included things like blood pressure, bone density, body temperature, regulation of the metabolic rate, and other things like cardiovascular conditioning, cholesterol levels, muscle mass and strength of muscles, and even things like hearing, vision, sex hormone levels, and immune function.

One of the things that came out of those studies was that psychological age had a great influence on biological age. So you have three kinds of aging: chronological age is when you were born, biological age is what your biomarker shows, and psychological age is what your biostat says.

WRIGHT

You call our prior conditioning a prison. What do you mean?

CHOPRA

We have certain expectations about the aging process. Women expect to become menopausal in their early forties. People think they should retire at the age of sixty-five and then go Florida and spend the rest of their life in so-called retirement. These expectations actually influence the very biology of aging. What we call normal aging is actually the hypnosis of our social conditioning. If you can bypass that social conditioning, then you're free to reset your own biological clock.

WRIGHT

Everyone told me that I was supposed to retire at sixty-five. I'm somewhat older than that and as a matter of fact, today is my birthday.

CHOPRA

Well happy birthday. You know, the fact is that you should be having fun all the time and always feel youthful. You should always feel that you are contributing to society. It's not the retirement, but it's the passion with which you're involved in the well being of your society, your community, or the world at large.

WRIGHT

Great things keep happening to me. I have two daughters; one was born when I was fifty. That has changed my life quite a bit. I feel a lot younger than I am.

CHOPRA

The more you associate with young people, the more you will respond to that biological expression.

WRIGHT

Dr. Chopra, you suggest viewing our bodies from the perspective of quantum physics. That seems somewhat technical. Will you tell us a little bit more about that?

CHOPRA

You see, on one level, your body is made up of flesh and bone. That's the material level but we know today that everything we consider matter is born of energy and information. By starting to think of our bodies as networks of energy information and even intelligence, we begin to shift our perspective. We don't think of our bodies so much as dense matter, but as vibrations of consciousness. Even though it sounds technical, everyone has had an experience with this so-called quantum body. After, for example, you do an intense workout, you feel a sense of energy in your body—a tingling sensation. You're actually experiencing what ancient wisdom traditions call the "vital force." The more you pay attention to this vital force inside your body, the more you will experience it as energy, information, and intelligence, and the more control you will have over its expressions.

WRIGHT

Does DNA have anything to do with that?

CHOPRA

DNA is the source of everything in our body. DNA is like the language that creates the molecules of our bodies. DNA is like a protein-making factory, but DNA doesn't give us the blueprint. When I build a house, I have to go to the factory to find the bricks, but having the bricks is not enough. I need to get an architect, who in his or her consciousness can create that blueprint. And that blueprint exists only in your spirit and consciousness—in your soul.

WRIGHT

I was interested in a statement from your book. You said that perceptions create reality. What perceptions must we change in order to reverse our biological image?

CHOPRA

You have to change three perceptions. First you have to get rid of the perceptions of aging itself. Most people believe that aging means disease and infirmities. You have to change that. You have to regard aging as an opportunity for personal growth and spiritual growth. You also have to regard it as an opportunity to express the wisdom of your experience and an opportunity to help others and lift them from ordinary and mundane experience to the kind of experiences you are capable of because you have much more experience than they do.

The second thing you have to change your perception of is your physical body. You have to start to experience it as information and energy—as a network of information and intelligence.

The third thing you have to change your perception on is the experience of dying. If you are the kind of person who is constantly running out of time, you will continue to run out of time. On the other hand, if you have a lot of time, and if you do everything with gusto and love and passion, then you will lose track of time. When you lose track of time, your body does not metabolize that experience.

WRIGHT

That is interesting. People who teach time management don't really teach the passion.

CHOPRA

No, no. Time management is such a restriction of time. Your biological clock starts to age much more rapidly. I think what you have to really do is live your life with passion so that time doesn't mean anything to you.

WRIGHT

That's a concept I've never heard.

CHOPRA

Well, there you are.

WRIGHT

You spend an entire chapter of your book on deep rest as an important part of the reversal of the aging process. What is "deep rest"?

CHOPRA

One of the most important mechanisms for renewal and survival is sleep. If you deprive an animal of sleep, then it ages very fast and dies prematurely. We live in a culture where most of our population has to resort to sleeping pills and tranquilizers in order to sleep. That doesn't bring natural rejuvenation and renewal. You know that you have had a good night's sleep when you wake up in the morning, feeling renewed, invigorated, and refreshed—like a baby does. So that's one kind of deep rest. That comes from deep sleep and from natural sleep. In the book I talk about how you go about making sure you get that.

The second deep rest comes from the experience of meditation, which is the ability to quiet your mind so you still your internal dialogue. When your internal dialogue is still, then you enter into a stage of deep rest. When your mind is agitated, your body is unable to rest.

WRIGHT

I have always heard of people who had bad eyesight and really didn't realize it until they went to the doctor and were fitted for lenses. I had that same experience some years ago. For several years I had not really enjoyed the deep sleep you're talking about. The doctor diagnosed me with sleep apnea. Now I sleep like a baby, and it makes a tremendous difference.

CHOPRA

Of course it does. You now have energy and the ability to concentrate and do things.

WRIGHT

Dr. Chopra, how much do eating habits have to do with aging? Can we change and reverse our biological age by what we eat?

CHOPRA

Yes, you can. One of the most important things to remember is that certain types of foods actually contain anti-aging compounds. There are many chemicals that are contained in certain foods that have an anti-aging effect. Most of these chemicals are derived from light. There's no way to bottle them—there are no pills you can take that will give you these chemicals. But they're contained in plants that are rich in color and derived from photosynthesis. Anything that is yellow, green, and red or has a lot of color, such as fruits and vegetables, contain a lot of these very powerful anti-aging chemicals.

In addition, you have to be careful not to put food in your body that is dead or has no life energy. So anything that comes in a can or has a label, qualifies for that. You have to expose your body to six tastes: sweet, sour, salt, bitter, pungent, and astringent because those are the codes of intelligence that allow us to access the deep intelligence of nature. Nature and what she gives to us in bounty is actually experienced through the sense of taste. In fact, the light chemicals—the anti-aging substances in food—create the six tastes.

WRIGHT

Some time ago, I was talking to one of the ladies in your office and she sent me an invitation to a symposium that you had in California. I was really interested. The title was *Exploring the Reality of Soul.*

CHOPRA

Well, I conducted the symposium, but we had some of the world's scientists, physicists, and biologists who were doing research in what is called, non-local intelligence—the intelligence of soul or spirit. You could say it is the intelligence that orchestrates the activity of the universe—

God, for example. Science and spirituality are now meeting together because by understanding how nature works and how the laws of nature work, we're beginning to get a glimpse of a deeper intelligence that people in spiritual traditions call divine, or God. I think this is a wonderful time to explore spirituality through science.

WRIGHT

She also sent me biographical information of the seven scientists who were with you. I have never read a list of seven more noted people in their industry.

CHOPRA

They are. The director of the Max Planck Institute, in Berlin, Germany, where quantum physics was discovered was there. Dr. Grossam was a professor of physics at the University of Oregon, and he talked about the quantum creativity of death and the survival of conscious after death. It was an extraordinary group of people.

WRIGHT

Dr. Chopra, with our *Stepping Stones to Success* book we're trying to encourage people to be better, live better, and be more fulfilled by listening to the examples of our guest authors. Is there anything or anyone in your life who has made a difference for you and has helped you to become a better person?

CHOPRA

The most important person in my life was my father. Every day he asked himself, "What can I do in thought, word, and deed to nurture every relationship I encounter just for today?" That has lived with me for my entire life.

WRIGHT

What do you think makes up a great mentor? Are there characteristics mentors seem to have in common?

CHOPRA

I think the most important attribute of a great mentor is that he or she teaches by example and not necessarily through words.

WRIGHT

When you consider the choices you've made down through the years, has faith played an important role?

CHOPRA

I think more than faith, curiosity, wonder, a sense of reference, and humility has. Now, if you want to call that faith, then, yes it has.

WRIGHT

In a divine being?

CHOPRA

In a greater intelligence—intelligence that is supreme, infinite, unbounded, and too mysterious for the finite mind to comprehend.

WRIGHT

If you could have a platform and tell our audience something you feel would help them and encourage them, what would you say?

CHOPRA

I would say that there are many techniques that come to us from ancient wisdom and tradition that allow us to tap into our inner resources and allow us to become beings who have intuition, creativity, vision, and a connection to that which is sacred. Finding that within ourselves, we have the means to enhance our well-being. Whether it's physical, emotional, or environmental, we have the means to resolve conflicts and get rid of war. We have the means to be really healthy. We have the means for being economically uplifted. That knowledge is the most important knowledge that exists.

WRIGHT

I have seen you on several primetime television shows down through the years where you have had the time to explain your theories and beliefs. How does someone like me experience this? Do we get it out of books?

CHOPRA

Books are tools that offer you a road map. Sit down every day, close your eyes, put your attention in your heart, and ask yourself two questions: who am I and what do I want? Then maintain a short period of stillness in body and mind as in prayer or meditation, and the door will open.

WRIGHT

So, you think that the intelligence comes from within. Do all of us have that capacity?

CHOPRA

Every child born has that capacity.

WRIGHT

That's fascinating. So, it doesn't take trickery or anything like that?

CHOPRA

No, it says in the Bible in the book of Psalms, "Be still and know that I am God"—Psalm 46:10.

WRIGHT

That's great advice.

I really do appreciate your being with us today. You are fascinating. I wish I could talk with you for the rest of the afternoon. I'm certain I am one of millions who would like to do that!

CHOPRA

Thank you, sir. It was a pleasure to talk with you!

WRIGHT

Today we have been talking with Dr. Deepak Chopra, founder of The Chopra Center. He has become the foremost pioneer in integrated medicine. We have found today that he really knows what he's talking about. After reading his book, *Grow Younger, Live Longer: 10 Steps to Reverse Aging*, I can tell you that I highly recommend it. I certainly hope you'll go out to your favorite book store and buy a copy.

Dr. Chopra, thank you so much for being with us today on *Roadmap to Success*.

CHOPRA

Thank you for having me, David.

About the Author

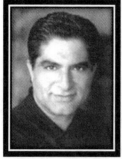

Deepak Chopra has written more than fifty books, which have been translated into many languages. He is also featured on many audio and videotape series, including five critically acclaimed programs on public television. He has also written novels and edited collections of spiritual poetry from India and Persia. In 1999, *Time* magazine selected Dr. Chopra as one of the Top 100 Icons and Heroes of the Century, describing him and "the poet-prophet of alternative medicine."

Dr. Deepak Chopra

The Chopra Center
2013 Costa del Mar Rd.
Carlsbad, CA 92009
info@chopra.com
www.chopra.com

Chapter Three

THE ART OF SUCCESS

MAYA CHRISTOBEL

DAVID WRIGHT (WRIGHT)

Today I'm talking with Maya Christobel. Maya has been in the field of psychotherapy and healing for the past thirty years. She is a graduate of Boston University and earned her master's degree and did her doctoral work in Developmental Psychology at Harvard University. She also did post-doctoral work in marriage and family systems in Cambridge, Massachusetts. Maya has worked in the corporate world and in private practice in Cambridge, Denver, New York City, Tulsa, and Maine where she raised her two daughters. Maya has developed a deeply spiritual perspective with regard to healing from trauma as individuals and as a collective. She says, "We can read all the self help books in the world, but true healing comes from opening the heart to life and love." The moment we ask the question "who am I and why am I here?" all possibilities open to us."

She is one of a handful of practitioners in the United States to use a biofeedback-based technology called Voice Stress Assessment as a way to rewire how we're hardwired in our neurology for repetitive dysfunctional patterns. "We've addressed the psychological and emotional effects of trauma over several decades," Maya says, "we can be triggered into old feelings and behaviors, repeating dysfunctional patterns over and over. We are now recognizing that each of us has a library of trauma, negative beliefs systems, pain, and fear catalogued in our neurology that needs to be released in order for us to become whole and healthy."

Maya teaches workshops and classes on empowerment and on rewriting our stories. She is currently taking a year to live as a "Gypsy", has sold most of what she owns and is learning to navigate her life through intuition and inspiration. She is a co-author of *Freeing Godiva: A Woman's Journey Toward Self-Empowerment.*

Maya welcome to *ROADMAP to Success.*

MAYA CHRISTOBEL (CHRISTOBEL)

Thank you very much, David.

WRIGHT

Most people find that it's important to have steps to follow toward a successful venture in business or even in relationships, and have a plan in place. Do you believe that this is important as a person takes responsibility to creating success in their life?

CHRISTOBEL

It is important for each of us to understand that we create everything in our lives, especially success. We are a "how-to culture." Most of the time we move toward solving a problem or attaining a dream, creating more money or love in our life by coming up with a plan, by coming up with the "to-do list" for how to achieve success. The mind loves lists. The mind loves goals. Lists are important and create an illusion of control that makes us feel comfortable. Yet, many times we fall short of that "to-do list" and reaching the dream slips away. We shake our heads in bewilderment, feeling we did all the "right" things, listened to all those amazing motivational speakers, and yet, somehow we failed to achieve our goal even with our five year goals in place and our ten point plan. Why do so many people find that they feel such a huge let down when this occurs?

When we have this let down or feeling of failure it is almost certain that we have tried to manifest in the outside world something that is not congruent with what we believe or how we feel on the inside. As within, so without. Our vision of ourselves as "successful" with the bank account, the thriving business, the fast car or great guy does not match our inner picture of ourselves. This lack of inner and outer alignment is the source for not achieving our goals.

Many of us simply fail to do what I think of as the "prep work" of really knowing who we are and being aligned with what we believe about ourselves, about our worth, or even considering if we truly feel we deserve what we want in life. It is essential to understand that what we are reaching to manifest in our lives—love, money, health, or happiness— necessarily depends on our knowing our own hearts and our own feelings about our authentic self. And first and foremost we have to know the difference between our authentic self and our persona, or adaptive self.

Let's say a child is born and is in love with painting and creating art. The child has innate talent and joy at being an artist. But they were born into a family that believes that art is not valuable and that being a doctor or a lawyer or making money is what is of value. The child most likely will abandon art as he or she grows and find themselves pleasing the parents and going to schools and studying law to conform, to please and to be acceptable.

Yet, as this child grows up, they long for more artistic expression and find that they are not as inspired by their career as they thought they would be. This is the adapted self. The true self, or essential nature of the child got buried under the rubble of cultural norms, family values and pressure. So understanding that what the true self wants requires knowing the difference between what we are inspired by, what we love, what we are passionate about and not what we believe we should do, or what is the right or acceptable path to success.

It is important to have a plan and all the steps to execute that plan, but the success of those plans entirely depends on those goals being congruent with our inner experience of ourselves. So, the number one tool for success is to "Know Thyself!" Taking the time to do the work of aligning our heart with our mind, our feelings with our thinking, and knowing deeply what inspires and moves us in life is equal to success in life.

WRIGHT

So many of us focus on managing and controlling our outer circumstances in order to be successful in life, yet you seem to feel that success is more dependent on what is happening on the inside of us rather than the outside. Will you speak a little more to our readers more about that?

CHRISTOBEL

I remember when the book The Secret came out, it took the world by storm. It took quantum physics, the power of positive thinking, visualization and affirmations and gave us an idea of how people who were worried about putting food on the table and raising their kids or trying to hold onto a job in our economy, can manifest their dreams. It took a lofty scientific and metaphysical system and made it accessible to everyone. The new idea, based on ancient wisdom, is that we each possess the power to create change and abundance in our life through our thoughts and where we focus our thoughts and how we generate an intention in our lives creates our reality.

This was a leap in awareness. But, as we began applying the ideas in daily life, we skipped an important step, in my opinion. Many failed to realize that our ideas for what we want in life need fuel behind the intention to propel it forward. That fuel is our feelings and emotions. Success depends on an idea that is aligned to the vibrational frequency of the "feeling of success" and an open and expressive heart. Without this fuel, success is either out of reach or short lived.

For instance, if you want to became famous or rich, which seems to be on everybody's to-do list in some form or another, if you don't love who you are, if you don't see the magnificence of your own being, if you don't have a sense of beauty in yourself, you are going to struggle to attain that recognition outside yourself because you don't feel that recognition on the inside. This alignment that has been spoken of for centuries is the true secret and the spiritual practice behind the art of success.

I remember talking to scores of people who started creating vision boards and they weren't visioning qualities of life or inner experience, they were envisioning outer experiences of accumulation—the dream house, the perfect partner. Others were envisioning making more money at their job or having a new job altogether, losing weight, or buying new clothes. They were envisioning something that had to do with physical reality being bigger and better, easier, or more comfortable. Most often we do this kind of external visioning because we don't sense that we have that abundant resourcefulness on the inside. We don't believe we are inherently great or big, that we are perfect, abundant, deserving and filled with worth and value. Our very being wants to express abundant joy, abundant happiness, or abundant love.

> We tend to project our inner lack of worth and self-love
> out into the world of accumulation and relationships.

Our culture has trained us to measure success by how much we have, how pretty we are, how thin, smart, educated and popular we are, what car we drive, what phone we have, who we know, where we went to school, and what neighborhood we live in. I am challenged to find persons who have all of the above and are happy, passionate, alive and inspired in their lives.

WRIGHT

So, Maya, how do you define success?

CHRISTOBEL

I sound really anti-American when ask this question. And in many ways I admit that how I see success is not aligned with the "American dream." Webster says this about success:

suc·cess/sək'ses/Noun
1. The accomplishment of an aim or purpose.
2. The attainment of popularity or profit.

David Rockefeller represents the prevailing opinion on success when he said that success requires training, discipline, and hard work. That may be true but unless our hard work for success in our lives is united with our soul's purpose for being on this planet, we have already missed the mark.

> If we are to truly succeed in life we must
> know our own soul and its unique expression.

If our wants, needs, dreams, and goals are informed by our soul's purpose, then we have access to joy and inspiration, which then drives whatever those choices are. It is inspiration that fans the flame and passion of our hearts, which is the force behind any true success in life. What kind of life we choose, where we live, the person we marry or don't marry, what kind of job we do or don't take, can be profoundly informed by asking one question: What truly inspires me and brings me the feeling of passion in life? The moment we stop and ask this question, is the moment when all things are possible.

If we can answer that for ourselves, then how we design that vision board will come from the wealth of inspired joy and being aligned with our soul. To ask this question, we must understand what inspiration is for each of us. Inspiration is linked to our own unique creativity, imagination, vision, and originality. To know what inspires us, we need to explore all of these qualities in our lives. And when there is that moment of feeling inspired—a moment of a distinct physical expression of awe and wonder at a sunset or a baby's smile that moves us—the end result is a deeper experience of our own heart.

Success is born in the heart.

Benjamin Disraeli said, "We are all born for love. It is the principle of existence and its only end." Love and the heart are synonymous. What would happen if when we ask ourselves about what a successful life would look like we were to see our life of success as only about love? If the things we reach for do not have love as a motive or an end then we might want to reconsider how we think.

If greed, fear of failure or scarcity is our motive, if showing up the neighbor, or puffing up our ego is the centerpiece to our drive for success, we can be assured that success will be short lived and empty in the end. If love of ourselves, our family, our world, if self-care and care for others or service to our community drives our desires, then we will find that we succeed beyond our expectations. There is another law that is more true than we know: "Do what you love and the money will follow". And the true result will be a joyful spirit and healthy body.

How many people of wealth or stature—those with all the things of life or the high powered job, big house, fame—do you know? They look happy but do they have healthy bodies, loving marriages, joyful children, creative lives? How many are overweight, sleep-deprived, alcoholic or addicted to prescription drugs, alone, divorced, ill, or dead prematurely from an unexpected heart attack at a young age? It is a harsh question to ask, but there is truth written on the canvas of a person's face and body that tells us all about what kind of success brings us joy and health and what kind brings us far from ourselves and others.

The mind seems to want something quite different than the heart. The mind is usually a wonderful mechanism for us to respond to the world that we live in, for problem-solving, for survival, but it is also the author of fear. Fear is not an emotion, but a reaction to a perception, belief, or a stimulus. We cannot make clear and strong decisions for success or direction in our life out of fear. So, many times we make decisions out of fear, not inspiration. And unless fear is a real saber-toothed tiger running right for us, these perceived fear-based thought forms load us up with adrenaline and then we make our decisions and strategies out of "reactivity," not "response" from the depth of our being.

What most people often fear is an illusion we have created out of our own projections. How many of us have had a dream or desire that we fail to even consider pursuing because we have the belief that we cannot do it or would never be able to obtain what we want? So, we never even try, let alone create a positive vision of the outcome we want or believe deeply that we deserve our vision.

We put huge amounts of energy into worrying or fretting that we don't have what it takes to manifest our dream rather than using that same amount of energy for the purpose of dreaming up our reality. That step from fear to dreaming our reality is bridged by an act of faith in ourselves and the strong belief that we do, in fact, deserve to have everything that brings joy to our lives. It also is an act of faith that there is a larger design in this life.

The Universe is a vast place filled with everything we could ever desire and limitless and abundant resources. There is more than enough to go around. Yet, our culture believes these resources are finite, has an end point and that there is never enough to go around. Enter - fighting for resources, greed, competition and the winner - loser mentality. Enter fear of not having enough.

There is an unseen force in the Universe that aligns to our life force and assists in creating and generating our options in life. Some call it coincidence, serendipity, kismet. Some call it grace, God, or spirit. It is the profound Universal Energy that is love and this love magnetizes to every loving act we create in our lives.

I had an amazing lesson with regards to manifestation. My dream was of going to Africa and learning about the white lions of Timbavati. My mind said the following avalanche of disclaimers: "You don't have the money, the time, the strength. You might get malaria, and will never make a seventeen-hour flight, your ankels will swell and you might get bitten by a snake—" Any one of these fears or thoughts could have snowballed into just shutting down the dream altogether and settling for a weekend at the lake with a Long Island Ice Tea.

I began meditating every day on seeing myself with the white lions in Africa, having more than enough money to get there and back and money to cover the time away from my psychology practice. I concentrated on feeling the sheer joy and exhilaration of being in Africa during each of my visualizations. I cut out photos of Africa, listened to African music and wrote down all of my desires for this trip.

Then I shared the dream with a group of women. The consensus was to create a blog and share my dream with the public and ask for support. A blog? That was a stretch, but I did it. On New Year's Day I launched www.whitelionswisdom.com, and on January 5 I had not only most of the finances I needed, but a first-class round-trip ticket to Johannesburg, South Africa. Five months later, I was sitting meditating with the white lions in Timbavati, walking among elephants, seeing the joyful faces of the South African people and never once cared about snakes or malaria or sunstroke. My life changed forever. My understanding about manifestation did, too.

We meet challenges or obstacles based upon what our mind thinks we need to react to, rather than responding from a heartfelt place. If we are responding from our hearts—from our inner most knowing—we calm our mind down and we can make really clear and strong decisions about how we create the life we really want. Our heart is an energy field far stronger than the mind.

"The heart's EMF (electro-magnetic field) is five thousand times more powerful than the electromagnetic field created by the brain and, in addition to its immense power, has subtle, non-local effects that travel within these forms of energy. Metaphorically, the heart is the sun, the pulsing, energetic centre of our biophysical "solar" system, and the brain is the Earth, one of the most important planets in our biophysical system." The vibrational frequency of the heart is energetically a magnet for what inspires us, physically manifesting it into our lives.

WRIGHT

You are really challenging the traditional business model—the Harvard MBA—and speaking about a much more feminine model of success. You are talking about success being heart-driven, not mind-driven. The masculine paradigm is struggling right now. I think we would all agree with that and it seems that you are looking at an archetypal principle that challenges our ideas of success.

CHRISTOBEL

Yes, we're challenging an historically masculine or patriarchal model of what success is or can be. We are all familiar with linking success to ideas like "relentless hard work is what reaches the goal," "no pain no gain," "grim determination," "intense ambition." I am not saying that having work ethics like these may not produce certain successful results in the workplace or in business and even, in some ways, relationship. But, I am challenging the concept of success as we link it to accumulation and "the bigger the better" model of our culture, especially all the models that result in power over others. This model comes with a price. These standards for reaching a goal often is what creates workaholics with singular focus but a limited capacity for intimacy, a drive that creates the "wake up on caffeine in the morning and go to sleep with a glass of wine to bring you down at night syndrome." This thinking about success is part of skyrocketing eating disorders, obesity, alcohol and drug addiction, divorce, and suicide.

Our culture has manifested more stress-related illnesses than any continent on the planet. Reaching a business or financial goal in this way is costly. Being driven by success for success's sake, being driven by fear of failure or the desire to have more, needs to be questioned as a stable model that is healthy for the person, for families, for society, and for the planet. This model of success can cost you your health and it can cost you your relationships. But most of all, it costs you your more authentic relationship with yourself—the most important relationship you can create in your lifetime.

Many of us are either in work that our parents told us they thought we should do, like being a doctor, or we fell into a direction in school because we had no other ideas, so we chose it by default. Or we've inherited a company from a family and now, after twenty years of running that company or that farm we are keeping a family legacy going and have no clue who we uniquely are. Doing the right thing does not need to exclude doing it to be happy. Maybe we have never asked ourselves whether we are doing work in the world that makes us truly happy.

How many of us are going to sleep at night and before closing our eyes ask, "What is my heart's desire for being alive on the planet? What brings me true happiness?" I think that as we get older we don't ask this question because we are too afraid the answer might not be truly aligned with what we have created already and it will require some sort of change or altering one's compass for living or navigating new waters in life. But by not asking the question early on in life, we eliminate the one factor that I believe is what leads us to success—happiness and joy. Joy is the result of being inspired, of sharing our hearts, living life for love.

One of the greatest tools for achieving success in our lives and determining what direction to go is our imagination. It is our creative spirit that, when let loose, can achieve anything.

WRIGHT

You speak a lot about a heart, understanding our heart's desire, and living from a place of inspiration and passion as an essential key to success in life. Would you elaborate on how we can each get in touch with that often elusive inner knowing?

CHRISTOBEL

Lau Tzu said that if we are truly whole in ourselves, all things will come to us. Wholeness is a feminine paradigm. Being whole, seeing the whole, working for the whole, and contributing to the whole are powerful motivational forces. There is an entire global paradigm shift going on. Our dominant masculine model informs us of almost everything—business or financial, health, or even relationships. We have been living in this patriarchal hierarchy and in the gender wars between masculine and feminine for centuries. Men are given higher salaries than women for doing the same job, men are the adventurers and women stay home with children. More profoundly, this hierarchy has produced more addiction, more child abuse, more sexual slavery and trafficking, more animal slaughter and degradation of our planet and her resources than any single virus or bacteria.

The patriarchal model is based on greed. We haven't made as much headway as you'd think in a lot of those areas and what's happening is the masculine model with our massive governmental, political, environmental, economic challenges are teetering and systems are not working as they once did. That is because the infrastructure or the heart behind these systems is not in place. This shifting and changing has made some room for the feminine model to come to the forefront. It is the feminine heart-based model that will, in fact, turn around the downward spiral the entire planet is in.

The feminine is a heart-based model. It is a model of inclusion, equality, interdependence, creativity, and love for all human beings and for the planet. It is a win - win perspective. It is not a model of greed and power. This feminine heart-based model sees intuition and instinct as just as informative as a mindful approach.

The largest number of small businesses that have started since we've hit economic hard times have been started by women. Women are collaborating more and more with one another. Cottage industries have provided creative ways for women to grow their families. There is a huge number of fatherless families and single-mother families. The feminine model is based on intuitions that create inspiration, which leads to creativity and success. These intuitions and instincts are based on feelings and emotions, gut instinct, dreaming up our reality and cooperation.

> A heart-based life is central to the health of any vision
> and the outcome of any dream.

The feminine model is more right-brained and the heart is accessed by the right brain and our emotional body. And emotions have gotten a consistently bad rap with regards to success. Americans have been raised with a deep, old belief that "men don't cry and women don't get angry." If a women gets angry she's a bitch, if a man cries he's a pushover. The truth is that anger or sadness are a true kind of passion. It is the fire of life. We all have these beliefs lingering in the psyche that lead us to a pervasive misconception that emotions are not good and thoughts are, and thoughts are more masculine and feelings more feminine and all models based on these beliefs are preferable.

Emotions and feelings are the doorway to the heart. When you have empathy for someone in trouble, have the ability to extend compassion and forgiveness you are motivated by your hear. When you see someone else's point of view, even if it is not your own, because you care to understand the person you are with you are living from an open heart. The capacity to know love, love of self and love of others, and to fully express that love in your life is a heart driven life. And love can also have the face of anger or ruthless honesty when it's appropriate in the face of injustice to self or another. All those passionate, fiery responses about right action and social justice tend to come from being heart-based and living inside one's self. And accessing the heart is be a big leap for many.

We have all been wounded by love, by family, or by disappointment and fear. So opening the heart leads us through the graveyard of all those experiences so we can first learn from them and then feel whatever we have not allowed ourselves to feel. Then we can forgive and release the story so we are free to express our true selves more fully. This is a real definition of being a warrior.

To achieve the mood of a warrior is not a simple matter. It is a revolution. To regard the lion and the water rats and our fellow men as equals is a magnificent act of a warrior's spirit. It takes power to do that.

—Carlos Castaneda

Today I read my astrology that comes to my inbox every morning. I could not say any more clearly what living from the heart looks like than what I read at 8am. My astrology for the day said, "Time to trust. Trust that others try to help you. Trust your urges to burst forward into some activities that are unlike you, but that come from the needs of your spirit. Trust that a flow exists in the universe. Trust that the unconscious lives deep within, guiding you with wonderful and powerful emotions. If you made a movie biography of yourself, what would you film? Those scenes are the ones to direct in real life. As you direct them, they become real."

If we access our hearts, we have to be willing to access our feelings. We have to express those feelings to self or others in writing, singing, chanting, even meditating. We must speak the truth, allowing ourselves to be unpopular and saying a big yes to our heart's desire. We have to be willing to feel for things, feel for others, feel about something, and that is very a different than react to, manage, think about, plan, and execute a five-year plan. The successful execution of a plan depends on the courageous expression of feelings and the access we have to our hearts desires.

Harnessing the energy of the heart is paramount in how we proceed or do not proceed as a planet, as a specie.

Accessing the heart means that we have to stop and take time to listen to what we feel and to ask ourselves daily, "How do I feel in my body? How do I feel about my life? How do I feel about myself? How do I feel about my work?" And if we answer, "Well, I'm bored or scared about being underpaid and resentful of my boss at work," or "I feel unloved by my wife," or if we are sad or lonely, then we are responsible for listening and then acting to change our life.

Andrew Harvey, the father of Sacred Activism and renowned author asked me a question once that changed my life. He said, "If you want to know what your true purpose is in the world, what you are passionate about, and what work you should be doing, then ask yourself, "What breaks your heart?" This is a brave question that leads to brave alterations of one's life. A heartfelt response to this question requires a necessary action.

> Taking responsibility to act on what we feel and know
> is the supreme fear of most unsuccessful people.

And it seems that there is an equation that goes something like this: You have to let go of what is not working in your life to make the room for what is more inspired to come in. It is the action of letting go of what does not work, with the possibility of not knowing what will take its place, that strikes fear in the hearts of those who resist change and resist the action of letting go. Most of us are far more comfortable having our ducks in a row before we burn a bridge. Being willing to not have money, be a little hungry, a little scared, and be a little insecure is about being open to the more probable outcome:

> By letting go of what makes us heart sick,
> we open to great opportunities rushing in.

> By holding on to what does not work in our lives,
> we can be assured that there will be no room
> for the miraculous or the surprising abundance of spirit.

So the question of "how do we access the heart" is a spiritual question. We're not asking a biological question, we're not even asking an emotional question, we're really asking a spiritual question because the heart is the center of how soulfully we are connected to ourselves, to the divine. Our spirit is the part of us that creates that plan for success in the first place and we can't access that part of ourselves if our heart, which is the voice of our spirit, is shut down, armored up, or hidden away because it's been damaged or is afraid. When we close our hearts we are basically creating a spiritual dilemma. For any one of us to live a balanced and harmonious life, authentically expressing the essence of who we are in all we do, we need to live with an open heart and converse with our feelings every day.

The first step is developing a healthy relationship to our own self love.

WRIGHT

It seems as if self-esteem is essential for success in life, if not a critical, component, part. How do we increase our sense of self-esteem and self-love and not move to a place of over inflation or grandiosity?

CHRISTOBEL

We were born a full expression of love. All the raw components for being fully human were perfectly intact. Compassion, empathy, love, passion, enthusiasm, industry, curiosity, joy, and imagination were all there. If you watch a child in a sandbox, with a puppy, watching the clouds, or making cities out of soap bubbles in the tub, each of us would recognize the perfection of a child. These wondrous qualities get tampered with through families, schools, and the cultural norms, so that as we grow up we either forget how to hold onto that essence or we get shamed or hurt enough to flip the switch and bury those qualities, replacing our true selves with an adaptation that is acceptable in the world around us.

> Opening the heart is about returning to these innate qualities,
> the qualities of the child.

There are some very visible people in the media who rose to such stardom because they were performers who had not lost the child within them and shine a little brighter because of it. Examples are Marilyn Monroe, Andy Kauffman, Julia Roberts, or even Will Smith or Robin Williams. There is a light in them. That is the child in them that is alive and well, accessible and expressive. And they became superstars.

In many ways, if we are looking at how to be successful in our world, how to be superstars in life, it is to access the heart of who we are and unearth the child in us that brings joy and inspiration and love to everything and everyone.

One of the most important ways to recreate a deep relationship with the essential child in us is play. Learn how to play, learn to allow yourself to be silly, remember how to giggle and laugh. The expression of playfulness opens the heart and releases all those qualities of the child, returning us to the capacity for awe, wonder, and sheer joy. It is from this place that we identify out heart's desire. And it is our heart's desire that creates action that leads to success. The game station, Wii, by Nintendo is a way to create family connection and play that is a great way to release the child in all of us.

We need to resurrect the part of us that is about four years old because those three-, four-, five-year-olds that we all used to be are the keepers of all of the wealth that we were born into the world to express. Most of us have turned off and dialed down and done all kinds of things to keep those parts of us that are beautiful and inspired and loving, safely out of sight in order to protect ourselves from perceived harm or shame or to conform to a world of expectations. What brings us joy is really what the child knows, more than the adult. And to have a healthy self-esteem, self-love, self-gratitude we must know who we authentically are.

Fully knowing ourselves is a process of remembering—remembering the unique, free, soulful parts of who we were born to be. We are surrounded by a multitude of societal distractions that are designed to keep us from knowing who we are. These distractions are so plentiful, mesmerizing, and anesthetizing that we begin to define ourselves by how we dress, by our stuff, the books we read and the movies we watch. We become identified with what we own—we are the car we drive, we are only pretty with Botox, the plump new lips and breasts—and these are nothing about who we are. We have been trained by the media to believe wholeheartedly in consuming as many goods and services as is possible in order to feel fulfilled. And we are an addicted society where we can drink, drug, sex and shop our way to feeling differently or feeling nothing. So, self-esteem is really about finding out really, truly who we are without the clothes, the drugs or the six-figure job.

> Self discovery is the most courageous trip
> we can take while we're alive.

WRIGHT

Let's talk about the energy or the frequency of success and what that means to creating road maps in our life for successful living. Will you speak to this question of energy?

CHRISTOBEL

Everything on the planet vibrates—rocks, trees, tables, jewelry, people, and places. Some places or things have that "feel good" energy and others can make you feel blue and out of sorts and you don't really know why. If a place or thing is not in tune with how you vibrate as a person—your energetic frequency—you will simply feel out of synch. Concepts and emotions also have a feel-good or a feel-bad frequency. Greed, fear, domination, strategies of power over another, manipulation, deceit all carry a negative energy or low vibrational frequency.

We have all heard someone in our lives tell us an out and out lie that is totally convincing, yet in our gut we feel that something is off. That is our feeling how out of synch the energy of the lie is to the truth. I am sure you can list numerous times you have been with a negative person and gone away not feeling well—feeling like the person is a "downer." And you may have felt just as many times when someone's enthusiasm, joy, or sweetness feels contagious and you simply feel better or vibrate at a higher frequency because you have spent time with him or her.

Gratitude, joy, love, appreciation, strategies of understanding and inclusion, and empathy and kindness carry a positive energy or high vibrational frequency. Gandhi is a bigger-than-life example of someone with a high frequency who changed everything around him. Millions of people who followed Gandhi did so not only because he said and did things that inspired them, but because he embodied a spirit of hope and calm, centered love. People felt better for being in his presence and then the frequency of his energy spread like a flame.

The highest vibrational frequency on the planet is a red rose, and rocks have a very dense, very different archaic energy; they're very low frequency. People who are angry and yelling have a very low frequency. People who are kissing and hugging and telling their partner how much they appreciate them create a positive field of energy around them. This energy draws to it similar energy.

Therefore, if we are looking at the idea of creating success in our lives, the frequency we bring to that goal will affect the result. For example, if I focus on manifesting love and abundance in my life but my thoughts are focused on how farfetched my dream is or how little I know or how scared I am or that I will fail, then these low frequency energies will simply limit or become the very obstacle to our achieving success. But, if I have the very same goal for success and instead bring joy, creativity, and positive, affirming feelings to the process, then the outcome will reflect, in direct proportion, the higher frequency that we express. I do believe that life begets life and what we put out we do get back in kind and what goes around really does come around.

"Be careful what you water your dreams with. Water them with worry and fear and you will produce weeds that choke the life from your dream. Water them with optimism and solutions and you will cultivate success. Always be on the lookout for ways to turn a problem into an opportunity for success. Always be on the lookout for ways to nurture your dream."

—Lao Tzu

And something we overlook at times is that, yes, we are responsible for the energy we possess and how we ourselves affect the outcome of generating success in our lives. But just as important are the people we surround ourselves with, where we live, and the kind of city we inhabit. If we live in city full of break-ins, rape and murder, or a home where fighting is going on all the time or employ people who are judgmental, negative, critical, and caustic, then these energies will limit our ability to succeed.

> Our lives are, in fact, a mirror of our
> environment and our surroundings.

If I bring to the idea of success the creation of joy and inspiration in my life and to touch humanity in a positive way, then that is a highly expansive success frequency that initiates an abundant response from the Universe.

If we are being centered, caring, hopeful, and passionate as we approach our desires for success and if we lead with the heart and let the mind be the supporter of the heart, then we will open up opportunities for success, for expression, creativity, for community, for companionship, and for creating a life that is full of love and abundance and all forms of wealth. This is very different than hitting the tarmac running with a Starbucks in hand and a to-do-list long enough to choke a horse so we can meet the day with that relentless grim determination toward being successful. If we wake up to the truth that success in life is—to live fully the true, joyful expression of our spirit without hesitation or fear—then there is simply nothing that we cannot achieve.

WRIGHT

Well, what an interesting conversation, I have learned a lot here. You have given me a lot to think about. I'm sure you've given our readers a lot to think about as well. I appreciate all this time you've taken with me to answer these questions.

About the Author

Maya Christobel has been in the field of psychotherapy, shamanism, and healing for the past thirty years. Harvard-trained, she is one of a handful of practitioners in the United States to use biofeedback-based technology, called Voice Stress Assessment, as a way to rewire how we are hardwired in our neurology for repetitive dysfunctional patterns. She teaches workshops and classes on empowerment and on rewriting our stories. She is a writing coach and has released a book on women's empowerment called *Freeing Godiva* through Insight Publications. She is working on her next book, *The Wake-up Call*.

Maya Christobel

Luna Consulting
405-639-6699
mayachristobel@gmail.com

Chapter Four

WHAT'S IN YOUR CLOSET?

CHARLES (CHUCK) BEAN

DAVID WRIGHT (WRIGHT)

I am speaking today with Mr. Charles (Chuck) Bean of Calgary Canada. This is the second time I have interviewed Chuck. His first contribution was to our book, *Success Simplified,* and I am excited to be talking with Chuck today as a contributor to our publication of *Roadmap to Success.*

Chuck is a Canadian-based consultant, trainer, and lecturer on the subject of leadership in business. His firm, Baxter Bean & Associates Inc., works with corporations and organizations worldwide. With more than thirty years of business experience, Chuck is a respected business leader and coach.

Chuck, welcome to *Roadmap to Success.*

BEAN

Hello, and thank you, David.

As you know, my focus is always on a business angle and today I would like to talk about four elements of business success that I see as foundational. So foundational in fact, that I coach every person I work with by saying if he or she can't operate with one of them and the person doesn't think he or she ever will, that the person had better find someone else to do it.

WRIGHT

Intriguing; what are they?

BEAN

The four are: technical expertise, business acumen, team management, and selling services.

Let me take you through them, if I may.

WRIGHT

Please do.

BEAN

First I will focus on technical expertise. The simple fact is that in order to be successful in a chosen business you have to be able to perform or deliver the offering with excellence. Regardless of whether you are a dentist or an accountant or you drill oil wells, if you don't know how to do it, you won't survive.

I know that this statement seems elementary, but it is surprising to see people go into business without knowing their business offering intimately. Or even worse, they don't have a passion for it. So they invest their money and they waffle around in complacency, eventually losing out in some way—financially or time, etc.

I am sure you have heard this one thousand times before: if you are going start a business, start a business that you understand. But there is more to it than that. Technical excellence requires continuous improvement. And it is not just continuous improvement, it is continuous reinvention.

WRIGHT

Chuck, I have never thought of that term in context. What do you mean by "continuous reinvention"?

BEAN

My experience has been that those people who are continuously reinventing themselves stay in a success position a lot longer that those who don't. Look at the music industry as a good example of where artists can be on top of their game and be knocked off in a heartbeat. Lots of people are successful, but very, very few sustain it. Yet there are a few. Madonna, David Bowe, U2, Sting, Annie Lennox, and Cher are amazing examples of musical success stories that have had amazingly long runs. They all have one thing in common—they continually reinvent themselves with new looks, trying different musical genres and more.

WRIGHT

So what does someone do to be sure that he or she is on the top of his or her game?

BEAN

A couple of things: when it comes to a business, ask yourself these questions:

1. Are you passionate about what the service or products or systems that you offer?
2. Are you practicing a continuous improvement strategy and being innovative? I know a great expression about innovation: "A pioneer is a person face down in the dirt with his back full of arrows." Pioneers get creamed! It is far smarter to take what you do and be innovative. And never, never think in terms of whether or not your competitors will do what you do. Think in terms of when. It is almost a proverb that if you are doing something great, you will be copied. The key for the successful businessperson is to not get sucked into believing that he or she is alone at the top.
3. Are you continuously reinventing yourself? Are you fresh and new or old and stale? Complacency is the same as mediocrity. Do you want to be mediocre?

WRIGHT

How do you know when to reinvent yourself? What about balance?

BEAN

Good question. If you have enough statistical information at your fingertips, you can develop a bell curve model that will show you when you have peaked, and then the decision should be to look for reinvention opportunities. Moving forward, you can track the peaks and then look for relevant patterns or previous ups and downs. From there you can determine the odds moving forward. It is just like watching the stock market, when you are up, sell and rebuild again.

Also, and very important, look to see if people are copying you; if so, it's time to reinvent. Finally, if nothing is clear, use a timeline. Review every eighteen months.

WRIGHT

Do you have anything else on this subject?

BEAN

Yes, one more. Avoid the flavor of the month. I know that I am saying reinvent yourself, but not every month; and not just to copy someone. Reinvent to improve. Reinvent *you*.

WRIGHT

So if people do all of these things it will make them successful?

BEAN

It will get them on the right track, yes. But there is no guarantee, mostly because technical expertise is a very proprietary thing. The successful businessperson has to have a differentiator—something that is unique to him or her—a special recipe or process that gives them an edge. And even more important, it needs to be scalable and duplicatable.

WRIGHT

You seem to be extra passionate about that point, Chuck. Why is that?

BEAN

The values of scaling and duplication provide both growth and expansion viability, and both will help the businessperson create more of a brand. Additionally, there is the need to recognize the difference between policy and process.

To grow a business successfully, we need many processes and few policies. Policies are designed to police and stop; processes are designed to enhance and grow. Policies are dead ends; processes are scalable and dulplicatable. Just look at your rule book. If there are a ton of items in it that are not scalable and duplicatable, you are too policy-driven.

WRIGHT

But, Chuck, aren't policies important?

BEAN

Not on my watch! Actually, I am kidding; but try to keep them to a minimum. Too many negative absolutes create an absolutely negative work environment.

WRIGHT

You mentioned business acumen as your second success point. When I think of business acumen I think of balance sheets and profit and loss statements. Is that we are talking about?

BEAN

Yes, of course it is important for a businessperson to know how to read and put the two together, but my favorite business acumen strategy is maximized utilization of assets or maximized asset deployment—something l like to call MAD management.

MAD means if you are spending money, be sure that what you are spending it on is used to the maximum. And before you spend a dime, be sure in your head or on paper that the expense will provide a return. If you are leasing something, it should be worn out at the term of the lease. If you are financing something, it needs to be exhausted at the term of the loan.

And it is also important to understand that there are two asset bases in a business: 1) fixed or hard assets: cash, fixtures, inventory, patents, proprietary value, customers, contracts, etc. and 2) soft assets: people, proprietary knowledge, and capability.

It is an interesting dichotomy that business leaders will say things like "our most important assets are our people," yet have no idea of what they are worth in concrete terms. How many people have a balance sheet that lists both the value of hard and soft assets?

Yet if you consider a typical company that would be moderately asset loaded, it is very likely that over the next ten years it will spend from two to ten times as much on direct people compensation as it will on hard asset purchases or leasing.

Put all of this together and you can quickly see how asset management can become a very leaky boat.

WRIGHT

Thanks, Chuck. I think I am feeling a bit sea sick right now. What can a person do about all of this to make sure he or she is doing the right thing?

BEAN

First, don't spend without a plan. It can be on the back of a cocktail napkin, but you still should want to see that there will be a return on investment before you take the leap.

Next, lease what depreciates, buy what appreciates. I learned this from a great boss many years ago who learned it from his father. This is seventy-five-year-old business acumen.

Consider preventative maintenance and continuous improvement strategies for all assets. It is not unusual to spend 5 to 10 percent of the total asset value on annual preventative maintenance for fixtures and equipment, yet soft assets can often be completely missed. Think of training and professional development as preventative maintenance for people and you can quickly see how training staff is critical to success and long-term viability, not to mention the peripheral benefits of loyalty, etc. So plan to spend 5 to 10 percent of salary on training for all staff.

And don't cut the training budget when things turn down. No sports coach is heard saying, "I am going to stop training until we start winning games." The same goes for business. Invest in your people.

WRIGHT

What else can fall under the heading of business acumen?

BEAN

There is so much, probably too much for this chapter; however, I would stress a few others.

Leverage yourself before you get into hot water. That's a big one. Arrange your credit facility as early on as possible and keep updating it. Banks have a funny way of wanting to lend money to people who don't need it and keeping it away from those who do. So don't wait until you need it. Get your credit facilities up and moving now. That being said, banks are great sources of inexpensive yet good advice. I have always said that if a bank will lend you money on your idea, it is probably a good idea. Use them as much as possible and don't be scared of rejection; go back again and again until you get it right.

Another important strategy that has nothing to do with business financially is "don't shoot the aliens."

WRIGHT

Okay, Chuck. I expect to hear unusual remarks from you; however, you've got me on that one. What on earth does that mean?

BEAN

It means that you shouldn't discredit or reject out of course something new. Just because you don't understand something, doesn't mean that it is wrong. Try to understand it. Again, this is another challenge that some businesspeople have—fear of change, fear of failure, and an inability to embrace new ideas. The most successful people I have ever met always keep an open mind.

I think I mentioned earlier on about the value of statistics, did I not?

WRIGHT

Yes you did mention that. How does this play into business acumen?

BEAN

It is a part of a trifecta, so to speak—statistics, patterns, and odds. I believe that the most successful people on the planet have an inherent belief in statistics and metrics—the patterns that have developed as a result and the odds of success that the patterns generate.

WRIGHT

Why are these important?

BEAN

If you think about it, running a small business is like riding a motorcycle. I used to ride a lot and when you ride, you can feel and see almost everything. You feel the environment, you hear the engine and feel the heat from the motor, you feel the road, you can see 360 degrees around you, the blinkers, etc. The fact is that you really only use one gauge, the speedometer, otherwise you ride entirely by your senses.

Running a big business, however, is like flying a jetliner. You have an extremely narrow window through which to see, otherwise everything is monitored by the gauges. You really can't feel a thing. The windshield is just there for show. There is very little feel and very much dependence on statistics, patterns, and odds. You're flying by gauges. In business, this means having key performance indicators (KPIs)

Taking the leap from the motorcycle to the jetliner is a major show of faith and talent. Very few people can do it well.

WRIGHT

Chuck, you mentioned team management as a critical success key. This seems very easy to add in, yet so many people have trouble with it.

BEAN

David, you are so right. I would say that this is the biggie. Lots of businesspeople fail on this one, mostly because they are too soft. I think I hear some hissing and booing, but I don't really care. Being a good manager is all about understanding the zone.

WRIGHT

What do you mean by "the zone"?

BEAN

My favorite example is a baseball team. It consists of a manager, trainers, scouts, and players. The role of the manager is to oversee, lead, inspire, and coach. Trainers are there to maximize potential and execute change in the players. Scouts are there to search out and recruit the best possible talent. And the players' job is to play their positions—their zones.

The manager has to watch his team members to determine if they are capable of playing in the zone based on a multitude of factors—skill, heart, intuition, focus, and intelligence. If he or she believes that a player is not able to fully execute within the zone, the manager brings in the trainers. If after the trainers have done their magic, things still aren't right, the manager then looks to the scouts and may trade or bench the player. It is pretty simple. It is a tough, fair system.

So if you are a business manager, you should be asking yourself if your team members are able to perform within their zone and if not, what needs to be done to make it work.

Once the team can work in the zone, the manager's job now becomes that of leader and inspirer, setting high expectations. And most importantly, the manager never, ever goes out on to the field to play the game. The role of management is getting people to do things, not do things themselves.

There is a great algorithm that comes into play that goes like this: Expectations create accountability. Accountability then delivers respect. Respect results in loyalty and loyalty moves people toward empowerment and motivation. The role of the leader is to set expectations that will motivate his or her team.

WRIGHT

That is it? That is the "secret sauce"?

BEAN

Heck no, there is a lot more, but let me explain the role of expectations first as the foundation of good team management. As mentioned, an important role of the leader is to set expectations and by setting expectations, an air of accountability for the team member and team is created. Expectations are a road map and, to a lesser degree, a vision and mission for the team. If you are a business leader ask yourself these questions: 1) Am I operating without comprehensive expectations that have been made clear to my team? 2) Have I lowered my expectations because I feel pressure from my team to do so?

These are important questions and I don't think I need to explain them any further. If you have answered either of these questions with a yes, you may have a problem.

Once the expectations have been made clear, accountability takes over; accountability creates a sense of self-value and gives people an opportunity to succeed. This is a fantastic way to create respect, loyalty, and finally, motivation. The more that you lay the foundation for people to succeed, the more respectful they will be, with that respect translating into loyalty. The ultimate payoff will be motivation, and the lasting value will be that team members will learn how to be self-motivated by creating their own sets of expectations going forward.

WRIGHT

This is interesting, Chuck. I never would have put this together like this. Using your sports comparisons, it strikes me that this is not unlike creating a playing field for success.

BEAN

I would agree, David. You see, structure attracts high-performance people and lack of structure attracts low-performance people.

WRIGHT

I agree, and I see what you are saying. With structure, people know the ropes, but without it, people can just lollygag around. Interesting. Chuck, you mentioned earlier that there is a lot more.

BEAN

Yes, and here are five additional items to consider.

One, the truth is that you have to like people. Seriously. If you don't like people and you are in a leadership job, you have picked the wrong career. Get out while you still can. As a leader, you will be constantly faced with the need to value diversity and if you don't like people, you will never make that work.

Again, this seems like a simple statement, yet as I think about it, I can remember people I have known who had a distaste for working with others.

There are many businesspeople who see employees as a necessary evil they would rather not have to deal with. I would put it this way: you don't make money from products, you make money from people.

Two, you have to pay them well, assuming of course that they are delivering on your expectations. One interesting thing about high performers is that they generally are not in it for the money. They often focus more on delivering excellence than wealth and as a result, they can quickly fall behind. I believe it is our role as leaders to ensure that they are adequately compensated for performance. Don't be cheap with your good people.

Three, you have to know who you can mentor, who you can coach, and who is simply trainable.

WRIGHT

What do you mean mentor, coach, and train?

BEAN

I believe that we can categorize the desire to learn and grow under those three headings and I use them loosely; but I believe the intent will be clear through the following: Trainable people are people who want to come to work, do a good job, and leave. They can execute tactics and processes. They will see their job as important, but not so important that they will want to move up, be managers, etc. As leaders we can teach them tactically and to a degree strategically, however, we should not expect much more out of them. Trainable people are *able*.

Coachable people can be taught to execute plans and are interested in supervising and driving processes. They will have a higher sense of desire to engage in running the organization. As leaders we can engage them in designing processes, and we can share both the ups and downs of being a leader. Coachable people are *willful* and *able*.

People who can be mentored are extraordinarily keen on learning and driving business. They are able to fully design processes, strategies, missions, and visions. They will strive to rise to the highest possible level. As leaders we can share everything with them, from the most difficult leadership challenges to the most rewarding and they will be more than engaged in moving things forward. I see people who can be mentored as *willing* and able.

WRIGHT

So what do you do if you only have trainable or coachable people on your team? Don't you want everyone to be mentorable?

BEAN

That is a great question. I say it this way: a car has four seats, but only one is for the driver. Great leadership means that we understand how to properly align our teams while effectively using the teams we have. We may only need one leader for every six or so others. In fact, if there are too many "drivers," things can stall.

What is critical is that you have a mix of people who are willing, willful, and able, rather than a mix of people who are not willing, and so on.

WRIGHT

Does this create any sort of strife?

BEAN

It can, and that leads into my next point being that we have to create competition among the team—friendly competition. If you want people to excel, having a goal with timelines and more importantly, a means of competing with others on an equal plane, is very important. Not everyone will want to be high performers, and even more so, very few will want to be record-breakers; however, what I have always said is that the best way to inspire performance is to allow competitive natures to permeate.

Here is my method: First, set a group of standards, goals, or targets for people to meet, be it financial or otherwise. Try to have more than one, so that more than just one person has a chance to succeed. Next, create an equal playing field either through having all individual goals the same or through indexing.

Once the goals have been set, report regularly on performance and post the results for everyone to see. What you will find is that almost nobody will want to be in the bottom half, and those who are will quickly take action to rise up. Over time you will actually raise your performance standards and those who continually fall well below the standard will either seek help for improvement or fall away. It may be a little tough love, but it is what it is.

WRIGHT

You mentioned two things: friendly competition and a group of standards or goals. What do you mean by that?

BEAN

Friendly competition means having targets that will not cause battles, and that will even allow team members to play together. For example, in baseball there is statistical reporting on every position that is indexed. There can be some strife in the team but, for the most part, the players all focus on the end game.

Regarding a group of standards, using sports again, baseball players will have a number of statistics wherein they can excel—RBIs, hits, hits with runners on, home runs, and field performance. Any one baseball player has the chance to be a star in a number of different categories.

WRIGHT

That is great, Chuck. I see it clearly. As I hear all of this, I can't help but think about the time commitment. It must take a lot of time to work with people if you want a high performing team.

BEAN

Yes sir, again! You must give people time to grow. If you are going to invest in people, it takes more than money, it takes time. My rule is that it will take eighteen months on average for a person to fully integrate into a new team or job. Some are faster, some are slower, but we should be willing to accept the eighteen-month rule. During the eighteen months, we must see forward movement. If they stall, show disinterest, or chronically underperform, then shorten the timeline. Remember that activities lead to results, so even if people are doing the wrong things, they are at least doing something.

WRIGHT

Just reflecting on what you have said, I can't help but think that team members could feel frustrated by some of this. Do you have a solution for that?

BEAN

Well, David, pain is not an option, but suffering is. I heard this from a fitness instructor and I think it is so very true. Hard work is almost always painful in some way, but we can reduce or eliminate the suffering and frustration through two simple steps:

First, as the leader, remember to explain the expectations and the conditions of the job when you first hire or engage someone in a position. We talked about expectations earlier on; however, conditions are something different. I recommend to many of my clients that they sit down and make a list—a *big* list—of everything that can make the job difficult or may cause problems. During the interview process, typically the final interview, lay them all out to the candidate so that it is perfectly clear where all frustrations may occur and how you expect them to respond to them. By doing this, you will stop frustration in its track.

The other step is more of a mental game, but it requires that people be educated about how to focus on the end game and the process, rather than the situation. We have covered this earlier I believe.

Let me add one final thought on this. Effective team leadership also means that the leader has to have the entire team pulling in the same direction and, as we all know, this can be difficult to do. I provide my clients with a statement they can share with their team and it goes like this:

I want you to think that we are a team of eight rowers in a boat pointed in one direction and I would like you to consider four scenarios.

- Scenario one – eight rowers, all rowing in the same direction.
- Scenario two – six rowers, rowing in the same direction, two seats empty.
- Scenario three – six rowers rowing in the same direction, two rowers with their ores out of the water.
- Scenario four – six rowers rowing in the same direction, two rowers rowing in the opposite direction.

Three of these examples are fine and one is unacceptable. So on this team you are free to row forward, you are free to leave, and you are free to pull your ores out until you feel comfortable about the direction; but you are not free to row in opposition. As a team, we must all be moving in the same direction, and if you are not, I would prefer that you leave.

WRIGHT

I agree with your thinking Chuck and I don't believe I have ever heard it stated as clearly before. I especially like the idea that people can pull out for a while, maybe needing to reenergize or regroup.

BEAN

Absolutely correct. What is interesting about this is those people who are resting will soon get the rhythm and get back in the water in the right direction; they just have a longer due diligence cycle.

WRIGHT

I get it. I see that your points about structure and performance all make sense. Your last point is about selling. You say that we must be able to sell our services. Would you explain?

BEAN

Sure. The final key is that you can have great technique, outstanding business sense, and a world class work team, but you will still have to sell something—sometimes it is a product, sometimes a service or sometimes an idea, but you have to sell it. Sales is critical to success.

WRIGHT

Two questions come to mind: first, would you provide a greater explanation of what sales is all about, and secondly, how does someone master all four of these skill sets that you laid out in the beginning?

BEAN

Let me answer them in order. First, what is "sales"? Sales is all about getting out to the potential client and selling three things: First, selling your idea, product, or service. Second, selling you, and not necessarily in that order, and thirdly selling you *providing* the idea. And we do that by providing proof and using persuasion.

WRIGHT

Would you break this down more?

BEAN

Sure, David. Generally, almost all of what we sell is concept and time-based. We sell ideas. They may be in solid form, like a tool or a fixture, or they may be intangible like advertising, but if you look at the base of all sales, we are selling ideas that maximize time. I have always said that people don't like to spend money to save or fix, they like to spend money to gain or enhance. And, people spend money to gain time.

So the first rule in sales is to understand your idea and what the features, benefits, value, and resulting effect will be if the client buys it. Nail down the idea and create a value proposition that supports it and ensure that it is time gainer. Also remember that all good lawyers argue their cases before they go to court. If you can't sell yourself on your idea, don't waste your time trying to sell it to someone else.

Next you have to sell *you*. You are a representative of your brand and if you are sharp, your clients will believe that your brand is sharp. Think of it this way: if you take a taste of something and it tastes bad, you will naturally assume that all of it is bad. Being a salesperson requires that you not taste bad.

Thirdly, you now have to sell your client on letting you execute the idea. I have seen it one hundred times where a salesperson will sell a client on an idea, then the client will go buy it elsewhere. What has happened is that the client was not sold on the salesperson or, even worse, the salesperson has failed to close the deal.

Selling ideas and people generally require a lot of proof and a bit of persuasion. Selling someone on taking action requires a bit of proof and a lot of persuasion. I am not going to get into the entirety of sales. As we all know, it would take an entirely new chapter. But it is important to understand that we all have to rely on more than just our offering to move a customer to buy. We have to rely on our own confidence and integrity to finish things.

I was working with the Chairman of a major tire retailer a few years ago and he told me this: "I put my cash where there is confidence," and nothing rings truer.

WRIGHT

But, Chuck, that is not all that sales is about is it—just the actual act of relating or collaborating with a client?

BEAN

Correct, there is more. Your service offering is also a critical piece to the puzzle. I tell all of my clients this: "be a tourist in your own business" and get a feel of what it is like to do business with yourself. Are you thrilled, or sick to your stomach? Sales is all about service. The best salespeople in the world are great servants, and the best servants are great salespeople!

It is fascinating that we will often commit significant resources to leadership and sales training and almost nothing to customer service and reception, yet the latter are critical customer touch points.

WRIGHT

Again I find myself reflecting on what you just said. I think you are right. Service is such a major part of our sales offering. If you can't serve me well, why should I do business with you?

So, Chuck, it seems like we are coming to a close. The second part of my earlier question was, how do we wrap all four of these skills together? Would you be able to provide me with some insight?

BEAN

Of course, David. I put it this way: First and foremost, every business leader should look out over his or her business and determine as to what degree of excellence he or she is delivering in the four areas. Rank one through ten or give yourself a percentage rating and, where you see the need for improvement, take action.

Secondly, and most importantly, give yourself a self-ranking on both your ability and interest in delivering excellence in the weak areas. If you are not interested in selling and serving, hire someone to do it. If you are not interested in providing technical excellence, find someone who is, and so on.

In this world, rarely does someone end up a success on his or her own. Often we need help through the difficult spots and it is a show of great leadership to recognize our weaknesses and gain help from others.

Finally, remember to be innovative. A leader's job is to lead change, be it an update, an upgrade, or and improvement. Great leaders inspire innovation, not just within themselves but with their people. Innovation can apply in all four of the core characteristics I have outlined today. If you want to inspire innovation, encourage your people to relate and associate, question the status quo, experiment with new and old ideas, and most importantly, network with and question others, especially in areas unrelated to your business.

David, I mentioned competition earlier as a means of inspiring greatness in one's team. I would like to ask you a question if I may. What does the leader do when he or she is top of class? What do leaders do when they are out in front of the pack and seemingly have no competition?

WRIGHT

That is a good question, Chuck. I guess they need to stay the course; but in thinking about what you have said earlier, would the answer be to reinvent themselves?

BEAN

Yes, reinvention is important. I also think, however, that the leader needs to find new competition. When people become best in class, they need to find a new class to compare to. If you are a best in class leader, stop comparing yourself to your direct competitors and start comparing yourself to different markets. For example, if you are best in class in oil and gas, compare your strategy to a best in class retailer such as Walmart. You will find a whole new and exciting ladder to climb.

All being said, I think I am out of gas now. I hope that this interview provided some insight for your readers into my ideas on business leadership.

WRIGHT

Plenty to digest and plenty to take action with. Chuck, thank you for participating in this project. I appreciate your time and I look forward to visiting with you again in the future.

I have been speaking with Charles (Chuck) Bean. Chuck is a Canadian-based consultant, trainer, and lecturer on the subject of leadership in business. His firm, Baxter Bean & Associates Inc., works with corporations and organizations worldwide. With more than thirty years of business experience, Chuck is a respected business leader and coach.

About the Author

Charles (Chuck) Bean is the President of Baxter Bean & Associates Inc. along with divisions, StandandCommand, Baxter Bean Creative, and Bean Dental. Bean's companies provide services in business coaching, consulting, and training in areas such as strategic planning, leadership development, sales development, communications, and teamwork. Chuck provides practical consulting and coaching, and his workshops and lectures are educational, informative, and always engaging! He works with business professionals and leaders around the world helping them grow their businesses quickly and profitably without giving up their personal lives and core values.

Charles (Chuck) Bean

Baxter Bean & Associates, Inc.
205, 5th Ave SW, Suite 3300
Calgary, Canada T2P 2V7
403-703-9525
chuck@baxterbean.com
baxterbean.com

Chapter Five

THE COACH PAUL CONNECTION

PAUL EDWARD

DAVID WRIGHT (WRIGHT)

Today we're talking to Dr. Paul Edward. Coach Paul, as he prefers to be called, is an award-winning author, coaching psychologist, and one of the world's leading experts in the field of personal and organizational development. His award-winning book, *Moving Forward: Turning Good Intentions Into Great Results by Discovering Yourself, Your Place, and Your Path,* has helped hundreds of people get unstuck and live better lives. A former corporate executive and Marine officer, Coach Paul's written work has appeared in the American Management Association's *Performance & Profits* e-newsletter, Monster.com, the *Entrepreneur & Self-Employed Business Journal, The San Diego Union-Tribune,* and the United States Naval Institute's *Proceedings* magazine.

Paul, welcome to *Roadmap to Success.*

PAUL EDWARD (EDWARD)

Thank you David, it's a pleasure to be here.

WRIGHT

So tell me, what is a coaching psychologist and how does that differ from a business coach or a therapist?

EDWARD

A coaching psychologist is a psychologist who is trained to help improve the personal and professional lives of people and organizations. We differ from therapists in the sense that therapists work with people who are, what we call, low functioning; whereas, coaching psychologists work with people who are high functioning and who want to achieve the next level of success. We also differ from business coaches in that we use some of the tools that psychologists use to help people live better lives and help organizations run better.

WRIGHT

How would a successful businessperson benefit from working with a coaching psychologist?

EDWARD

One of the biggest benefits of working with a coaching psychologist is that you get the best of business coaching and personal development. Most businesspeople know that if they want to move forward professionally they must also improve their personal lives. By working with a coaching psychologist, you get to work on both sides of your life so that you can make sustaining progress in all areas.

WRIGHT

In your book, *Moving Forward,* you talk about the *five foundations of personal success*; do those same foundations apply to business success as well?

EDWARD

They certainly do. Those five foundations are self-awareness, synchronization, connection, deliberation, and adaptability. *Self-awareness* means knowing who you are, down to the psychological level. *Synchronization,* the second foundation, means designing a life that fits who you are. The third foundation, *Connection,* means being connected to the right people. Then the fourth foundation is *Deliberation,* which means being intentional about the choices and decisions you make, so that they support your objectives and goals. The fifth foundation is *Adaptability,* which means being flexible enough to respond to the dynamic nature of life and the world around you.

If we look at those same foundations from a business perspective, we see that they align very nicely. *Self-awareness* is having an understanding of your core business values, your products, services, and your customers. *Synchronicity is* ensuring that your business practices and processes support your core business values, products, services, and customers. *Connection* is developing strong internal cohesion among your employees, having strong strategic alliances and supplier relationships, and being a valued partner to your customers. *Deliberation is* making strategic and operational plans that support your core business objectives. *Adaptability is* continually surveying the dynamic nature of your industry and your clients' needs to deliver long-term results.

WRIGHT

In your experience, which of these five foundations do most business leaders struggle with achieving?

EDWARD

The one foundation that most business leaders struggle with is *connection.* Remember, *connection* is about developing strong relationships with the right people. There is a lot of truth in the saying, "It's lonely at the top." Unfortunately, the skills that take most business leaders to the top of their organizations aren't the same skills they need to develop healthy, supportive relationships. Also, if you add organizational politics, trust, competition, time pressures, and the need for confidentiality, it's easy to see why business leaders struggle with developing meaningful relationships."

WRIGHT

So how do you help business leaders overcome those obstacles and get connected?

EDWARD

The first thing we help them do is form, what I call, a *Fan Club*. A *Fan Club* is a group of people who have made a formal commitment to *support* and help you achieve *your* objectives.

Let me tell you a story to illustrate this: When I was starting my career in the financial services industry, I was approached by leaders of one of our two political parties to run for a local congressional seat. After thinking about it for a couple of days, I went to see my boss and mentor and asked what he thought about the idea. I still remember his words to this day. He said, "If you're going to go into any leadership position, particularly one that has a lot of power and influence, you need to have at least five people in your life who will be able to tell you the truth and support you in achieving your goals." What he was telling me then is the same thing I tell people now: Every leader needs a Fan Club.

So we help business leaders identify their potential Fan Club members and then help them recruit these people into their Fan Clubs. Once they do this, the lives of the business leaders change. They go from feeling isolated and alone to supported and part of a larger community. It's one of the most rewarding aspects of what we do at Life-Changing Coaching.

WRIGHT

So in creating a success road map, what are the key concepts that business leaders need to keep in mind?

EDWARD

When creating that success road map, one of the things that is really important for business leaders to keep in mind is the foundation of *Deliberation*. Leaders need to be very intentional about where they are going and intentional about how they plan on getting there. Steven Covey calls this "beginning with the end in mind" and he's right.

The first concept business leaders need to consider is that they need to be very clear about their goals and objectives. We help business leaders accomplish this by taking them through a formalized, step-by-step process that helps them clarify their goals, prioritize them, and then develop specific plans to achieve them. These plans include action items with dates and check points to help keep them on track.

The second concept business leaders need to keep in mind is that they can't do everything at once. They need to focus on the things they can reasonably accomplish given the time and resources available to them. The foundation of *Deliberation* is not just about intentionality, it is also about developing a disciplined focus so that business leaders avoid the common mistake of attempting to focus on so many things that they end up accomplishing nothing.

WRIGHT

So what makes your approach so unique?

EDWARD

We like to differentiate ourselves from the self-help genre. We are really an *other's help* company. We strongly believe in that third foundation of *Connection* and that you cannot make sustaining progress in life without having a community of supportive people around you. You can make short-term progress and go pretty far by yourself, but you cannot sustain that trajectory over a long period of time without people to support you. So we are unashamedly about connecting with others and helping people develop communities that allow them to have a long-term approach to success and continue moving forward.

WRIGHT

Sounds a little like the people who do networking. Is that what you're talking about—networking and relationship-building?

EDWARD

Yes, it is. One of my mentors is Ivan Meisner. He founded Business Networking International (BNI). The organization's members do four or five billion dollars' worth of business referrals each year. Or look at Starbucks; what did they do to build their business? It wasn't just that they offered gourmet coffee—they brought back the front porch that has been missing in a lot of Americans' lives. With organizations like BNI and Starbucks you have this place where you can go and you can be in a community with other people. Their success has a lot to do with providing a place of belonging. That's what we help people do at Life-Changing Coaching—both in their personal and professional lives.

WRIGHT

So what made you realize this concept was lacking in the business world?

EDWARD

I was commissioned as a second lieutenant in the Marine Corps. The Marine Corps teaches esprit de corps—camaraderie—because teamwork is essential if you are going to survive in a combat situation. We went into combat in Desert Storm during the first Gulf War and that combat made us all very close. That was when I learned about being a part of a community and how important it was for success.

When I came back home, I left the Marine Corps and went into the civilian world to discover that people showed up at eight o'clock, when work started, and at five o'clock, everybody was gone. That was it; there was no connection. Having experienced the camaraderie of the Marine Corps, I noticed the lack of community in the civilian world and realized how greatly everyone would benefit by reintroducing this concept of community into their work lives.

WRIGHT

It used to be a running joke, where I grew up, that if you were at the courthouse at four-thirty, you'd be trampled to death. But I never thought about how this affected our connectedness. That is new to me.

EDWARD

Yes, I'm glad you can see that because it was one of the things that was a glaring problem, in my opinion. When I was in the Marine Corps, we had workdays too, but at the end of the workday you would have some kind of social interaction with the people you worked with.

WRIGHT

Were there any other valuable lessons you learned from your time in the United States Marine Corps that have contributed to your success or the successes of others?

EDWARD

I think another key lesson I learned in the Marine Corps is the idea of looking at leadership as a profession. A lot of times we just look at leadership as a title and not as a profession; we do not change our behaviors with the higher position. Many people who are promoted never have the chance to take formal leadership training. My initial obligation to the Marine Corps was four years, yet two of those years were spent training on how to be a leader.

Think about that ratio. The Marine Corps believes that the profession of leadership is so important that it devotes 50 percent of the time it has to training people how to be good leaders.

More companies need to adopt this philosophy. Too often they blame the employees, when really they should be looking at the leaders of those employees and training them how to be better leaders.

WRIGHT

They're probably not looking for many field commissions then, are they?

EDWARD

No, but when you look at the civilian world, most managers start out as supervisors and are then promoted. They never have the opportunity to attend a class or learn anything about how to effectively use their new responsibilities. Eventually they continue to be promoted and become CEOs with no formal leadership education.

WRIGHT

In your opinion, is there a correlation between personal and professional success?

EDWARD

Yes, my research and experience with leaders shows that when you look at people who have had long-term professional success, they will tell you that they would not have succeeded if it were not for their personal support. Nine times out of ten they'll point to one or two people who have been there throughout their careers and served as mentors to encourage and guide them. It all comes back to that Fan Club and knowing that if you are not supported in your personal life, then you will probably not be strong enough to prevail in your career.

WRIGHT

A wise man once told me that if you are walking down a country road and see a turtle sitting on top of a fencepost, you can bet that he didn't get up there by himself. Would you tell me who are your role models and what did you learn from them?

EDWARD

My three biggest role models are Abraham Lincoln, Martin Luther, and Charles Blake.

Abraham Lincoln taught me that if you're going to be a leader, you have to be willing to lead, even when half of the people you lead think what you are doing is wrong. I call that the courage of leadership—the courage to stand behind your convictions. I've learned a lot about that because visionary leadership is often ahead of what people can see, and so you must have that insight and courage to stay in your resolve. Staying with your vision is important but when variables change, we must stay adaptable and change with them without losing that original vision.

My second role model is Martin Luther because he taught me the value of continuing education. He started out as a lawyer, which at the time was a lifetime of learning. Then he switched and became a theologian, which was another lifetime of learning. If you read some of his biographical works, you'll see that even up to the day he died, he was always looking to learn and grow. He was constantly seeking to develop and change the world around him. For me that was very encouraging.

My third role model is Charles Blake. He is the presiding bishop of the largest African-American church denomination in the world, the Church of God in Christ. Bishop Blake has taught me the value of integrity. In these days of scandal after scandal of high-profile leaders, he has lived a life of honesty and humility. I've known him all my life and he has been a shining example of someone who practices what he preaches and has been doing so for more than forty years. That is inspiring!

WRIGHT

Well, this has been a great conversation, Paul. I've learned a lot here today and I've been taking notes.

EDWARD

Thanks David, I appreciate it; I've enjoyed it too.

WRIGHT

Today we have been talking with Paul Edward. Coach Paul is an author, a coaching psychologist, and an expert in the field of personal and organizational development. He helps hundreds of people get unstuck and live better lives.

Paul, thank you so much for being with us today on *Roadmap to Success*.

EDWARD

Thank you David.

About the Author

Coach Paul has been in the people and organizational development business for more than twenty-five years. Clients like working with him because of his warmth, sense of humor, and ability to help them unravel and solve their most difficult challenges.

Coach Paul uses a blend of leadership theory, philosophy, and psychology to help clients:

- Discover and develop their unique talents
- Make meaningful connections with the right people
- Clarify their objectives
- Create easy-to-follow road maps
- Begin making sustainable progress

After graduating from the University of Southern California, Coach Paul became a commissioned officer in the United States Marine Corps, where he led Marines in peacetime and in combat during the First Persian Gulf War. After the Marines, he worked in various management and executive positions in the private sector.

He is now a coaching psychologist, leadership consultant, professional speaker, and award-winning writer.

In addition to having a BS, MA, and PhD, Coach Paul is also a Certified Corporate Coach and a Certified Type Professional. He is married, has two sons, and lives in the Southern California area where he says the weather is the same and the people are different.

Dr. Paul Edward

Life-Changing Coaching
8333 Foothill Blvd., Suite 106
Rancho Cucamonga, CA 91730
909-457-8280

Chapter Six

CHARTING THE COURSE

MARISHKA GLYNNE

DAVID WRIGHT (WRIGHT)

Today we're talking with Marishka Glynne. Marishka is an intuitive motivator who helps clients generate the success they seek in their business and personal lives. Several decades of high-end achievement in business have given her a rigorous background in the professional and interpersonal issues at the heart of every successful organization. Substantial training has helped her access the wisdom clients need to turn their dreams into concrete reality.

Marishka, welcome to *Roadmap to Success*.

MARISHKA GLYNNE (MARISHKA)

Thank you, David.

WRIGHT

So why have you chosen to write a chapter called "Charting the Course" in a book titled *Roadmap to Success*?

MARISHKA

When my voyage started, the seas were calm, the sun was shining, the wind was softly blowing, and it seemed that nothing could go wrong. The boat was moving steadily through the water, heading out to sea. When the wind picked up, I needed to reset the sails but I couldn't find a winch handle. As the wind speed increased, it was evident that I needed less sail but I didn't know how to adjust it. The boat was heeling over, water started to come into the cockpit and I panicked, not knowing what to do next. The sails were billowing and luffing, and making a terrifying noise. Even worse, I couldn't see the shore, couldn't read the compass because it was getting dark, and I couldn't find the light switch! Then I woke up and I found myself in a sweat. Looking around me, I realized it was just a dream, but the dream warned me that I needed help.

All of us individually and collectively are slowly inching towards the "Great Unknown." No one escapes this fact. We try not to think about it by keeping busy. For example, we take care of our families, our careers, and ourselves, and most of us feel very comfortable with our routine; we don't want to "rock the boat." When something out of the ordinary happens and our "boat" gets rocked hard, we are shaken and we want to know where do we go from here—what's next? We get frustrated, antsy, and we can't sleep. We need to take control again. We need to take action and take positive steps to get us back to feeling confident about where we are and where we're heading.

My husband's passion is sailing and we have a thirty-one-foot C&C Corvette. It was designed with such elegant lines and is so sturdy that it sails beautifully, even in heavy weather. At first I had no desire to sail, but within a short period of time I got the "bug." I had the desire to sail, but when the boat started to heel (that's the term for tipping to one side), it scared me. Now, for a true sailor, this is the "ultimate sailing," so in order for me to be relaxed and enjoy my new venture I needed to do something that would bring me peace of mind—I had to chart my course. Where did I want to go and where was I going to start? The beginning for me was to take professional sailing classes and learn everything I could so that I would be an accomplished sailor. I wanted to enjoy my journey, not just sit there biting my nails the whole time and anticipating the fear of what could, would, or should be happening.

I did everything I could to prepare for that adventure, and for my efforts I got second place the first time I entered the Lady Helmsmen's

Race! My wants and my desires were being fulfilled—I had charted my course, set the sail, and was ready to have that boat heel over—I was in control again!

WRIGHT

So what does this have to do with a road map to success?

MARISHKA

There comes a time in most people's lives when we ask ourselves, "Is that all there is?" It's strange how we can do the same thing day in and day out for years and then we need change. You know what I mean—the time when we've had enough, we're mentally exhausted, and we need space for ourselves to "veg out." Have you ever done this? Did it feel good? I have done it several times and it felt good to me—not thinking about yesterday, today, or tomorrow, no schedules, and no cares.

After a while inactivity becomes boring and we become lethargic, and sometimes even depressed. We may even begin to crave the "outside" world. Where is everyone, what are they doing, what am I missing? You may ask, "How did I get to this stage in my life? Was it by accident, coincidence, or maybe even a fluke?" Everything in life happens for a reason. There is a road map, even though you may never have planned it. Life is not about discovering—it's about re-discovering and looking at things from a different angle, a different perspective. Your map has always been there from the beginning and the destinations are limitless. The question is where do *you* want to go? Success isn't about reaching the destination—it's about the journey.

> If you don't have a dream, how are you going to make a dream come true?
>
> —Oscar Hammerstein

WRIGHT

How do we choose our destination?

MARISHKA

You've got to have a dream! When we are children, we are carefree and we have dreams and we have visions. We want to be "someone"—a pirate, a prince, a princess, a fireman, a doctor, a teacher—whatever our imagination brings to mind. There are so many role models out there. We are creative with our fantasies and we role-play. We are curious, inquisitive, and we are like sponges—always wanting to learn and try new things.

When my grandson was six years old, he was in love with dinosaurs. He could sit and draw and color them for hours. He has such a passion for them that he knows all their names and all the individual characteristics of each one.

Slowly, his interests started to shift and then his biggest passion became Lego. He loved it and he was so proud when he completed a Lego model designed for ages eight to twelve years, and he wanted no help from others. He looked at the finished product on the box and persevered until he eventually built what looked good to him and proudly showed his accomplishments. He loves gadgets; he has a lot of patience, and is good at putting things together. These are skills that will encourage him to see what he loves to do and where his passion lies. His parents are teaching him from an early age to experiment and try different things—nothing is the "wrong way."

Have you noticed that as we get older we start listening to others, and we start second-guessing our dreams and our ideas? We may even begin to drift from what we want in order to please others by doing what they want. It's easy to fall into this trap. We wonder what others will say and what will they think? We begin to sway in the wind.

Dr. Mehmet Oz says that people with passion and dreams live seven to ten years longer, and they have a better quality of life. He explains that if you stop dreaming for any reason (e.g., being laid off, retirement, empty nest), you can suffer from apoptosis, a medical term describing a condition of your brain believing you've outgrown your usefulness. The brain sends a message to the body that it is no longer needed and people will begin mentally and/or physically self-destructing. This can happen at any age. The cure is to be connected to your passion, which gives you renewed energy, enthusiasm, vitality, and creativity. From that place, create the life of your dreams. There is the dream you have for life and then there's the dream of what life has for you. When they meet, it is beautiful.

Have you ever been on a sailboat?

WRIGHT

Not a big one, just a catamaran.

MARISHKA

Life is very much like sailing, we decide where we want to go, we chart the course, set the sails, adjust the compass, and we're ready for the ride. Eventually we arrive at our destination, but the adrenaline and thrill is in the experiences and the lessons we learn along the way.

Our life adventure begins by adjusting our compass. Below is the acronym NWES and what the letters stand for:

N is for new,
W is for want,
E is for effort,
S is for success.

New—We begin with uncharted territory; every time we set sail it's a new adventure and new circumstances. It will always be different from what we have experienced before. The winds may be stronger or lighter, the waves may be higher or calmer; as is true in life, and nothing stays the same. When starting something new, we need a plan, a map—we need to chart our course. If we have no plan, in time we meander, we get frustrated, angry, and fearful. Where do you want to go? Where do your dreams want to take you? Do you have a timeframe—one year, five year, even ten years? What are the key areas of your life you would like to venture into? Is it your health, your career, your relationships, finances, self-worth? When one area is out of kilter, it eventually affects the others. We need to have balance in all areas of our lives. How do we balance them?

Your health is most important. Are you getting proper nourishment? Are you getting proper sleep. How is your mental state—emotional or spiritual? Are you preoccupied and have you so much on your mind that you are overwhelmed? Without your health, if something goes wrong along the way you will have neither the strength nor endurance to continue.

What about your career—are you happy with your present choice? Have you outgrown your job? Are you looking for something more challenging? The sooner you face your reality, the sooner you can set sail. Stop procrastinating, embrace fear, it's only a benchmark to let you know that you are ready to take the next step. Remember that FEAR is only False Evidence Appearing Real. Which direction are you heading for? Are you running away or are you running toward?

How are your relationships—partner, spouse, family, or friends? Support is necessary in life. When you come across that storm, is there someone you can lean on—someone you can talk to? We're all connected; we all want to feel that we belong. Who will you call with an SOS or a mayday? Who is your "life jacket"?

How are your finances? You don't have to be a millionaire to enjoy sailing, there are big yachts and there are smaller yachts, they all take you on the water. You may enjoy a little more comfort being on the bigger yacht, but that is a choice you have to make. How much money is enough for you? What is your style—luxury, adventurous, or are you a diehard?

How healthy is your feeling of self-worth? Do you value who you are? Do you feel good about how far you have come? What experiences and lessons have you learned in life that have made you feel strong, confident, and invincible? Do you believe that you have what it takes to make the trip? Are you flexible when it comes to those last-minute decisions? Are you ready to batten down the hatches when a storm arrives unexpectedly?

When you know the area in your life that you want to chart, you begin by setting the sails. When you hoist the sails, you steer into the wind. If you steer too far to port (the left side), or starboard (the right side), it's going to require tremendous strength to get the sails up the mast and it's going to take you longer to start your journey.

Once the sails are up, you set the course to your destination, but you have to steer according to the direction that the wind is blowing. Too much wind will blow the sails over too far and you may take on water. Too little wind and you won't even get to the starting line. Just the right wind, the right helm (the steering), and proper management of the sails will give you the smooth sailing you are looking for.

The wind is what powers the sails; you can't just sit there and do nothing, you must be flexible. Watch the compass and adjust the sails in order to get to your destination. The more you go off course, the longer it will take to reach your goal. This is the same as in our lives—we need the wind, which is the passion that drives us, we need to be flexible, we need to be in control, and we need to keep the vision, which is our destination.

Want—How passionate are you about this trip and how badly do you want it? What kind of an attitude do you have? Are you anticipating this new venture or is it just another ho-hum day? Are you excited and do you expect wonderful things along the way? Do you look forward to positive things or do you dwell on all the things that could go wrong?

This is a trip that you have planned for a while, why are you second-guessing yourself? How many times in life do you keep going over and over the same situation and end up spinning your wheels with no success? So many of us spend so much energy and time on the past that we forget to enjoy the present. What are you doing to fulfill your wants and needs? What is your passion? Know that anything is possible. Do you have a map? Can you see your destination?

Effort—If you don't make the effort and take that next step forward, you might as well put your feet in quicksand and just stand there. Life is about taking action, and it's about being alive and kicking. All you have to do is make the effort.

When my granddaughter was eight years old, she was fascinated with sailing. She would talk about it daily and look at pictures of where she wanted to go and what she wanted to do. This kept her goal alive. She made the effort and took the time to plan a day or a night on the boat, then packed her clothes, her favorite foods, and her water. Coming on the boat was a lot of fun for her—sleeping on it, having breakfast in the morning, enjoying the sunrise, and saying good morning to the ducks and the loons that would come by. Marveled at how easy it was to steer the boat, she enjoyed being the captain at the helm, watching the compass and paying attention to which way the wind was blowing. She made the effort and enrolled in sailing classes on her summer holidays so she could enjoy her sailing even more.

It's interesting that when we're young we are fearless, there are no barriers, the sky is the limit, and we want to do things we have never done before. We are like sponges, soaking up all those new adventures that are there to be explored. What is stopping you from making the effort?

Success—Finally we've arrived! After all the planning, the excitement, the anxiety, and the emotions of the journey, we have reached our destination. What area of your life have you been working on? Was it health, career, relationship, finances, and/or self-worth? How does it feel? How has this journey affected your personal or business growth? Notice your emotions when you are feeling good or on top of the world. Do you feel confident, hopeful, motivated, inspired, and do you have a feeling of self-empowerment? We've all had these feelings at one time or another in our lives. Think back on how you felt. Was it easy to make the effort to do things?

Everything you do will be easier if you feel positive about yourself and do things you enjoy and have fun doing. In order for you to be in alignment with yourself you must feel comfortable and love who you are. Enjoy being in the moment, it's a good place to be, but also plan for the future, have dreams, become adventurous and prepare for smooth sailing.

WRIGHT

So why do some of us choose to do nothing or have difficulty choosing a destination?

MARISHKA

There are usually two possible answers to that question. It could be limited beliefs or it could be negative emotions.

WRIGHT

How do limited beliefs affect us?

MARISHKA

Were you told as a child that you would never make it, that you were not good enough, or that you offered very little value to the world? It could have been your parents, your teachers, and/or even your friends who told you this. These are negative statements that others have made and you believed them. What was their motive in saying these things to you? Was it jealousy—were they trying to show themselves to be superior to you? Perhaps they didn't know any better and they were just passing on to you what they were taught. What they did was instill their beliefs into you.

Are you using limited beliefs as an excuse or a crutch in order to not move forward and/or to shield yourself from the pain of failure? Limited beliefs are the boundaries you set for yourself. You have the power to change what you don't want. In order to let go of limiting beliefs and get past the barrier preventing you from moving forward, you must address them and then take action.

A way of releasing limited beliefs is to look back on your life and see how far you've come. Think of things you have said or done that have made you feel good about yourself. How did these actions affect your life? Were you empowered? Did you become more confident? In what way have they enhanced your life? This shows that you are capable of making your own decisions, you have made it, you are good enough, and you do add value to the world.

WRIGHT

How do negative emotions affect us?

MARISHKA

Emotions are the driving force of everything you do. Become aware of them. What emotions do you have when things aren't going your way? Take the time and become aware of them. Ask yourself, "How do I feel?" Do you feel anger, fear, sadness, guilt, jealousy? Are these all familiar to you? These are called negative emotions and are a signal or a red flag to make you aware that something is not balanced in your life—you need to make changes. We can get so wrapped up in our negative emotions that they begin to consume us and we lose sight of the horizon. We may even get to the point where we just want to jump ship. This is why we have lifejackets on board when we set sail—we all need life jackets when we go through stormy weather.

WRIGHT

How do we get rid of these negative emotions?

MARISHKA

I want you to close your eyes and think back to a time when you had one of these emotions. For example, let's take anger. Remember a time when you felt very angry. Think about that situation and ask yourself what was going on, what were you doing, how old were you, what caused you to be so angry? Now ask yourself the question, Why? Why did you have to go through that emotion and what lesson did you have to learn—how did that experience change you?

When you look back and connect the dots; it may have been that very situation that has caused you to be where you are today. Are you a better person for it? In what way did that emotion help you to grow and learn more about yourself and others? Do you still feel angry about the event or was it a blessing? If your negative emotion is still there, you must continue to look for another lesson and blessing. Sometimes we can learn many lessons from one experience.

WRIGHT

Will you give us some examples of how that would work for us?

MARISHKA

Many of my clients had anger toward their parents or their school teachers. They were yelled at regardless of what they did or they were never praised when they did something that was special. They were not chosen to do certain things and they felt unappreciated. By asking what lessons were learned from those experiences, many responded that it had made them stronger in order to survive in life. They learned to be resourceful and depend on themselves, realizing that at times people may be fickle or have other commitments and may not always be there when you need them. They learned early in life that some people have their own agenda, they're self-centered and selfish. Because of their negative experiences, my clients learned to have compassion and treat people and children with kindness. They speak in a softer voice, praise accomplishments, and encourage and acknowledge their individual strengths and authenticity. The anger they experienced was really a blessing because now they are aware of how damaging it is to hurt someone. Negative emotions teach us to have empathy, humility, and compassion for others.

Do you treat others differently now because of what you have learned from those experiences? Are you kinder, wiser, and more mature? Many things can be learned through these negative emotions. Living life is like sailing. The waters may be calm and yet at other times those waves can become pretty choppy, depending on how strong the wind is. Release the negative emotions; there is always a rainbow at the end of the storm.

WRIGHT

How about another example that is a blessing in disguise?

MARISHKA

A relationship creates a roller coaster of emotions. Unfortunately, when it ends, whether it's a marriage, friendship or just living together, we all go through a gamut of negative emotions—anger, fear, guilt, jealousy, and so on. We may even get to a point where we are so consumed by these emotions that we literally make ourselves sick. You must be honest with yourself and reflect on the relationship. In looking back, were there signals you chose to ignore or issues you didn't want to confront? Were you outgrowing each other and slowly drifting apart? Did you start having different interests? Did one of you become a workaholic so that you didn't have to face reality?

We use so much energy trying to maintain something that makes us unhappy and miserable; in time it just gets progressively worse. We are so focused on projecting an image that everything is wonderful, meanwhile, we could be doing so much more with our lives and making ourselves happier by either being alone or meeting someone else.

When a separation finally occurs, do some evaluating. Ask yourself why you had to go through that relationship? What was the lesson you needed to learn from that experience, what was the blessing? Think back to the time when you decided to get involved. What was the attraction? Why did you go into this relationship? Were you looking to escape reality and fell in love with the fantasy? Did it bring you financial security? Were you looking for a family unit or did you want to start your own family? Think of everything that happened during your time together and how those experiences made an impact on your life. In what way have you changed? Are you a stronger, more confident person? Did this relationship have an effect on your career? Did you move up the ladder of success or did you make a complete change? Did it offer you the opportunity and flexibility to travel or travel more? Do you now have a better understanding of what you want and/or what you don't want? Did this relationship help you to become a better judge of character?

Not everyone is meant to be in our lives forever. It's all about the journey, learning about who you are, setting goals, and living your dreams.

WRIGHT

You spoke earlier about the journey and the areas of our lives that we may need to work on. Will you expand a bit on that?

MARISHKA

Some of the areas that we may want to work on are health, career, relationships, and finances.

Health—Being totally healthy is when you are balanced on every level—physical, mental, emotional, and spiritual. When your health is not the best, eventually it is going to cause discomfort and compromise the immune system. Make an effort to eliminate the problem and create a healthy future. Exercise, even if it's just walking twenty minutes a day. Eat nutritious meals and get proper sleep. When you are feeling down, do something that is going to change the energy and make you happy. You may want to listen to music, set new goals, sing. Did you know that singing has been proven by researchers at Newcastle University in the United Kingdom to boost the immune system, promote optimism, and improve physical health by increasing breathing capacity? Be aware of what is going on in your life and you'll be able to make changes, adapt, and improve your health.

Career—When it comes to your career, what do you really want? Is it money or prestige? Do you want to change your job or do you need to change your entire career? Tap into your dreams and your imagination. What would you do if you had everything you wanted? What makes you tick? What is your passion? We all have a calling or a path in life; if you follow your passion, it is going to be effortless and you will enjoy the journey. But if it's an uphill battle, you eventually need to take a different path. Do you enjoy what you're doing or do you take a lot of time off or call in sick?

Success happens when you feel fulfilled, focus on what you really want, and take action to get it.

Relationships—Relationships are like a battery—there has to be a positive and a negative in order for them to work. Some of us try hard to be compatible, but over time this can become difficult because none of us are perfect and there are sure to be things that will annoy us.

At first it may feel good having the other person make the decisions, be the leader or the nurturer, but over time (it usually takes about six months), the blinders of "honeymoon bliss" will come off and that person may get tired, burned out, frustrated and angry, which will cause friction in the relationship. Don't take things for granted—learn how to get along. Develop good relationship skills. Share experiences together, communicate, express yourselves, have fun, laugh together, and compliment each other. We all have flaws; none of us are perfect. The question is: which flaw can you tolerate and live with? Relationships are all about give and take. The secret is to find balance.

You may take a lot of sailing classes but if you don't get on the boat and practice those skills, you are never going to experience and learn to get better. You have the power to change; you hold the key to your happiness.

Making changes takes effort, so step out of your comfort zone. This is the time for you to move forward, keep your vision, and stop dwelling on the negative. Put energy into making it better, and ask yourself why you have a relationship with this person. Think back to all the reasons you were attracted to him (or her). If you try too hard it's just going to burn you out. Search your heart, make the change, and go for what you want.

Finances—When it comes to finances, we all need a little monetary help from time to time; money gives you the freedom to do what you want in life. In a land of wealth and opportunity and in an age of unlimited freedom, attaining wealth is a matter of choice and determination and is even a sign of personal achievement. To begin, you must know what you really want and believe it with all your heart and soul. Ask yourself if you are getting paid fairly for your skills and what your job is worth. Should you ask for a raise or look elsewhere? Should you spend less than you make and pay off your credit cards? Those pieces of plastic are so easy to use and it's easy to forget that it represents real money spent every time you use them.

Save a percentage of your salary every month. It doesn't have to be big, it's called "paying yourself first." You will be surprised how much it adds up by the end of the year. Make a budget so you can set goals for spending and saving. If you don't budget, you lose track of where your money is going, you just keep spending, and eventually it will become a problem. Money is a resource or a tool to be managed wisely. Money is neither evil nor is it the source of happiness. It may be used to achieve your dreams and priorities and increases your choices but it also increases your responsibility.

Develop a desire to have wealth consciousness (being aware of money), to have money, and use money to reflect your values and your priorities. Take responsibility for how you handle money. Addictions to shopping, drama, power, sex, or the need to have the newest gadget will eventually destroy your freedom of choice and your ability to handle money responsibly. Review your insurance coverage and have an updated will. Seek experts and professionals when investing. You can decide to have a healthy, exciting, and profitable relationship with money, but choose wisely.

WRIGHT

Sounds like a plan! Where do I start?

MARISHKA

Once you have confronted each of the above areas in your life, you will have created the foundation for "your road map to success." Every day, every moment, you are creating your destiny. You have a choice—you can just let it happen or you can choose to create your destiny with feelings, intention, and joy.

You must be motivated, take time out alone in order to clear the mind and get rid of the mind chatter. This creates a vacuum that will enable you to be aware and see new opportunities. Focus on what you want and need. Write down three things that you want to achieve daily and make it happen, read them out loud to bring life to them. Meditate every day or just take some quiet time for yourself. Get in touch with that inner voice, make it your best friend and allow it to guide you when others around you are saying you're crazy or you can't do that. Write in a journal daily expressing all the thoughts going through your mind and pay attention to your dreams. Look at pictures that make you see the end result of your achievement, and see yourself living the lifestyle you would lead if money were no object.

Practice every day, create a moving picture of all the things that you would be, do, and have when your goals are realized. Allow it to become so real in your mind that you actually experience the feeling of joy and freedom. Stay positive and become aware of opportunities; you will begin to notice an increase in the prosperity you are attracting.

Create opportunities for yourself to bring happiness, joy, laughter, prosperity, and better health into your life. Call your friends, talk to people, sign up for classes, dance, and volunteer in your community. Join local organizations such as Rotary, Toastmasters, Chamber of Commerce, or groups of people working toward the same goals. Be creative, have a makeover, be self-motivating. Observe when you get distracted and then put yourself back on track. Be productive, do one thing each day that makes you feel you've accomplished something, even if it's just making someone smile. Reward yourself for accomplishments, even if it is just your favorite coffee.

Be grateful and always say thank you. What are you thankful for right now? Look for something, even if it's just the beautiful sunshine or the rain that will make the grass grow. Believe in miracles and in yourself; what you believe becomes your reality. Trust that you can achieve anything. Let yourself really live with passion and gratitude on the edge of your comfort zone. Live your heart's desire. You can transform all your possibilities into reality.

Have you ever heard the expression "keep your chin up"? There is a reason for that. I want you to put your chin up about one inch above the norm and try to be angry, sad, or depressed. It's impossible. Now put your chin down and look at the floor and try to be angry, sad, or depressed. It's much easier. When you are feeling down and you need a quick little pick-me-upper, put your chin up!

Think, Dream, Believe, and Trust. Walk proud with your head held high. Create the life you were meant to live. You are someone who is truly *amazing!*

I wish you happy sailing.

WRIGHT

Well, what a great conversation. I always enjoy talking with you, Marishka.

MARISHKA

Thank you, David, it's always a pleasure talking with you, too.

WRIGHT

Today I have been talking with Marishka Glynne. Marishka is an intuitive motivator who helps her clients generate the success they seek in business and in their personal lives. Her consulting practice includes personal consultations, coaching, keynote presentations to business groups, and writing projects aimed at helping people tap into their own inner strength and insight.

> There's no thrill in easy sailing
> when the skies are clear and blue.
> There's no joy in merely doing
> things which anyone can do.
> But there is some satisfaction
> that is mighty sweet to take;
> when you reach a destination
> that you never thought you'd make.
> —Anonymous

Marishka, thank you so much for being with us today on *Roadmap to Success.*

MARISHKA

Thank you, David. It was my pleasure.

About the Author

Marishka Glynne is an intuitive consultant who helps clients generate the success they seek in their business and personal lives.

Several decades of high-end achievement in the banking industry have given her a rigorous background in the professional and inter-personal issues at the heart of every successful business. Substantial training in numerology, palm energy, tarot, neurolinguistic programming, Hawaiian Huna, time line empowerment, and hypnosis has helped her access the wisdom clients need to turn their dreams into a concrete reality.

Marishka's consulting practice includes personal consultations and coaching, key-note presentations to business groups, and writing projects aimed at helping people tap into their own inner insight. To learn more about how she can help you get more traction on issues that have been holding you back, visit her website at the address given below.

Marishka Glynne, MNLP, MTLT, MHt, CTC

Xanadu Associates
99 Bronte Road, Suite 224
Oakville, Ontario, L6L 3B7, Canada
905-847-9890
marishka@marishka.ca
www.marishka.ca

SOLVING PEOPLE PROBLEMS CAN IMPROVE THE BOTTOM LINE

LINDA M. DUFFY

DAVID WRIGHT (WRIGHT)

Today I'm talking with Linda M. Duffy. Linda is a Certified Senior Professional Human Resources Practitioner and a Certified Practitioner of Neuro Linguistic Programming. Linda earned a BA in Sociology and Political Science from Occidental College and is a member of the Delta Mu Delta Honor Society through Webster University where she will receive her MBA in early 2012.

Linda, welcome to ROADMAP to Success.

LINDA DUFFY (DUFFY)

Thanks, David; it's nice to be here.

WRIGHT

How did you get started in human resources?

DUFFY

To be honest, it could be said that I fell into it. When I graduated from Occidental College, two of my professors strongly encouraged me to continue my education, earn a PhD, and teach. I applied to programs and received scholarships and stipends to go to The University of Chicago and Northwestern, both great schools. I deferred for a year. In that year, I ended up answering an ad for a position, then called "personnel clerk" and, as they say, the rest is history.

Within eight months I was promoted to a new position and, seven months later, I was promoted to be the company's first personnel manager. I knew I was very good at studying, so I used to do crazy things like take the California Labor Code home and read it. I attended every seminar I could, and I joined human resources associations to increase my HR knowledge. During this early part of my career, I also learned that what was important to key executives at the company was anything that increased revenue or improved the bottom line.

I remained with the company for more than thirteen years, and I was in the right place at the right time. My employment with that company afforded me some incredible exposure to issues involving human resources, risk management, and legal issues, and it was in a heavy manufacturing environment, which was important experience.

Since then I've worked at companies in different industries, giving me well-rounded knowledge to assist business owners. I've built HR and administrative infrastructures, and I've recruited in various industries. I've helped organizations successfully navigate the many challenges with mergers and acquisitions work, and I've been in companies that have either been rapidly growing or dramatically downsizing. I also have been part of the IPO process as a couple of companies became public entities.

All of this experience has taught me many lessons, developed me as a leader, and helps me today as a business consultant and trusted advisor to my clients.

WRIGHT

What led you to start your own consulting firm?

DUFFY

I was working in a marketing company, and I felt that it was the last piece of the puzzle I needed to learn before starting my own firm. I learned a remarkable amount of information on how to market my business and how to market myself in my business. I had always been very entrepreneurial by nature, and once I added that last piece to the puzzle I began to think about starting my own firm.

One day I was at lunch with my friend and mentor Jan, who said, "You know, you're never going to be happy until you are doing your own thing." To her it was obvious that I should start my own business, and she gave me the support and confidence I needed to take the first step. At that point, my energy became focused on what type of business I wanted and what services I would offer.

I saw a need for smaller and mid-sized companies to have access to more strategic level human resources advice. Many smaller companies have administrative level HR people or someone designated to wear multiple hats like the controller or an office manager. They are doing finance on Mondays and facilities on Tuesdays. When Wednesday comes along, they have to do HR work but don't have any knowledge or experience. That's okay for transactional tasks such as processing paperwork, but the founder needs someone to trust on a strategic level to help him or her solve the company's people problems. Founders can hire attorneys, but they can be expensive and often don't have practical real-world experience in a corporate environment.

I continually get feedback that my clients appreciate my practical advice. Instead of saying, "Here are the legal risks involved, and you'll have to make a business decision," I advise them how I would handle the situation based on best practices developed during more than twenty years of hands-on experience.

I guess that's a long way of saying that I started my business because I wanted to help companies that can't afford a strategic human capital professional on a full-time basis, but who see the value in having that partnership with an outside trusted advisor. My clients are passionate about their businesses and products, and they have expertise in manufacturing, engineering, accounting, sales, marketing, service, operations, and other functions. They just need a resource they can call to talk about people issues when they arise.

WRIGHT

What kinds of people challenges do your clients consult with you about?

DUFFY

Anything people-related. People are essential to every company, and payroll is often the largest line item in the budget. Yet, many executives don't devote the same attention to their people as they do to other areas of their business. I can't think of anything more critical to business success than investing time in your people.

My practice is focused on four main areas: recruiting, consulting, training, and mentoring. Often, my engagements start by auditing the human resources function for legal compliance and then best practices. Once owners or CEOs can sleep better knowing they are handling HR matters the correct way, I'm invited to help with other people-related challenges.

There are usually two main challenges: first and foremost, how to hire the right people and secondly, how to manage their performance once they are on board. Most companies hire too quickly and fire too slowly. The truth is, this should be reversed—managers should be slower to hire and should fire much more quickly than most of them do.

WRIGHT

What is the secret to hiring the right people?

DUFFY

For me, the key is starting with your outcome in mind, meaning where are you headed as a business? I've seen probably more than fifty thousand resumes in my career and hired more than fifteen hundred people. Some of those reported directly to me when I was in leadership roles, many worked with me in companies, and now they work for my clients' organizations. It doesn't matter what the position is or what the industry is, it all starts by getting clarity about where you are going as a business and then hiring the people who can help get you there. It sounds really basic, David, but I've found that many small businesses, and even some larger ones, don't take the time to get that clarity up front, both regarding where the company is headed during the next one to three years and secondly, clarity about the specific deliverables employees need to achieve to help the business succeed.

Getting that clarity about the business is important because it makes a difference in the employees you need to hire. Many candidates appear qualified on paper, but they may not be a good cultural fit. For example, if someone has worked only at large, publicly-traded companies, it might be difficult to fit into a smaller, family-owned business. In a larger firm, that person's position would most likely be specialized, and he or she generally would have access to greater resources. Moreover, some companies have a culture of risk-taking, while some are more conservative. Some are fast-paced, while others are more methodical. Understanding those cultural nuances is important when determining whether a new person will fit.

Similarly, you don't go out and hire a bunch of great athletes and then decide what sport to play, right? That would be backward. You could end up with a tennis player, a soccer star, a right-fielder, and a quarterback, and that's not going to make you very competitive in whatever game you play. If you're going to play baseball, you need someone who can play each position and bat in order to be successful. It's important to know what your outcome is so you know what success looks like in each position. And, it's critical to keep your culture in mind to ensure the people you hire will be a great fit with the rest of your team.

The same is true for the competitive landscape of the business world. The tool we use with our clients to get clarity about their business goals and what the newly hired employee must do to be successful is called a Success Profile™. (Readers can download a sample Success Profile from my Web site: www.EthosHCS.com.)

WRIGHT

Is a Success Profile like a job description?

DUFFY

There are certainly elements that are similar, but job descriptions are usually a static list of tasks with no link to the company's business objectives. The Success Profile contains specific and measurable deliverables that the newly hired employee must achieve to be successful. It is a dynamic document tied to the company's business objectives.

If you ask most hiring managers what they're looking for in their newly hired employee, they tend to list job qualifications such as having a college degree, having a certain number of years' experience in that exact industry, and then a list of attributes like self-motivation and being a team player. And, that's just for the receptionist—the list gets longer as you move up the organization. What we do is work with them to shift their thinking so they become focused on what candidates need to do once they come on board.

For example, it seems managers want everyone to have a college degree, and when asked why, they're sometimes stumped. If you're going to hire a CEO to start up a company, you might automatically say that he or she must have a college degree. But I think everyone would agree that Bill Gates and Steve Jobs have had successful careers, and they are both college dropouts.

Going back to the receptionist for a second, what the hiring manager really wants is to ensure that the receptionist can use proper verbal and written communication skills in order to draft e-mails and to speak with customers on the phone in a manner that reflects professionally on the organization. So, it's not about what the person has, but what the person will do with his or her skills and experience that makes a difference.

Using our Success Profile process requires hiring managers to focus on those outcomes rather than qualifications. I'm a huge fan of education, but we can all think of college grads who can't write a coherent thought. We can also think of people without a formal education who speak and write beautifully.

I developed the Success Profile process because it helps shift a manager's focus to what the employee must *do* to be successful. The process of developing the Success Profile starts with one key question: what will this newly hired employee need to do in the next twelve to twenty-four months to be successful? Asked another way: when I come back in six or twelve months and ask how Joe is doing, and you reply that Joe is a rock star, what has Joe done during that time to make you a raving fan? Those types of questions help the manager get clarity about the achievements needed to support the business plan.

The Success Profile itself contains different sections including a company overview, a summary of the position, how it fits into the organizational structure, and, most importantly, the smart goals and deliverables that will support the business plan. Of course, it also addresses some of the nuances of what will make someone successful in the particular position in terms of the cultural fit within that organization.

Let me give you a quick example of what I mean by that. Recently we did a search for one of our clients—a cell phone company. The position was for a human resources director. The Success Profile included a deliverable that said, "Within 180 days, work with the recruiter and director of training and planning to develop an ongoing process for new employees to A) quickly ramp them up to full productivity, B) provide an understanding of the company's goals, mission, vision, values, policies, and procedures, and C) ensure their successful integration into the company's culture."

When we first sat with the hiring manager to develop a Success Profile, he was insistent that the candidate have a certain number of years of retail experience. While retail experience would be helpful, what we felt was critical was finding someone who, first, could develop the culture and communicate with remote employees and, second, support the growth of the organization from twenty-five to forty stores in one year. This client had twenty-five stores across five different states. The plan was to open another eighteen stores. Finding somebody with retail experience in a large retail store, where all of the employees worked under one roof, wouldn't necessarily help this person be successful. It would be much easier to take someone who had remotely recruited, trained, and managed employees, and who had supported an organization through rapid growth, and teach them retail, rather than the other way around.

In the end, we found someone who had done all of those things in a retail setting so the client was ecstatic. But, the critical part of the process was the initial identification of where the business was moving and what needed to be done in the next one, two, or three years to support that business plan.

WRIGHT

After you have the Success Profile developed, what comes next?

DUFFY

There are two parts: knowing how to source and recruit candidates, and knowing how to properly interview to identify the right talent and cultural fit.

WRIGHT

Tell me more about sourcing and recruiting candidates.

DUFFY

Most of the people I come across who are struggling with hiring are struggling because they don't know how to recruit and source candidates. They only know how to hire the people they already know, so they look around and find a friend, a family member, someone they know from church, or maybe they're introduced to someone who needs a job.

If a business doesn't expand its network and go out and find the right people for the right positions, it's going to end up with unhappy and unproductive employees and a high level of turnover. What company leaders need to do is get that clarity up front about where they are headed and then focus on what the employees must do to be successful.

It's important to train internal recruiters to actually source candidates so they can identify candidates who may be passive and not actually looking for a new opportunity. You may be able to entice them to leave their current employer if you're offering a great opportunity. Many internal recruiters and hiring managers only know how to post an ad on a job board and sort through resumes.

When we source candidates for our clients, we use different techniques including researching and profiling companies within the same standard industrial classification (SIC) code, and then we find ways to connect with people within those organizations. This can be through cold-calling, online tools like LinkedIn, or general networking. We also use our extensive personal networks to help spread the word to get referrals.

In the case of the HR director mentioned earlier, the candidate who was ultimately hired wasn't looking. She had been at the same company for more than eight years and was happy. We found her on LinkedIn, approached her, and began a dialogue to see if she or someone she knew might be interested. We were able to show her how this might be a great opportunity for her, and, in her case, that meant leaving a manager level position in a larger organization for a director level position in a smaller organization where she would have a seat at the table with the other executives. It was a win for her because she had the opportunity to step into a higher level strategic role, and the company benefitted by being able to leverage her larger company experience as they grew. She wasn't actively seeking employment, so we would never have found her by just posting an ad and sorting through people who responded.

WRIGHT

Do you ever post recruiting ads on job boards? Are they ever successful?

DUFFY

Yes, they can be when they're well written and actually enticing to prospective employees. The trick is to not just rely on a job description and call it an "ad." Many companies post a job description on a job board, but it just lists all the tasks and qualifications needed for the job. Again, that doesn't cut it in a competitive business environment because that's not attractive to potential candidates. An effective ad is so much more. It needs to attract top performers by describing the opportunity, the projects they will work on, and the way their role factors into the company's strategy and success. Top performers want to make a difference, not just collect a paycheck.

When using ads, you also want to think about where to post them. You can use general job boards like Monster and CareerBuilder, or you can use niche boards that target a more narrowly defined group. Besides writing a great ad, you want to place it where your target audience will see it.

WRIGHT

You mentioned interviewing. What makes a great interview?

DUFFY

The best interviews are more like conversations where you and the candidate get to know each other. It's important to train your managers and recruiters and anyone else involved in the process to know how to ask open-ended, behavior-based, questions instead of yes/no questions. The trap that many interviewers fall into is talking too much instead of listening. They get nervous or they want to make sure that the candidate understands what they want, so they spend an hour telling the candidate about the job. A better approach is to ask the candidate questions to understand their experience and way of thinking so you can judge whether you feel it's a mutually good fit.

You want to make sure you can weed out the people who are good at interviewing and getting jobs for the people who will actually be good at doing the job. Again, it sounds like a simple distinction, but it's an important one.

Let's go back to the example of the Success Profile deliverable I mentioned for the human resources director. I could just ask, "Have you ever developed an orientation process for newly hired employees?" However, that can be easily answered yes or no. A better way of asking the question would be, "Will you tell me about a time you developed an orientation process for newly hired remote employees in a retail environment?" Assuming the candidate can provide such an example, there are many follow-up questions that can be asked, including:

- What types of challenges did you experience and how did you overcome them?
- With whom did you collaborate?
- How long did it take you to develop and implement the process?
- How did you measure the success of the program?

By asking these types of open-ended, behavioral questions, it's easy to determine whether the candidate actually did the work and how he or she approached the project.

Many people have difficulty interviewing because they become nervous or they're not sure what to ask. Preparation is key, and it takes practice. When we teach our clients how to interview, we help them focus on each of the deliverables in the Success Profile. If you've already identified what you expect the newly hired employees to do to be successful, you just need to develop questions based on each one of those deliverables. After that, it's just a matter of practicing until you're comfortable asking questions in a conversational manner.

WRIGHT

Does the Success Profile play a role once the employee comes on board?

DUFFY

Absolutely. It's a performance management tool and a road map for success. Candidates love it because they have clarity about what is expected of them. In fact, many candidates will self-select out of the recruiting process in early stages if the Success Profile doesn't describe what they like to do or what they believe will be a good personal fit. Managers love it because it provides a tool they can use to evaluate how the employees are performing. Either they are meeting those deliverables or not, but everybody has clarity about what is expected. That's why I don't like job descriptions—they are static and not tied to business objectives. Job descriptions, in my opinion, are generally obsolete before the ink dries.

Ideally, everyone in the company should have a Success Profile with deliverables that align with the overall company goals. It should be reviewed and updated as business conditions change, and at a minimum, once per year. It can be done at the time of a formal performance review or whatever feedback system the company uses. That's the best way to ensure that everyone is moving forward in the same direction.

That's another lesson I learned early in my career—it's important to make sure everyone in the company has individual goals aligned with the company's goals. We had a great process we used at one company where the executive team would meet on a regular basis to set the overall company direction. We maintained a rolling, six-quarter business plan that we reviewed monthly. Once we established the organization's goals, each of us went back to our respective departments to set individual goals for ourselves and the members of our team that would support those top level strategic goals. As we began to recruit new people, we knew what they would need to do to be successful in our department and the overall organization.

That process became the basis for the Success Profile, and it ensured that everyone in the company was in alignment and focused on success from day one.

WRIGHT

Some companies use assessments in hiring or managing employees. How do you feel about assessments?

DUFFY

I think they can be very useful if they're used correctly and if they are validated as a tool. You have to remember that there are certain legal restrictions on which types of tests and assessment tools can be used in certain environments. I also think people have to be wary of letting them become a crutch. We have some clients who have approached us about using assessments, but it's usually because they're not comfortable asking the right interview questions. Sometimes it's because they've had a lot of turnover in the past, and they don't feel confident that they can actually identify a candidate who will be successful in their environment. We encourage them to invest in training and developing their managers, rather than relying on a "test" of some sort.

Having said that, there is one tool in particular that we use a lot with our clients—the DiSC® assessment. The version we use is published by Inscape Publishing. They have been developing assessments for more than thirty years. The DiSC assessment is based on the 1920s work of a psychologist named William Moulton Marston. In his book, *Emotions of Normal People*, published in 1928, Marston identified what he called four "primary emotions" and their associated behavioral responses. Today, the DiSC assessment labels these four primary behavioral responses as Dominance, Influence, Steadiness, and Conscientiousness. Every person has all four styles within them; however, we tend to be more comfortable exhibiting behaviors associated with one or two of the styles. The DiSC is more of a behavioral assessment rather than a personality assessment that some companies use in hiring.

The DiSC is not a validated tool for hiring, but it's something that could help round out your selection and placement process. Suppose you have a group of candidates you're considering for an opening. You might be able to identify who might be the best fit within the organization or who might be able to round out a team if you're trying to put people together for projects. It should not be used to predict who is or isn't qualified for a type of job, but it's often useful as one additional piece of information in your selection process.

We also use it with our clients for team-building and coaching. There are a few different DiSC assessments that we use, one of which is designed for managers to help them grow as leaders and managers. We use another DiSC assessment, the Everything DiSC® Workplace profile, as the basis for training and building teams. Both teach people how to identify their own behavioral style, quickly recognize others' styles, and then how to close a communication gap if one exists. It's an effective tool in any relationship and it can improve relationships with managers, direct reports, and co-workers.

David, what I have found is that most people come from their own behavioral and communication style. They believe that everybody thinks the same way they do and has the same rules for their values. Then you get in the real world and you find out that's not always the case. Teaching them about DiSC increases their understanding that there are multiple ways to evaluate and respond to situations. It fosters great teamwork and reduces conflict and communication problems within an organization.

WRIGHT

You said earlier that managers are quick to hire and too slow to fire. What did you mean?

DUFFY

Most of the managers we deal with struggle with filling an opening. They feel pressured to hire because work isn't getting done or they might be paying overtime to get it done. They turn to the person closest to them or slip into the "get me a body syndrome" where if you can fog a mirror, you get the job.

Often this results in disaster because they haven't taken their time to identify the right candidates or ensure they'll be a good cultural fit. Unfortunately, once they're on board, the manager is reluctant to fire them because they'll be back to the same problem. If they're getting any level of productivity out of the employee, they figure it's better than none. Sometimes months and years go by before the problem is addressed. The employee isn't meeting expectations, but managers aren't sure how to handle it. Consequently, they do nothing.

Managers are people, too, and their emotions play a role in their decision-making. Often they ignore problems hoping they'll go away without needing to have a difficult conversation, or maybe they buy into the employee's story about how he or she is going to try harder or do better. Let's face it—it's hard for many of us to be critical of others, especially if we like them or we're afraid criticism will worsen the relationship.

But as time goes by, and without improvement in the performance, another less visible problem has developed: other employees begin to question the effectiveness of that manager. I often receive calls where managers will say, "I've got this problem employee," and they don't know how to handle it. As I start asking questions about the situation, I'll find out that the employee has been there five or six years. When I ask how long there has been a performance problem, I often hear that the problem has been there from the beginning and nothing has been done to resolve it.

There was actually a situation that occurred early in my career, and I learned an important lesson. My company had hired a new production manager named Chinh. She came into an environment where there was an existing workforce, and she replaced another production manager. There was one employee named Sally who worked in that department and had been in the company for a very long time. She was well-liked by everybody else on the team, but she had a tremendous attendance problem.

After a few weeks on the job, Chinh came to me and said, "I don't know what to do. I feel that if I fire Sally, everybody is going to hate me." Coaching Sally and using progressive disciplinary steps with her had resulted in no improvement. Sally felt she could get away with her bad attendance because she had been getting away with it for years.

Finally, one day Chinh decided to do what she felt was right and fire Sally. She was concerned about the response from the rest of the workforce, but exactly the opposite than what she feared happened. Instead of the employees disliking her for taking that action, they actually came to her and expressed how happy they were that someone finally did something about the problem. The level of respect that the employees had for Chinh went up dramatically because it was the first time somebody actually addressed the problem. The teamwork and productivity in the department increased after Sally was gone. This taught me that when you don't address a problem, such as a performance issue, you not only accept the poor performance of one employee, but it can actually lower the performance overall because of the effect it has on everyone else. It also taught me that people respect leaders who can make a tough decision.

Perhaps you recall that in 2007, Gallup did a poll of more than one million employees. It was found that the number one factor in determining how long employees stay in a job and how productive they are in that position is determined by the relationship they have with their immediate supervisor. Employees can definitely affect the bottom line, when they are dissatisfied, through poor productivity and higher turnover. That's why it's important that managers are trained, mentored, and coached in management and leadership areas. The sooner they learn how to hire the right people and quickly address performance issues that arise, the more successful the company will be.

WRIGHT

You seem passionate about what you do. What do you like the best about your role?

DUFFY

For me it's all about making a difference in someone's life each day—personally or professionally. I love solving problems and making connections for people.

Just today, before taking this call, I helped a client solve one of his people problems. Unfortunately, he needed to let an employee go because his business has downsized. As a small employer, his company doesn't have a full-time human capital professional on staff, so the company relies on me to help its leaders through those difficult decisions and processes. On that same call, I learned the company was having some technical problems, and I was able to connect them with the CEO of an IT company who can help. My client was happy. I also referred business to the IT professional, so he's happy, too. Even better, that CEO is looking to hire someone, and I introduced him to someone in my network who is looking for an IT job. I think he will be a great fit for the IT CEO's organization, so I'm hoping that works out.

Days like those I enjoy the most—I can help people solve their problems and put people together who can help each other. If I can make a difference in someone's life, I've had a great day.

WRIGHT

Today I have been talking with Linda Duffy, founder and president of Ethos Human Capital Solutions. Known as The People Problem Solver, Linda and her firm work with corporate clients to help them get the right people, systems, and culture in place to achieve their business goals.

Linda, thank you for talking with our readers today about your *ROADMAP to Success.*

DUFFY

Thanks so much for having me, David. I appreciate it, and I had a great time talking with you.

About the Author

Linda M. Duffy, founder and president of Ethos Human Capital Solutions, has parlayed twenty years of executive human capital experience into a thriving business that provides recruiting, consulting, training, and career transition services. Known as The People Problem Solver®, Linda and her firm provide strategic human resource solutions that help corporations attract and retain top talent, solve complex people problems, develop leaders to peak performers, and mentor professionals through career transitions. Some of the industries they serve are high-tech, manufacturing, professional services, as well as nonprofit organizations. Ethos Human Capital Solutions works with founder- and CEO-led businesses and specializes in proving support for rapid growth, downsizing, and mergers/acquisitions.

Linda M. Duffy

Ethos Human Capital Solutions
949-525-0138
Linda@EthosHCS.com
www.EthosHCS.com

Chapter Eight

BUILDING HIGH VALUE RELATIONSHIPS

RANDY NOE

DAVID WRIGHT (WRIGHT)

Today I'm talking with Randy Noe. Randy specializes in building high-value relationships for executive leadership and career development. With more than twenty years' senior leadership, operations, and finance experience, Randy brings business perspective and best practices from working with thousands of C level and vice president executives. He led the regional financial valuation practice for a major global accounting tax advisory firm, directed mergers and acquisitions for a public software company, treasury operations for a $500 million manufacturing and retail company, and has participated in numerous complex transactions in excess of $1 billion.

He understands the pressures business leaders face because he has been there. He speaks their language and knows the drivers that create and sustain business value. Randy has coached executives from global companies to small business enterprises for clients including Accenture, Cisco Systems, Edwards Lifesciences, Honeywell, Philips, Quest Software, and Thomson Reuters. Randy is a Chartered Financial Analyst and holds an MBA in Finance from the University of Southern California and a Bachelor of Arts degree in Psychology from San Diego State University.

Randy, welcome to *ROADMAP to Success*.

RANDY NOE (NOE)
Thank you, David, glad to be here.

WRIGHT
So how do you define and measure business success?

NOE
From a strictly valuation and analytical standpoint, there are five drivers that create and sustain business value. The first is growth, the top line revenue, including the overall trend and the rate of acceleration. The second is the profitability that comes from increases in revenue and/or reduced expenses. The third driver is the riskiness of projected cash flows. The more predictable and reliable the projected cash flows, the lower the discount rate that is applied and the higher the value. The fourth driver is operational control—having the ability to set strategy and direction of the business, which also includes efficiency from a functioning and engaged workforce. The last factor that drives value is marketability of the stock, which includes the financial condition of the company, liquidity, leverage, and the ability to readily obtain financing, as well as corporate branding and how the company is viewed by its customers and the community.

Each of these value driver variables individually and in combination influences pricing multiples and discount rates for projected cash flows, and facilitates a comparative analysis for benchmarking with other companies. They are results that are derived and optimized from having a successful overall business strategy. The heart of the business needs to be addressed and understood as well.

WRIGHT
What do you see as key elements in the most successful business strategies?

NOE
I've worked with hundreds of companies; I've seen good ones and bad ones, big ones and small ones. I've also had the pleasure of working closely with executive leaders including many impressive inspirational people as well as some dysfunctional types and everything in between. The key differentiators I have experienced are really twofold—the leadership and the culture of the business. One of my fundamental basic assertions is that relationships are assets, and cultivating high value relationships is a strategy. This includes the attention and intention to a core value of connectedness and the behavior and attitude mind-set to enable healthy relationships with customers, employees, and all invested stakeholders.

What works for fostering individual relationships extends to the collective whole, too.

WRIGHT

Can the value of relationships be defined or measured?

NOE

Human beings are wonderfully complex and there are a myriad of qualitative factors in our relationships. We must be careful not to label, judge, or put anyone in a defined box.

If we see and treat human beings as disposable assets like computers, they will have a limited useful life. We'll get a short-term return, as they will work hard for us then burn out every two or three years. We'll have a lot of churn with high employee turnover.

Let's consider the same value drivers to businesses and how they might apply to our relationships. Let's look at growth. Does this relationship enable our growth? Are we learning, being affirmed, encouraged, moving forward in a healthy way?

Let's look at profitability, the next business value driver. Is this relationship generating revenue, or providing referrals? You don't need all of the above, any will contribute value to a relationship. Someone could be sending a flow of referrals yet we don't grow otherwise because we don't see each other often.

The predictability or riskiness of the projected cash flow of the business can also be considered for relationships as well. Is the relationship stable, or emotionally volatile with a negative cycle of pushing each other's buttons? Is there a foundation of reliability, consistency, integrity, authenticity, and trustworthiness?

Operational control is not to be confused with command and control or domination of another. It is more akin to efficiency or flow of the relationship, or effectiveness in communication. Are we communicating clearly and cleanly, really listening to each other?

Lastly, when we think about marketability, does this relationship mutually enhance our reputation, our branding? Is it valuable to know or be associated with each other in the marketplace?

Any of these factors provide value to a relationship. Relationships do not need to have all factors to be valuable to us. An absence or deficiency in a factor can sometimes be offset by a strong connection in other factors. However, if all factors are absent or negative, the relationship should be evaluated. Some relationships are unproductive with low value and low utility. Others can detract value by draining our energy, consuming time and other resources.

WRIGHT

What are the characteristics of the most successful organizational cultures?

NOE

The most successful cultures have clarity across the organization. We all know who we are, what we want, and where we want to go. We have shared values, particularly integrity, client service focus, work ethic, trust, and mutual respect. We also have clarity as individuals. Aligned with the common overall vision and mission of the business, I also know who I am, what I want to accomplish, and where I want to go with my individual contribution to the success of the business.

Interdependent relationships and interactions are the key to successful cultures. An internal culture of collegiality fosters camaraderie, encouragement, truth-telling, and leveraging of individual and team strengths.

WRIGHT

So how do we assess our own business culture or leadership brand?

NOE

Our business, leadership, or personal brand is not just what we say and assert. It's also how we say it and how we display it. Even more important is how the market sees, perceives, experiences, and interacts with us. For example, we can assert to the market that we are a turnaround specialist, but if people perceive us as an angry, condescending jerk, then that's our brand.

The mission of any individual or business is combining what we love to do with what the market wants. I can assess or learn about my brand by listening to the market. I can ask people around me—customers, employees and others—how they see me and what my special genius work is from their experience and interactions. If we're receptive to feedback, the market will often give us gifts, revealing some things we may not know or appreciate otherwise.

Other clues are available from the market as well. How easy or how hard is it to recruit and retain employees? What do people say about us when they leave the room or the company?

WRIGHT

What do you think are the characteristics of the most successful leaders?

NOE

I ask my clients often to reflect on the best leaders they have ever worked for and what made them so great. The best leaders are visionaries who are able to balance the big picture and longer-term strategic objectives with short-term tactical execution. They're very comfortable with ambiguity and navigating change. They have an adaptable leadership style appropriate to situational, group, or individual needs.

In addition, best leaders are very self-aware, not to be confused with either self-absorbed or self-centered. It is easy for others to see them. They lead with authenticity—being the best they can be and not a poor imitation of someone else. This is who I am no matter what others think. They drop the ego and veneer and lead by telling the truth from both the head and the heart. They are able to be vulnerable without giving up their empowerment. They have very positive self-talk and a healthy, contagious enthusiasm that attracts. They're also curious, continuous learners.

They empower others around them, they provide clear vision and direction then get out of the way and let their people proceed. They trust, even love their people. They have empathy for others. Empathy is not "how is your dog?" It is about genuinely caring about the hopes and dreams of people working with and for them.

Once employees know you care they will take a hill for you. And they'll take the next one, too. Leaders with empathy are perceived as different and it's really impressive and emboldening to experience it.

WRIGHT

Can empathy be developed?

NOE

Yes! The encouraging thing about empathy is that while some have a preference to lead with feelings and the heart, empathy itself is a core element of emotional intelligence that can indeed be developed. As we become more and more successful as leaders, our need for additional technical knowledge and skill decreases—attaining another certification adds less incremental value over time, whereas our social- and self-awareness can improve day by day for the rest of our lives.

Empathy can be improved by growing our own self-awareness. This includes understanding the underlying factors that drive our behavior, our life experiences and personality preferences, our beliefs, values and perceptions, motivations, and attitude. With motivation to be a leader, empathy is being curious about what factors are driving someone else's behavior. It's not diagnosing per se. Rather, it's being curious. When I observe changes in people's behavior, I wonder. Has something happened in their life experience? Are they tired, adapting out of preference, not engaging their strengths? I wonder if they've been poked in a value or a belief, or maybe they haven't been recognized lately. Then, using a leadership style that is appropriate to the person and the situation, to check in and connect.

WRIGHT

What can we learn from the least effective organizational cultures and leaders?

NOE

Well, one thing we often learn when I ask clients to tell me about the worst leader they've ever worked for is that we carry them around with us. They are still very much a part of our life experience, and easy to recall fairly quickly for many people. The key is what can we learn from them? Also, we can stop giving them power by moving them off to the side instead of keeping them in front of us where we continue stumbling and tripping over them.

The least effective or worst cultures tend to be internally competitive. Everyone is out for themselves. Relationships are compromised in a command-and-control environment, with hyper rapid turnover that inhibits the investment in getting to know people.

The behavior and attitude mind-set of the least effective or worst leaders is self-focused. This is often evidenced by emotional volatility or inconsistency, hidden agendas, selective memory, and insecure, defensive, and overly critical behaviors. Worst leaders are often described as overly critical micromanagers, fixed in their positions, very narrow-minded, and closed to receiving input and feedback. They treat people as disposable assets. They are condescending toward others and play favorites.

Internally competitive cultures without shared vision results in people moving in different directions, making it hard to move forward, less productive, and inefficient with more distractions.

WRIGHT

What core leadership practices enable greatest sustainable business success?

NOE

There are four core research and success-based leadership practices I use with my clients. The first is continuous learning, which uses concepts of Otto Scharmer's Theory U and The Presencing Institute. It's about slowing down and opening up the mind, the heart, and the will. We also need to suspend voices of judgment, cynicism, and fear, letting go so that we can be liberated to move forward.

Next is positivity. There has been some impressive research from Barbara Frederickson in North Carolina and Martin Seligman in Pennsylvania, among others. Positivity has several dimensions that can be developed and understood. What gives us joy? For what are we grateful? What gives us serenity, what interests draw us in? What gives us hope looking forward? What makes us proud? What makes us laugh? What inspires us? Being open and being positive are related. The two feed each other and create an upward spiral for individuals and organizations.

Third is a solutions focus. Here I refer to some incredible cutting edge research coming from the neuro-leadership community. David Rock and others are translators of the research and leadership applications. This includes what we give our attention, how we relate to each other, and our ability to quiet the mind to generate new insights.

The fourth practice is emotional intelligence. Research by Daniel Goleman and others build upon self-awareness and drivers of behavior. Self-regulation is a key factor, the ability to not give power away to anything or anyone to hijack our life. This enables us to stay motivated and be the leader we aspire to be. We can be empathetic and curious about what is driving another individual's behavior, and develop social skills to lead many. The ability to both calm and quiet the mind are characteristics of best leaders as well. Self-regulation is the ability to calm the mind, whereas quieting the mind is the ability to focus.

You can engage any and all of these practices by yourself, but there is one additional critical piece—connectedness. Merging these practices with each other, and more importantly, having high value relationships more rapidly accelerate the upward spiral toward finding new insights and innovative solutions.

WRIGHT

So what is the starting point for enabling collective and individual success?

NOE

The starting point in terms of process is counterintuitive—the starting point is to stop. There are two traps that affect organizations and individuals: One is running a hundred miles an hour trying to do a hundred things a day, busy doing the same things over and over. Pick your metaphor, running the rat race or on a treadmill or like a bull charging the streets of Pamplona, we download with tunnel vision and apply past solutions to new problems. This very day, many people woke up tired and hit the snooze alarm. When it went off again, we hit it again, and again, until finally there is no more time, and before we've even put our feet on the floor we do something like Fred Flintstone driving his car—we hit the ground running. If we don't see ourselves doing that, we can go on like that for how long? For how many days, or how many years are we running?

The other trap is the opposite. Instead of doing and doing all the time and never thinking, it's thinking, thinking, thinking but never doing anything. With analysis paralysis, we worry about the future, regret the past, and thereby miss living in the present. Depending on how we compartmentalize our lives, we could actually have both going on simultaneously.

We start by stopping, and slowing ourselves down. Instead of trying to press or force a mountain to move, we walk toward it. We open up to receive incoming new ideas, to solutions, and let others into our life. One executive shared that she was fiercely independent and the key to her success was learning to let others in and not trying to do everything herself. We can build alliances with people who have subject matter expertise that can complement us with their sales, marketing, finance, IT, organizational development, or human resources acumen. We can foster a culture of supportive relationships with peer coaching, feedback, and feed forward.

I learned this myself in my own transition experience: When you try and navigate the change curve by doing things all by yourself, you can find yourself hitting bottom. I experienced isolation and it's one of the worst words in the English language. We are not alone, and it's important to plant people on our calendar. We have healthy, valued relationships that fill our life and affirm and lift the spirit. Engaging the change curve, then, is also about slowing down to engage the learning and growth that is happening, not trying to force, press, or avoid it by zip-lining across it, or making it so deep by going it alone.

WRIGHT

What are some of the greatest challenges and hurdles to overcome?

NOE

In order to open up we need to confront some natural resisters. The first is to suspend our voice of judgment. We tell ourselves we know everything and have all the answers. We need to open up to the possibility that maybe there is something else out there. When I meet someone who takes an adamant stance, I let them know I appreciate their passionate position, and while I may or may not agree with them I shift the focus by asking them now that they have that part of their life figured out, what are they curious to learn about next?

Another challenge is to listen to others around us. I could think for the rest of my life and never come up with an answer by myself, but if I listen to different perspectives and world views of others, I can get an insight that fits just like a piece of the jigsaw puzzle; I would have never seen it otherwise. These insights don't just come from predictable sources like trusted advisors, consultants, or subject matter experts. They can come from anywhere at any time—from the person behind the counter at Starbucks or a toll booth operator reminding us to have a nice day or from our kids when they remind us that we need to take breaks.

We also need to learn to let go of whatever is holding us back from running our very best race. We need to forgive people who have hurt us in the past and stop giving them space in the present or the future. Instead of letting others push our buttons, we need to grow our capacity to self-regulate and not give power to anyone to hijack our life. Sometimes like moths we stick to the source of our anxiety. We can't get beyond it because we can't see it.

We need to let go of emotional baggage we've been holding on to—anger, disappointment, envy, hyper-competitiveness, and adamant stances. It's like holding beach balls underwater, we can hold them as long as we want but it's really hard to swim that way.

Another challenge is trying to look beyond the present and see too far down the road. When I have tunnel vision, I drive by new ideas, new relationships, and even miss seeing the miracles that happen all day long. Why is it so important to have absolute certainty about the future? I can learn to embrace uncertainty, keeping the big picture in mind. I can understand and accept that I don't know what I don't know, and that's okay.

WRIGHT

So how does executive leadership coaching enable business success?

NOE

Successful executive coaching starts with the context itself—the current challenges, changes, and leadership issues. We need to define what we want to achieve. What's going on with our personal effectiveness? Do we want more influence? Are we morphing or stepping up to a new role? Do we need better team alignment? Are we navigating an industry or company change?

Next is readiness—the desire and willingness of the individual to do something about it. If you can't see it, you can't address it, and if you're unwilling to change you're not ready for coaching.

A client was preparing for a very important meeting and asked for coaching support. As we sat across the table from each other, she leaned in toward me, crossed her arms, and told me she had been getting a lot of feedback that she was coming off aggressive. I interrupted her flow and asked her to freeze. I then asked how that behavior had been working for her, and shared that was exactly how I was experiencing her in that moment. I then asked her what she loved about her job. I watched her lean back into her chair as she reflected on the question. Her whole body shifted, along with her behavior. From that point on she began to engage her life from that standpoint. She realized tremendous success in the meeting, and got exactly what she wanted to accomplish and where she wanted to go. It was impressive to see her catch this for herself.

Then there is connectedness—is this the right chemistry relationship, the right coach who can provide the safe environment? David, what I do is meet people right where they are. I hold a mirror for them and create a safe environment for learning and growth. I encourage with a core value of tolerance, loving people in our differences. We do not all have to be the same.

I listen, ask curious questions, challenge assumptions, see possibilities, explore options, and look at things from a different point of view. Are we seeking to help and empower others, or seeking followers? Are we leading with our positivity or with our adamant positions? Are we able to be open and vulnerable without giving up our empowerment? Are we loving and being loved, letting others into our life? Are we dog-paddling in the river right now, or rolling over and floating? Are we living from a joy-to-joy experience, or from worry to worry?

I don't fix, change, or save anyone, though sometimes I catch them. If someone wants to swim in the rapids, I don't jump in with him or her. I stand on the shoreline and extend my hand out toward the person, or sometimes just wave. Whenever there is an "a-ha" breakthrough moment, I encourage my clients to be gentle with themselves and not beat themselves up wishing they'd known ten years ago. I tell them to be grateful they know it now and that they hadn't learned it ten years from now.

I believe nothing is ironic or coincidental. We just see the connections and the connectedness in relationships. In my view, nothing is more fulfilling in business and life than the value of emerging and enduring friendships. And that will drive business value, leadership, and personal success.

WRIGHT

Well, what a great conversation, Randy. I have really learned a lot; I've been taking copious notes here. I can apply this to my own business and I really do appreciate all the time you've taken with me to answer these questions. Our readers are really going to get a lot of information from this chapter and it's going to be a tremendous asset to our book.

NOE

David, it has been a real pleasure. In cultivating high value relationships, we start with our first conversation and off we go.

WRIGHT

Today I have been talking with Randy Noe. Randy brings business perspective and best practices from working with thousands of C-level and VP executives. He understands the pressures business leaders face because he's been there, he speaks their language, and he knows the drivers that create and sustain business value. I'm listening to him today, but you had the opportunity to read what he had to say.

Randy, thank you so much for being with us today on *ROADMAP to Success*.

NOE

Thank you very much, David.

About the Author

Randy Noe builds high-value relationships for executive leadership and career development. With more than twenty years' senior leadership, operations, and finance experience, Randy brings business perspective and best practices from working with thousands of C-level and VP executives. He understands the pressures business leaders face because he's been there, he speaks their language, and knows the drivers that create and sustain business value. Randy led the Regional Financial Valuation practice for a major global accounting/tax advisory firm, directed mergers and acquisitions for a public software company, treasury operations for a $500 million manufacturing and retail company, and participated in numerous complex $1 billion transactions.

Randy has coached executives from global companies to small business enterprises for clients including Accenture, Cisco Systems, Edwards Lifesciences, Honeywell, McGladrey, Philips, Quest Software, and Thomson Reuters.

Randy Noe

Randy Noe Coaching
Encinitas, CA 92024
760-650-6586
randy@randynoe.com
www.randynoe.com

THE FOUR CHANNELS:

ALL YOU ARE IS ALL YOU NEED

HOLLY LATTY-MANN, PHD

DAVID WRIGHT (WRIGHT)

Today, I am talking with Holly Latty-Mann. Dr. Latty-Mann is the president and co-founder (with the late Dr. Jim Farr) of The Leadership Trust®. Imagine a software application with an accompanying user manual for becoming wildly self-aware and successful that we humanoids could download and run. This user-friendly transformation program offers four applications representing our Four Channels™ through which we operate to unleash our full human potential—Mind, Body, Emotions, and Spirit. It would scan for malware and other viruses in our bio-computer, correct them, and load in the turnaround performance applications. When we use our Master Channel™ (Spirit), it becomes our virtual road map to success. Until these downloadable applications become available, enjoy this chapter on the anatomy of your success.

Dr. Latty-Mann, welcome to *Roadmap to Success*.

You are a psychologist, yet your primary work is helping leaders become successful. How did that happen, and how much personal development must someone in a corporate environment undergo to achieve success in leadership roles?

HOLLY LATTY-MANN (LATTY-MANN)

Leadership is all about relationships and the quality of your relationships is a function of the nature of your personality, which, of course, is the work of psychologists. So, whatever gets tweaked in your personality through personal development will influence every arena of your life. It's just another way of saying, "Wherever you go, there you are!"

Following my internship in clinical psychology, I chose to work in the leadership industry because it offers the opportunity to impact more people in one fell swoop due to a leader's far-reaching influence on those around him or her, whether good or bad. This includes family members of not only the leader in question, but also the family members of those within the leader's sphere of influence. It truly has a ripple effect, and changing harmful ripples into positive ones is the work of both psychologists and those involved in helping leaders become successful.

When a person goes home after having been demoralized at work, that person may take it out on his or her spouse and children. I saw that happen in my own family growing up, and I hear it repeatedly in my leadership workshops. If I can help an executive experience more meaningful and harmonious relationships both at work and at home, I am vicariously improving the quality of life of all the people he or she influences.

So it stands to reason that the need for personal development for people in leadership roles is fundamental. The way I look at leadership development is through the lens of self-awareness, of which the focus is on one's mind, body, and emotions; I say you can't get much more personal than that. *Think about it:* mind, body, and emotions—put it all together, and you've got yourself a personality, and that becomes your delivery system. If people don't like your delivery system, they won't be following your lead. (They may not marry you, either, for that matter.)

Speaking of marriage, work affects home, and home affects work. Some people attempt to compartmentalize their life and think that they can separate their home life from their work life. You can't fool yourself this way. Work does indeed affect home and vice versa, and the degree to which we acknowledge this is also a function of self-awareness.

Leaders, like anyone else, need to do inventory. Whatever beliefs are in their head are creating a pattern of how they treat people. Once people catch on to the notion that *what they put out there comes back in kind,* they become more mindful of how they are being perceived by others. I call it the Boomerang Effect™, and it's as close to a psychological law of the universe as physics is to the physical world. If you're basically supportive of others in all your interactions, you're essentially creating a supportive environment for yourself, as people are more inclined to respond to you in kind. I should add that this is one reason why selfish people tend to be the most unhappy people of all out there.

While some people might want to argue that great leadership is all about being a great visionary, it still remains that a leader with a great vision must inspire and motivate everyone to support the company vision. This once again puts the focus back onto relationships and the need for managing others' perceptions of them. This is personal development at its best.

WRIGHT

Your internship at Duke Medical Center apparently played a major role in your holistic, integrative approach for people seeking wholeness and happiness. How did this experience inspire the way you developed models for success for those beyond a hospital setting?

LATTY-MANN

First of all, the medical model is an excellent model for attaining success in any setting. Rather than focusing predominantly on a person's physical health, I was looking at my work with people outside of the medical field as being in the business of promoting personality and relationship health.

Physicians know that if they can diagnose the problem, then they can apply the corresponding treatment plan. So if those of us in the helping profession, like the authors in this book, can "diagnose" what is *not working*, which takes a good dose of self-awareness, we can start to figure out what *does work*. It is why, for example, AA says the first step in owning one's problem is to state that he or she is an alcoholic. So in the case of relationship health, if someone can recognize he or she is a Dysfunctional Pleaser™, and say, "I have the disease to please," then this person is now in a position to figure out what to do about it.

Little did I know back when I was a part of a grassroots initiative for holistic, integrative medicine at Duke that these principles would set the stage for how I would help others achieve success more expediently. This was beyond anything I had ever experienced in the more traditional settings. While it was easy to appreciate how mind, body, and emotions all worked together toward optimal physical health, it was during this time I took Duke's holistic (mind, body, and spirit) findings and applied them to what I had gleaned from my doctoral programs in both social and clinical psychology.

I also knew to search for root cause in distressed relationships rather than simply treat the symptoms of discord. And while it was clear to me how the degree of self-awareness was a major factor in healing, it had an intuitive appeal that the same model could likewise be applied toward increasing life satisfaction or success.

Other than with patients, I had also been using holistic models helping couples in intimate relationships determine what beliefs (we're talking about the mind here), what facial gestures (e.g., the body), and what emotions (both expressed and hidden) were at play in their discord.

Duke was giving me the spirit piece that was missing in doctoral programs. Fortunately, society was starting to soften to words like spirituality back in the mid to late 1990s. The medical industry and hospitals like Duke were promoting their "mind, body, and spirit" model for promoting physical well-being.

So it was truly serendipitous that following my internship I found a behavioral science firm that trained leaders using these same holistic principles Duke espoused with patients and that I was using with couples.

It was another good turn of events to discover early on in this leadership training facility that the CEO (the late Dr. Jim Farr) and I shared remarkably similar ideologies with enough discrepancies to make for spirited discourse leading to theoretical and methodological tweaks. So it wasn't long before we were working alongside each other almost like two mad scientists creating new models while preserving our own individual contributions.

I'd like to add that when I was invited to be interviewed for a chapter in your project, *Roadmap to Success*, I knew it was important to share these basic and expanded self-awareness models for others to benefit in their journey toward attaining their definition of success.

WRIGHT

What are the specifics of this holistic, integrative approach that these self-awareness models offer to promote optimal life satisfaction?

LATTY-MANN

Let's start with what I call the granddaddy or grandmama self-awareness model. It is synonymous with the "mind, body, emotions, and spirit" holistic model. I refer to these as the Four Channels with spirit being the Master Channel. While we can describe each component or channel individually, all work within each channel is to be done within the context of the remaining channels. And when there is proper alignment in place among the three channels of mind, body, and emotions, we humans are operating at our best. More accurately, we're operating from our Master Channel, or spirit, when these three lesser channels are in alignment with one another. So, no matter what our "stuff," when we are operating from our spiritual essence, we don't get triggered by others' remarks or behaviors. Neither do we generate or entertain negativity from outside sources for long.

My friend and co-founding business partner, Jim Farr, offered a compelling visual for this holistic model. I will therefore ask that you imagine three circles on top of one another, like a snowman. Now label each circle going from the top to the bottom using the words Mind, Body, and Emotions. Now put a large circle to the left of this holistic "snowman," and label it Spirit. What you envision should look similar to the following model:

Because self-awareness is key to a happy and successful life, we have to acknowledge in this model that there is an unaware side of us that creates havoc. With this in mind, note the long line down the center of the three circles. Everything to the right of the line represents your awareness, and everything to the left represents unawareness. Now let's look at each of these three channels from an awareness versus an unawareness perspective.

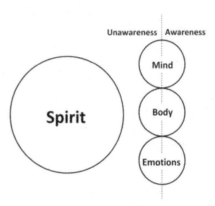

Because both sides of the mind have programs dictating our future actions, it's important that we become aware of previously unaware programs that are acting like saboteurs to our otherwise good intentions. *Now how does one become aware of that of which he or she is unaware?* Better put: *how can you know what you don't know?* It's not that hard when we are operating from heightened self-awareness, but too often, people are operating from automaticity rather than through choice—somewhat like a robot. For example, when we choose not to hear negative feedback because our feelings have been hurt, we've missed a chance to grow our self-awareness. Out of habit, we defend ourselves from an observation we don't like, which sends a strong message to the mind to stay as is.

If we look at our body within the same manner of its having an aware and unaware side, it's amazing how few people are aware of how they are being perceived by others. If some people knew the scowl that stays on their face at work or at home, they could better appreciate that people are often responding to how they look rather than what's being said. So that would be an unawareness piece. Ralph Waldo Emerson said, "What you are speaks so loudly, I cannot hear

> *"What you are speaks so loudly, I cannot hear what you're saying."*
> ~Ralph Waldo Emerson

what you're saying."

Much of our body language and facial expressions are simply learned, yet according to research, people are placing some 55 percent of their attention on the speaker's body while listening, with another 38 percent of their attention going to the tone of voice, and only 7 percent is actually focused on the speaker's words. It's important that we pay special attention to how we're physically coming across to people. For example, we may feel relaxed with our arms folded but that could be sending a message that we are closed off.

As for emotions, we may be aware that we are angry, but how often in the midst of feeling angry are we aware that it is really a cover for hurt, fear, or sadness? Once we become aware of that of which we had been unaware, we can now go about the business of turning it around. Self-awareness is the first step. If we don't know, we can't fix, and if we keep doing what we've been doing, we'll keep getting what we've been getting.

The integrative aspect to this model has two-fold significance. For one, it speaks loudly to our need to integrate harmoniously our mind, body, and emotions via our Master Channel (Spirit), our source of all good. Secondly, upon choosing that direction with our free will, only then can we enjoy the harmonious integration of our work life, home life, and social life. It is through this power of choice that we can ultimately discover with a genuine sense of reverence that *all we are is all we need.*

WRIGHT

Your research on attachment theory makes a clear argument that our early childhood experiences influence the quality of our relationships later on in life. Please elaborate on that within the context of this model.

LATTY-MANN

Great leaders, or for that matter, great lovers, are not born. They are made. It all boils down to the choices we make throughout our life, which are influenced by how we view ourselves and others. At a very young age, we create a view of how safe it is to navigate out there as well as how loveable we are, and often these two programs are mutually reinforcing. They play out into our romantic relationships later on in life as well as how we interact with others at work. This is all based on how we as kids interpreted the events surrounding us during our early years.

Attachment theory holds that children tend to develop a certain attachment style in response to the way parents engage them based on their own style, which can be described as secure, intrusive, anxious, avoidant, negligent, unpredictable, abusive, etc. These styles create the basis for an adult romantic attachment style later on in life. It further influences how they engage others in non-intimate settings. Depending on how extreme or how secure versus insecure one's style, such patterns can affect the quality of one's relationships for a lifetime, unless he or she learns to act out of choice.

Go back to the self-awareness model with the Four Channels and pretend that someone just received negative feedback. Depending upon attachment style and therefore certain beliefs about self and others that are an intrinsic part of each style, there will be predictable reactions in alignment with that style. If the person in question operates predominantly out of a secure attachment style, then there is a greater likelihood he or she will be responding out of choice and therefore will likely handle the negative feedback more appropriately and grow from it.

The beliefs in the unaware part of the mind of someone with an insecure attachment style are attached to negative emotion. And depending on how much negative energy is housed there, that can explain why some people are more easily triggered by negative comments than others.

Through self-awareness, we can start to get rid of some of the negative energy that seems to fuel the degree of negative reaction to whatever it was we didn't like. This entails being mindful in the moment when someone disrupts our otherwise neutral state of mind. Instead of shutting down or arguing, perhaps the new behavior that requires mental re-wiring is simply asking the source of the negative comment for clarification in a factual, non-emotional way. It may also entail our being aware that our anger is actually covering up our hurt by that comment and that it's best not to act on the anger but rather own the hurt and manage the anger.

For those interested in how early family dynamics can play out in leadership roles at work, certain issues from *Harvard Business Review* (when Tom Stewart was editor) speak to how our response to our early family dynamics indeed determine, in large part, how successfully we cope and manage important relationships at work.

Although it is usually not necessary to remember certain events that happened early in life, it can offer insight and thus be helpful in our quest to make changes. Otherwise, being aware of when we first find ourselves feeling negative allows for insightful introspection and a chance to change.

Because your reality is a function of your choices, the real question here becomes whether or not you choose to act on your chance to change.

WRIGHT

You mention your own intensive personal work in your bio. What early life experiences led you to your own road map to success and ultimately to a career helping others?

LATTY-MANN

From the time I first became aware of a profession called psychology in which you help people remove what's bad in their life in order to create what's good, I could not imagine doing anything else. But my dad tried to discourage me by telling me he'd never known a psychologist who did not need a psychologist and that they were all nuts. I somehow remained undaunted. But interestingly, I actually fit the very description my dad used to describe psychologists—I needed a psychologist but didn't know it. In other words, I was unaware.

Let me give an example from my unaware years. I grew up with the role of peacemaker in my family. I can even remember my father complimenting me for not saying a word when there was significant family dissension. Of course, I fit the description of a Dysfunctional Pleaser with the disease to please. But if you had asked me as a late adolescent or young adult the truth of how I saw my life, I would have said that there are a lot of jerks taking advantage of my goodness. The truth of my life was that I was still playing out tapes and programs and beliefs that worked when I was a little girl growing up in an alcoholic family where I worked hard not to rock the boat. I did not learn appropriate self-assertiveness in my home environment. Outside of my home environment, I could be either under or overly assertive or simply dysfunctional at times. In my high school years, I became consistently nice, which was not *cool*. Too often I simply did not claim those things that were rightfully mine or speak my truth.

Leaving for college gave me new ground to practice. Once I started noticing that the so-called jerks would not pick on certain other people in my social circle, I started noticing the difference between those people and myself. I stopped operating on automatic and started becoming mindful of the messages my behaviors were putting out there and the subtle messages that were teaching people how to treat me. I was able to say, "Okay, that worked then, but now is now, and this no longer works for me." I started acting on my observations, engaging in some trial-and-error behaviors in order to develop healthier self-assertiveness skills. I finally found my voice to assert my truth in the moment when others were taking advantage of my pleaser role. I started looking at myself from the other side of the fence, so to speak, and could see what others were seeing and then own that which was not working.

It was through my personal development work that I came to appreciate that every growth spurt was a function of self-awareness and that I could only help others to the degree to which I had developed myself. In other words, how could I know where to shine the light onto a path if I had not traveled there before? Practiced long enough, paths become roads and super freeways.

So it was my own personal journey in self-awareness that gave me multiple models, concepts, anecdotes, and metaphors to share with others on their road to whatever they define as success.

We define where we are, where we want to be, and we create a road map to getting there. It's called a discrepancy or gap analysis, and it takes self-awareness to define what's missing as well as what it will take to attract the end product. What old

> *You just can't steer a parked car.*

behaviors must I let go of and what new behaviors must I put out there in order to get what I want?

But knowing how is not enough. It takes action. You just can't steer a parked car.

WRIGHT

You have said that self-awareness is the cornerstone for ultimate success. How so?

LATTY-MANN

When I say self-awareness, I'm talking about being aware of how we use our thoughts and feelings and body to create appropriate perceptions in others as we take action or choose not to take action. This is another way of saying *that I am the instrument of my leadership* or the instrument of my "loveship," depending on the nature of my social environment. Most people would agree that success is a function of what we do or say or what we don't do or don't say at any given time and in any given situation. So it's mighty hard to talk about success without making reference to one of these four channels—mind, body, emotions, and spirit.

All behaviors emanate from an intention that comes from a thought. Sometimes thoughts come from a negative feeling, and sometimes thoughts create the negative feeling. Likewise, positive thoughts and emotions are positively correlated as well. It's a scientific fact that the nature of our thoughts and emotions can dictate whether our healing is expedited or not.

One reason nurturing our faith (spirit) or ideology can help us heal is because it teaches us how to reconceptualize or reframe our current health challenges. We can reframe a diagnosis as a wake-up call to change unhealthy life patterns. We can orchestrate and direct at will how we will respond to whatever our health issue (i.e., we can go bitter or better). We can also take the lazy way out and stay in our comfort zone doing whatever we've always done. At least there are no surprises if we continue settling for mediocrity.

My mantra is mind, body, and emotions. Put it all together and that becomes my personality, which is my delivery system. It's the nature of my delivery system or how I deliver my communications that determines if my relationships are high quality or not. The better I find my relationships and life, the more in alignment my mind, body, and emotions. If I don't like what I'm experiencing in life, then my job is to figure out what's not working and go about the business of turning it around.

So, self-awareness, in part, means that I need to be aware of what programs, tapes, and beliefs I have created in what I call my bio-computer, or mind. If something in my life is amiss, as programmer of my bio-computer, I very likely inserted a belief in there at a time when that belief may have actually worked. My job is to become aware of what is attracting unwanted circumstances. Often times our circumstances are responding to the subtleties of our behaviors, which are always responding to our thought patterns. What may have worked at an earlier time in our life could now have detrimental effects if we don't change our thoughts and thus our behavioral responses in accordance with our changing circumstances.

Some people have a thought that people are guilty until proven innocent, and if they would change that belief to "people are innocent until proven guilty," they would find over time an entirely different set of friends and life circumstances. Thoughts attract certain people into your life because your thoughts dictate behaviors, and certain people respond to certain behaviors.

When someone has achieved a significant amount of self-awareness, he or she has actually become *highly other-aware*. It is only upon understanding what makes you tick that you can fully appreciate what makes others tick. So essentially it all starts with self, and if we don't know, we can't fix. And if we don't learn how to love and accept ourselves, it's even harder to do that with others.

WRIGHT

If self-awareness is so pivotal to achieving success, then in what ways are people unaware? Also, what are some of the ways people keep themselves from becoming aware?

LATTY-MANN

Many people seem to know more about cooking or cars than they do about themselves. A self-awareness handbook would make for a great *User's Manual for Humans.*

One way in which people are unaware has to do with their being unaware of their self-limiting beliefs. Some people may know they like controlling things, but they may not realize just how pronounced their need is to control people and things in order to feel safe. Or some people may have a belief that to be vulnerable or tender is to be weak but may not realize it is this belief that has left them unable to engage on a deep, meaningful, human level with the one they love most in this world. It's one thing to have certain beliefs, but if we don't connect those beliefs to the undesirable circumstances currently facing us in our life, then nothing will change.

In my own case, I had developed self-limiting beliefs that I must make others happy, that I was responsible for others' happiness and so forth. This allowed me to build up resentment over time because I was left feeling unappreciated or unvalued or unimportant. In my state of unawareness, I would end up reacting to my own subconscious, false belief of being "unvalued, unimportant, and unappreciated," yet would blame others for my feeling bad. In the example above, I had nobody to blame but myself because I set myself up for disappointment by operating on not only a self-limiting belief but a false one as well, which when taken to an extreme can be self-destructive.

Then there are the unnecessary needs—the need to be right, the need to win—a variation of self-limiting beliefs. When coupled with the false belief of not measuring up or not good enough, you get angry when someone suggests that you are not doing something right. If you're operating from self-awareness when this suggestion is made, you can learn the basis of the shared observation in a factual, adult manner and then take corrective action, if necessary.

Unaware people miss multiple opportunities for growth because in anger they either shut down or lash out, bringing to a close what could have been a meaningful discussion. But let's say that the other person is saying something intentionally hurtful, then what? Once again, if we're operating out of self-awareness, we can put it in proper perspective and not play the other side of their game or get hooked by their melodrama. So being in the moment is the only way we can catch ourselves being unaware (e.g., being angry, bored, cynical, confused, aggravated) in time to change it before it does the relationship some damage.

The harder we resist being perceived as unlovable, unworthy, not measuring up, not good enough, we stand the chance of being perceived the very way we don't want to be. That's why it's important to take that journey within and learn what our stuff is all about; only then do we own it and therefore get to manage it. Otherwise, it remains in our subconscious as negative energy, easily triggered, and too often raising its ugly head to sabotage our otherwise good intentions and efforts.

By moving our energy into our fear source (i.e., admitting our personal challenges and areas in need of improvement), we discover that those vulnerabilities do not define us; but rather, they make us human and we begin connecting more meaningfully with the rest of the human race. It is in giving up control that we get control. It is in owning our weakness that we dismantle the power it once had over us, thereby allowing us to turn that stumbling block into a steppingstone.

WRIGHT

What are the biggest challenges that keep people from unleashing their full human potential?

LATTY-MANN

The biggest challenge is FEAR—False Evidence Appearing Real. Too often we contaminate our current moment or distort our reality from past failures, criticisms, regrets, resentments, and remorse. Other than gravity and mortality, our limitations are pretty much self-imposed.

But what about fears that tend to hang over us like a cloud as we contemplate the economy or unstable job market? Because we tend to attract the very thing we fear, which is related to Jung's "what you resist persists," it's time for a thought transplant. Norman Vincent Peale said you can change your thoughts and change your world. This comes from a man who learned how to consistently hold onto positive thoughts and who massaged thoughts into things. His secret

> *"What you resist persists."*
> ~Carl Jung

was to act as if his thoughts were true. Therefore, we must be mindful to create positive energy around that which we seek.

If we have a job interview coming up, we get to envision our opportunity to share what we can do to help this company grow because of our unique gifts and talents. We get to envision that the interviewer will surely like us, and vice versa. Likewise, envisioning what can go wrong will almost with certainty lead us to engage in ways that will sabotage our efforts. The what if's can either hurt us or help us, depending on how we fashion the possibilities that are in store for us.

Just as some people view the world through rose-colored lenses, others may view the world through depressive lenses. Either way may be a distortion, yet one way is certain to lead to behaviors that confirm victory as opposed to defeat. Interpretation determines the quality of our journey, given the science behind self-fulfilling prophecies. As Henry Ford said, "Whether you believe you can or can't, it's true."

> *"Whether you believe you can or can't, it's true."*
> ~Henry Ford

Another way to prepare our path for unleashing our full human potential is to expect any new behavior designed to capture the victor's cup will likely not feel good at first. We're essentially stretching some new psychological muscles in preparation for a new action that can bring forth a new outcome.

There's only one problem. A new behavior does not tend to feel comfortable, which is exactly why we've been doing the old behavior for as long as we have. That's why we call it our comfort zone. And just because the power zone resides outside of the comfort zone, does not mean we get to enjoy the sense of power upon leaving the comfort zone. Instead, we get to experience the pain of rewiring. Imagine our neurotransmitters firing only to have the doors at the receptor sites slam shut at the point of entry. That's a picture of the pain of reprogramming. The good news is that it takes a minimum of twenty-one to thirty days for you to jell a new behavior, if you are consistently mindful to stay in the moment and catch yourself reacting out of old patterns.

Reacting is an automatic behavior. Responding is a deliberate behavior. When we are mindful in the moment, we can operate from choice and respond best to whatever stimulus or challenge comes our way. Reacting can also be in response to a negative feeling that we interpret as, "Don't take action; it won't work" or "They won't pick me or hire me." Our job is to become aware of predominant negative emotions as well as self-limiting beliefs that are dictating how we perceive our world because this is what we are actually responding to rather than the reality of what may be actually happening to us. It is our interpretation that holds us back. So, if we don't inventory to identify and then change those programs that are no longer serving us well, nothing will change.

I've mentioned how important it is to be in the moment to catch ourselves falling into negativity. Unless you are in the moment and operating from a self-aware place, it is easy to automatically engage in compensatory behaviors when you start feeling negative. Compensatory behaviors lead us down a path that takes us from our opportunities—from being our best. Exactly how do compensatory behaviors work and what does this mean?

Simply stated, when our stuff gets triggered (e.g., not good enough or not valued), we end up feeling an intense negative emotion. When left unchecked, it causes us to engage in a compensatory behavior to disprove our stuff. So if I have a need to be right because I am a slave to my negative energy and false belief of not being good enough, and you point out a flaw in my work, I will likely engage in a compensatory behavior to prove how good I am and how wrong you are. The problem with compensatory behaviors is that they tend to discredit us because we're operating out of negativity and fear and insecurity.

There is always an upside and a downside to compensatory behaviors. The upside is the person feels vindicated somehow by upstaging the other person. The downside is that people almost always end up feeling the same negative emotions that caused them to engage in the compensatory behavior in the first place—not good enough and unvalued—because of how others reacted to their negative, compensatory behavior. This is exactly what Carl Jung meant by "what we resist persists."

Compensatory behaviors almost always hold us back from unleashing our full human potential. With self-awareness, we start understanding what triggers us and can start managing our stuff before we find ourselves in an angry or negative place.

People tend to think, when someone makes them angry, that there is a direct relationship between what the person said or did and their state of anger. This is not entirely true. We can only feel anger if we have a program in our subconscious related to what we perceive as the offensive stimulus. When we discover what our "stuff" is that gets triggered, we help neutralize our "stuff" by refusing to react to the triggers that would normally activate it. We stop reinforcing old, ineffective behaviors. Better yet, we replace them with new behaviors that encourage pushing our potential to peak performance. The work it takes to *reprogram* explains why we just can't go to the next higher level without going to the next deeper level.

> *We just can't go to the next higher level without going to the next deeper level.*

WRIGHT

How do people know if they are making progress in the change process and how might they expedite change?

LATTY-MANN

> "Some people mature while others just have birthdays." My mother says this when she observes someone who would do well to engage in the change process.

Sometimes we have to go through a bad place to get to a good place. Not all change is painful, but whenever we are changing an old behavioral pattern that no longer serves us well, the experience of playing out the new replacement behavior at first will not feel all that natural. So, if it feels uncomfortable trying on your new behaviors, you're still rewiring and therefore changing. Assuming you are finding more harmony and life satisfaction due to even small subtle changes, that's an indicator you're changing in the right direction.

Look for these three dimensions within any change process: *frequency, duration, and intensity.* Let's say someone is quitting smoking and is keeping a journal on the experience. I would suggest the person keep a running tab on how often the cravings surface (frequency), how long each one lasts (duration), and on a scale from one to ten, how bad was the craving (intensity).

I had a short rotation at Duke Medical Center in the Smoker's Cessation Consult Service and would tell my cardiology patients that if they refrain from smoking for the length of time it would otherwise take to smoke a cigarette, the craving would go away. Over time the cravings would completely disappear, but during the interim, the charts would show a downward spiral on all three dimensions. One can do this with anger management or any other identified psychological construct.

"Fake it 'til you make it!" It's not being unauthentic if you act "as if" you've already made the change. That's because you are being mindful of your motivation behind the contrived behavior. It is also giving your mental wiring a rehearsal of what it's going to be like. Sometimes when we're acting "as if," people notice and comment. The positive reinforcement expedites our change because the shared observations make us more mindful of what we are doing.

Change typically takes place in various stages that we can easily describe, and it's not always a smooth, linear progression we experience. We can go back and forth as the effort to change challenges us. The first step is always self-awareness, given we can only change something we have identified as a problem. But even if someone were to say, "Hi, my name is Jennifer, and I'm an alcoholic," change won't necessarily follow the declaration. We have to acknowledge responsibility for it. So even if Jennifer were to say, ". . . and I am responsible for making this change," she is going to have to take action and assert her truth about what has to happen to eliminate problem drinking. It's that action (abstinence) that alcoholics call recovery and success, all the while acknowledging relapse is always a possibility, which is true for almost any change process.

Another way to chart our progress in the change process is to know a little something about how change functions in stages, which is a more practical model than simply a description of change. This four-stage change model I learned from the late Dr. Jim Farr takes place as follows:

1) Unconscious Incompetency
2) Conscious Incompetency
3) Conscious Competency
4) Unconscious Competency

The first stage is dormant, whereby we are not yet aware of the nature of the problem (Unconscious Incompetency). We simply are feeling out of alignment with ourselves.

Once we identify a specific problem area, we have moved from Stage One to Stage Two or from Unconscious Incompetency to Conscious Incompetency. An example of identifying a problem could be, "I hear myself say in response to an unreasonable request, 'No problem,' when my gut says, 'No way!'"

To move from Stage Two to Stage Three or from Conscious Incompetency to Conscious Competency, it is a matter of creating operational definitions of the change that is to take place. Using the above example, it could be "I will only say 'yes' when I mean 'yes,' and 'no' when I mean 'no.'" In order to move to the fourth and final stage of change, Unconscious Competency, it takes practice, practice, practice. While research has shown it takes twenty-one to thirty days to jell a new behavior, if it is not consistently practiced in a mindful way, it will take longer.

Change is unique to the nature of the problem behavior and the person in charge of the change. Don't count on others to notice and compliment you. Refuse to feel discouraged if you know you're putting out that new behavior. Sometimes people have to experience the consistency of your new behavior to recognize it. It's nice to receive a kind word, but remember: you're the one in charge here, and you don't need others' approval.

Sometimes you'll feel like you have an angel whispering in your ear encouraging you to put out the new behavior, while the devil is whispering in your other ear to be lazy and indulge yourself. What you need to do is simple—feed the angel, and starve the devil. You'll soon be operating out of unconscious competency.

Remember, you are master of your fate, captain of your destiny, executor of your existence, and nobody and nothing can affect your experiential universe but you. That's because you have a free will endowed with the power of choice.

When I start a leadership workshop, I ask people, "How many of you believe you can change?" If anyone says, "No," I tell that person I cannot help him or her. Leaders, like anyone else, have no power over anybody else to make them do anything. I say this in the sense that people decide what they will and won't do. Leaders can only motivate and inspire. So, while it is easier to change with the help of a trusted coach, leader, or friend, you essentially remain the prime motivator to stay on track with whatever your identified goals in life.

Envisioning the final product expedites change. How will it look and feel? Use all your senses in this vision of what you are seeking to accomplish—the sights, the sounds, the smells, the feelings, the whole enchilada. Bask in the glory of it all. Make your acceptance speech. Take a bow.

WRIGHT

References to mind, body, and spirit permeate a plethora of literature promoting optimal health and well-being. You speak of the Master Channel as providing a road map to success, yet how do we know when we're operating from our spiritual essence, and what can we do to actively nurture this part of ourselves to where it becomes a natural part of our being?

LATTY-MANN

I believe there are numerous writers, theologians, and theorists representing multitudinous ways to help us humans create a spiritually enriched life. Many of us are saying essentially the same thing using different words and angles, and that is a good thing because no one or no one way can likely appeal to everyone.

When I consider how strongly drawn I was to my co-founding partner's holistic model showing spirit as this large circle to the left of the three smaller circles (mind, body, and emotion), I saw it representing the wherewithal we have to orchestrate and direct our thoughts and beliefs and emotions. It was for me a model of how I aspired to practice my Christian faith, and I have since heard from many others who espouse a different faith say the same. It's not about who is right or wrong, it's all about finding a model that works for you, then live it to the betterment of both self and humankind.

It takes being in the moment and being mindful to engage life in an optimal way. Children tend to naturally do this until the socialization process suggests they need to be someone other than who they are. Then years later they pay for a course or find some other means of enlightenment to return to who they authentically are at their central core. Perhaps that's why we call it a journey. That's why I say we can't go to the next higher level until we go to the next deeper level.

When I was a little girl growing up with an alcoholic father and would find myself in the middle of a family scene of turmoil and utter distress, I practiced being mindful of the role of spirit in my life without really knowing that. As mentioned, children up to a certain age tend to have some natural rhythms with this sort of thing. Living with little predictability was stressful because at any moment my father would start a fight, usually with my brother, and sometimes with my mother. He invariably was the instigator, no matter how hard we would try to steer clear of his path.

The way I coped was by pretending I was the protagonist in a movie—a child who made the most and the best of a sometimes agonizingly sad or scary situation. I would behave as if I were being watched by an audience on television, admiring this small, young child for handling nobly such a pathetically unfortunate situation. I was aware I was pretending, so it worked beautifully as a coping mechanism. Best of all, it made me mindful of how I responded, and as such, I did not provoke my father to continue his ranting and raging. In fact, I somehow knew to feel sorry for him. I somehow knew he was acting out of his own pain and misery, although never was the source obvious to me as a child, as our lifestyle was one of relative privilege. It was from these moments of wonderment that I wanted to find a way to help people be happy "when I grew up."

I share this example from my childhood to show that there isn't the need for complexity to nurture the connection to one's spirit. It can be as simple as unblocking blocked lovingness or learning to love and honor oneself in a healthy manner. We learn how to treat and honor others once we have practiced the same with ourselves. It can work the other way, too. By being gentle with others, we may find it easier to likewise be gentle with ourselves. There is a natural flow in the human connectedness factor, if we would just experience the connection rather than think it.

Another way to nurture the connection to our Master Channel has to do with getting comfortable with what I call the Humanistic Law of Polarities™, whereby it is in giving that we receive. When we give up control, we get it. It truly can feel like a leap of faith because at times it does seem to defy logic. We hear of how a leader's credibility skyrocketed upon admitting a mistake. It is in making ourselves vulnerable that we attain a quiet power within. All such "polarity" experiences lead to that sense of social knowingness, which then forms the basis of how we can navigate through life with our "engines purring," despite the occasional wrong turns and potholes in the road.

Holistically speaking, every time we are mindful to revere our mind by nurturing thoughts that are more inclined to create good, we are enhancing our pathway to our spiritual essence, which increases the likelihood of further growth and inner peace. Nurturing behaviors that keep us more consistently connected to our Master Channel also entails identifying viruses in our bio-computer (mind) as the first step in a *mental exorcism.*

Mental and emotional viruses come in many forms, including not being an approachable person, handling criticism poorly, speaking poorly of others or ourselves, withholding our truth about the situation, not admitting we don't know, refusing to forgive, etc.

It's easy to identify a virus. The next time you catch yourself feeling negative, do some inventory. Identify that virus and gently evict it from your life. The irony of psychological viruses is that we tend to blame the people we infect. In other words, they were simply reacting to our "stuff" with their stuff, but we can only see theirs. Drawing from a scripture in the Bible, if we remove the log from our eye, we can then see what was only a speck in the other person's eye (Matthew 7:5).

When we are operating from our Master Channel, our spirit, we are orchestrating and directing at will to our mind, body, and emotions to bring these three aspects of who we are into alignment. This entails deleting those aforementioned viruses. When coming from spirit, we are more aware and thus in control of our thoughts and emotions sitting on the launching pad ready to take off in response to others.

Nurturing the means to one's spiritual essence takes on a voice of calm and reason with messages so sound and clear that it becomes a sixth sense to trust that inner voice of knowingness. There is an appropriate voice and behavior for every situation, whereby even aggression has its virtues when the circumstances call for it. We are at peace that we did the right thing when our behaviors come from that source of all knowingness, our Master Channel.

Even if current circumstances may not be as favorable as we would like, we can choose our attitude about this particular chapter in our life. As the Buddhist would say, "If you don't have what you want, then want what you have." This attitude helps keep us from getting in our own way in our quest for betterment. It instills patience, hope, faith, and optimism. Better yet, if you don't have what you want, then envision whatever your quest with childlike enthusiasm. Such a state of mind often times produces insights into what action you must take to get you there.

Picture a clock ticking away in the midst of a thunderstorm, and now you've got the picture of what you can develop through mindfulness. Visualize no more unnecessary ruminating, vacillating, second-guessing, or beating yourself up for inadvertent mistakes. Does that mean no more mistakes? No, it means we've cultivated within ourselves a spirituality whereby we can simultaneously be appropriately self-accepting and self-disciplining. We can weed from our lives those relationships or indulgences that have the capacity to inflict damage or harm. We can now see when misery is optional. We learn to be gentle with ourselves, yet push and strive for excellence. As we hit that balance that tells us we're on the right path, we foster hope with a backbone. When we allow ourselves to feel good reading these words, we are operating from our Master Channel, our master road map to success.

About the Author

Dr. Holly Latty-Mann, co-founder and president of The Leadership Trust®, is a well established authority in the leadership and "loveship" industries. Armed with two doctorates in psychology with her dissertation on mate selection, plus years of global success helping thousands of executives achieve breakthroughs via self-awareness processes, Holly nevertheless claims it is the combination of her grounded faith and intensive personal work that gives her an extra edge in her role as change agent. Holly's involvement on a grassroots committee for holistic, integrative medicine while interning at Duke Medical Center inspired her to rework this medical model to help people everywhere achieve breakthrough success.

Outside of her work role, Holly is passionate about animal welfare, her rescue cat Romeow, hiking and biking her favorite trails, and foreign travel. She says all these translate into a total sense of childlike freedom, joy, and one big smile!

Dr. Holly Latty-Mann

The Leadership Trust®
New Hope Court
1502 West NC Hwy 54, Ste. 403
Durham, NC 27707
919-401-8648
888-313-2570
Fax: 919-401-8649
drlatty@leadershiptrust.org
www.leadershiptrust.org

Chapter Ten

AN INTERVIEW WITH

DR. KENNETH BLANCHARD

DAVID WRIGHT (WRIGHT)

Few people have created a positive impact on the day-to-day management of people and companies more than Dr. Kenneth Blanchard, who is known around the world simply as Ken, a prominent, gregarious, sought-after author, speaker, and business consultant. Ken is universally characterized by friends, colleagues, and clients as one of the most insightful, powerful, and compassionate men in business today. Ken's impact as a writer is far-reaching. His phenomenal best-selling book, *The One Minute Manager*®, coauthored with Spencer Johnson, has sold more than thirteen million copies worldwide and has been translated into more than twenty-five languages. Ken is Chairman and "Chief Spiritual Officer" of the Ken Blanchard Companies. The organization's focus is to energize organizations around the world with customized training in bottom line business strategies based on the simple yet powerful principles inspired by Ken's best-selling books.

Dr. Blanchard, welcome to *Roadmap to Success*.

DR. KEN BLANCHARD (BLANCHARD)

Well, it's nice to talk with you, David. It's good to be here.

WRIGHT

I must tell you that preparing for your interview took quite a bit more time than usual. The scope of your life's work and your business, the Ken Blanchard Companies, would make for a dozen fascinating interviews. Before we dive into the specifics of some of your projects and strategies, will you give our readers a brief synopsis of your life—how you came to be the Ken Blanchard we all know and respect?

BLANCHARD

Well, I'll tell you, David, I think life is what you do when you are planning on doing something else. I think that was John Lennon's line. I never intended to do what I have been doing. In fact, all my professors in college told me that I couldn't write. I wanted to do college work, which I did, and they said, "You had better be an administrator." So I decided I was going to be a Dean of Students. I was provisionally accepted into my master's degree program and then provisionally accepted at Cornell because I never could take any of those standardized tests.

I took the college boards four times and finally got 502 in English. I don't have a test-taking mind. I ended up in a university in Athens, Ohio, in 1966 as an Administrative Assistant to the Dean of the Business School. When I got there, he said, "Ken, I want you to teach a course. I want all my deans to teach." I had never thought about teaching because they said I couldn't write, and teachers had to publish.

He put me in the manager's department. I've taken enough bad courses in my day and I wasn't going to teach one. I really prepared and had a wonderful time with the students. I was chosen as one of the top ten teachers on the campus coming out of the chute. I just had a marvelous time.

A colleague by the name of Paul Hersey was chairman of the Management Department. He wasn't real friendly to me initially because the Dean had led me into his department, but I heard he was a great teacher. He taught organizational behavior and leadership. So I said, "Can I sit in on your course next semester?"

"Nobody audits my courses," he replied. "If you want to take it for credit, you're welcome."

I couldn't believe it. I had a doctoral degree and he wanted me to take his course for credit, so I signed up. The registrar didn't know what to do with me because I already had a doctorate, but I wrote the papers and took the course, and it was great.

In June 1967, Hersey came into my office and said, "Ken, I've been teaching in this field for ten years. I think I'm better than anybody, but I can't write. I'm a nervous wreck, and I'd love to write a textbook with somebody. Would you write one with me?"

I said, "We ought to be a great team. You can't write and I'm not supposed to be able to, so let's do it!"

Thus began this great career of writing and teaching. We wrote a textbook called *Management of Organizational Behavior: Utilizing Human Resources*. It just came out in its eighth edition last year and has sold more than any other textbook in that area over the years. It's been nearly thirty-five years since that book came out. I quit my administrative job, became a professor, and ended up working my way up the ranks.

I obtained a sabbatical leave and went to California for one year twenty-five years ago. I ended up meeting Spencer Johnson at a cocktail party. He wrote children's books—a wonderful series called *Value Tales for Kids* including, *The Value of Courage: The Story of Jackie Robinson*, and *The Value of Believing In Yourself: The Story Louis Pasteur*. My wife, Margie, met him first and said, "You guys ought to write a children's book for managers because they won't read anything else."

That was my introduction to Spencer. So, *The One Minute Manager* was really a kid's book for big people. That is a long way from saying that my career was well planned.

WRIGHT

Ken, what and/or who were your early influences in the areas of business, leadership, and success? In other words, who shaped you in your early years?

BLANCHARD

My father had a great effect on me. He was retired as an admiral in the Navy and had a wonderful philosophy. I remember when I was elected to president of the seventh grade, and I came home all pumped up. My father said, "Son, it's great that you're the president of the seventh grade, but now that you have that leadership position, don't ever use it. Great leaders are followed because people respect them and like them, not because they have power." That was a wonderful lesson for me early on. He was just a great model for me. I got a lot from him.

Then I had this wonderful opportunity in the mid 1980s to write a book with Norman Vincent Peale. He wrote *The Power of Positive Thinking*. I met him when he was eighty-six years old when we were asked to write a book on ethics together, *The Power of Ethical Management: Integrity Pays, You Don't Have to Cheat to Win*. It didn't matter what we were writing together, I learned so much from him, and he just built the positive stuff I learned from my mother.

When I was born, my mother said that I laughed before I cried, I danced before I walked, and I smiled before I frowned. So that, on top of Norman Vincent Peale's influence, really affected me as I focused on what I could do to train leaders. How do you make them positive? How do you make them realize that it's not about them, it's about whom they are serving? It's not about their position, it's about what they can do to help other people win.

So, I'd say my mother and father, then Norman Vincent Peale, had a tremendous effect on me.

WRIGHT

I can imagine. I read a summary of your undergraduate and graduate degrees. I had assumed you studied Business Administration, Marketing Management, and related courses. Instead, at Cornell you studied Government and Philosophy. You received your master's from Colgate in Sociology and Counseling and your PhD from Cornell in Educational Administration and Leadership. Why did you choose this course of study? How has it affected your writing and consulting?

BLANCHARD

Well, again, it wasn't really well planned out. I originally went to Colgate to get a master's degree in Education because I was going to be a Dean of Students over men. I had been a government major because it was the best department at Cornell in the Liberal Arts School. It was exciting. We would study what the people were doing at the league governments. And then, the Philosophy Department was great. I just loved the philosophical arguments. I wasn't a great student in terms of getting grades, but I'm a total learner. I would sit there and listen, and I would really soak it in.

When I went over to Colgate and took some education courses; they were awful. They were boring. The second week, I was sitting at the bar at the Colgate Inn saying, "I can't believe I've been here two years for this." This is just the way the Lord works—sitting next to me in the bar was a young sociology professor who had just gotten his PhD at Illinois. He was staying at the Inn. I was moaning and groaning about what I was doing, and he said, "Why don't you come and major with me in Sociology? It's really exciting."

"I can do that?" I asked.

He said, "Yes."

I knew they would probably let me do whatever I wanted the first week. Suddenly, I switched out of Education and went with Warren Ramshaw. He had a tremendous affect on me. He retired a few years ago as the leading professor at Colgate in the Arts and Sciences, and got me interested in leadership and organizations. That's why I got a master's in Sociology.

The reason I went into Educational Administration and Leadership? It was a doctoral program I could get into because I knew the guy heading up the program. He said, "The greatest thing about Cornell is that you will be in a School of Education. It's not very big, so you don't have to take many Education courses, and you can take stuff all over the place."

There was a marvelous man by the name of Don McCarty who ended up going on to be the Dean of the School of Education, Wisconsin. He had an effect on my life, but I was always just searching around. My mission statement is: to be a loving teacher and example of simple truths that help myself and others to awaken the presence of God in our lives. The reason I mention "God" is that I believe the biggest addiction in the world is the human ego, but I'm really into simple truth. I used to tell people I was trying to get the B.S. out of the Behavioral Sciences.

WRIGHT

I can't help but think when you mentioned your father, and how he just bottomed-lined it for you about leadership.

BLANCHARD

Yes.

WRIGHT

Years and years ago when I went to a conference in Texas, a man I met, Paul Myers, told me, "David, if you think you're a leader, and you look around and no one is following you, you're just out for a walk."

BLANCHARD

Well, you'd get a kick—I'm just reaching over to pick up a picture of Paul Myers on my desk. He's a good friend, and he's a part of our Center for FaithWalk Leadership, where we're trying to challenge and equip people to lead like Jesus. It's non-profit. I tell people I'm not an evangelist because we've got enough trouble with the Christians we have, we don't need any more new ones. But, this is a picture of Paul on top of a mountain, and there's another picture below of him under the sea with stingrays. It says, "Attitude is Everything. Whether you're on the top of the mountain or the bottom of the sea, true happiness is achieved by accepting God's promises, and by having a biblically positive frame of mind. Your attitude is everything." Isn't that something?

WRIGHT

He's a fine, fine man. He helped me tremendously.

I want to get a sense from you about your success journey. Many people know you best from *The One Minute Manager* books you coauthored with Spencer Johnson. Would you consider these books as a high water mark for you, or have you defined success for yourself in different terms?

BLANCHARD

Well, *The One Minute Manager* was an absurdly successful book, so quickly that I found I couldn't take credit for it. It was published around the time when I really got on my own spiritual journey and started to try to find out what the real meaning of life and success was. That's been a wonderful journey for me.

The problem with most people is they think their self-worth is a function of their performance plus the opinion of others. The minute you think that is what your self-worth is, your self-worth is up for grabs every day because your performance is going to fluctuate on a day-to-day basis. People are fickle. Their opinions are going to go up and down. You need to ground your self-worth in the unconditional love that God has ready for us, and that really grew out of the unbelievable success of *The One Minute Manager*. When I started to realize where all that came from, that's how I got involved in the ministry I mentioned. Paul Myers is a part of it. As I started to read the Bible, I realized that everything I've ever written about or taught, Jesus did. You know, He did it with twelve incompetent guys that he hired. The only guy with much education was Judas, and he was His only turnover problem.

WRIGHT

Right.

BLANCHARD

It was a really interesting thing. What I see in people is not only do they think their self-worth is a function of their performance plus the opinion of others, but they measure their success on the amount of accumulation of wealth, on recognition, power, and status. I think those are nice success items. There's nothing wrong with those, as long as you don't define your life by that. What I think you need to focus on rather than success is what Bob Buford, in his book *Halftime,* calls significance—you know, moving from success to significance.

I think the opposite of accumulation of wealth is generosity. I wrote a book called *The Generosity Factor* with Truett Cathy, who is the founder of Chick-fil-A, one of the most generous men I've ever met in my life. I thought we needed to have a model of generosity. It's not only your treasure, but it's time and talent. Truett and I added *touch* as a fourth one.

The opposite of recognition is service. I think you become an adult when you realize you're here to serve rather than to be served. Finally, the opposite of power and status is loving relationships. Take Mother Teresa, as an example. She couldn't have cared less about recognition, power, and status because she was focused on generosity, service, and loving relationships, but she got all of that earthly stuff. If you focus on the earthly, such as money, recognition, and power, you're never going to get to significance. But if you focus on significance, you'll be amazed at how much success can come your way.

WRIGHT

I spoke with Truett Cathy recently and was impressed by what a down-to-earth good man he seems to be. When my friends found out that I had talked to him they said, "Boy, he must be a great Christian man, but he's rich." I said, "Well, to put his faith into perspective, by closing on Sunday it cost him $500 million a year." He lives his faith, doesn't he?

BLANCHARD

Absolutely, but he still outsells everybody else.

WRIGHT

That's right.

BLANCHARD

Chick-fil-A was chosen as the number one quick service restaurant in Los Angeles. They only have five restaurants here and they've only been here for a year.

WRIGHT

The simplest market scheme, I told him, tripped me up. I walked by the first Chick-fil-A I had ever seen, and some girl came out with chicken stuck on toothpicks and handed me one; I just grabbed it and ate it, it's history from there on.

BLANCHARD

Yes, I think so. It's really special. It is so important that people understand generosity, service, and loving relationships because too many people are running around like a bunch of peacocks. You even see pastors who say, how many in your congregation? Authors, how many books have you sold? Business, what's your profit margin? What's your sales? The reality is that's all well and good, but I think what you need to focus on is relationships. I think if business did that more and we got Wall Street off our backs with all the short-term evaluation, we'd be a lot better off.

WRIGHT

Absolutely. There seems to be a clear theme that winds through many of your books that have to do with success in business and organizations.

It is how people are treated by management and how they feel about their value to a company. Is this an accurate observation? If so, can you elaborate on it?

BLANCHARD

Yes, it's a very accurate observation. See, I think the profit is the applause you get for taking care of your customers and creating a motivating environment for your people. Very often people think that business is only about your bottom line. But no, that happens to be the result of creating raving fan customers, which I've described with Sheldon Bowles in our book, *Raving Fans*. Customers want to brag about you, if you create an environment where people can be gung-ho and committed. You've got to take care of your customers and your people, and then your cash register is going to go ka-ching! and you can make some big bucks.

WRIGHT

I noticed that your professional title with the Ken Blanchard Companies is somewhat unique—Chairman and Chief Spiritual Officer. What does your title mean to you personally and to your company? How does it affect the books you choose to write?

BLANCHARD

I remember having lunch with Max DuPree one time. He is the legendary Chairman of Herman Miller. Max wrote a wonderful book called *Leadership Is An Art*. I asked him, "What's your job?"

"I basically work in the vision area," he replied.

"Well, what do you do?" I asked.

He said, "I'm like a third grade teacher. I say our vision and values over, and over, and over again until people get it right, right, right."

I decided from that, I was going to become the Chief Spiritual Officer, which means I would be working in the vision, values, and energy part of our business.

I ended up leaving a morning message every day for everybody in our company. We have about 275 to 300 around the country, in Canada, and the U.K. Then we have partners in about thirty nations.

I leave a voice mail every morning, and I do three things on that as Chief Spiritual Officer. One, people tell me who we need to pray for. Two, people tell me who we need to praise—our unsung heroes and people like that. And then three, I leave an inspirational morning message. I really am the cheerleader—the energy bunny—in our company, and the reminder of why we're here and what we're trying to do.

We think that our business in the Ken Blanchard Companies is to help people to lead at a higher level, and help individuals and organizations. Our mission statement is to unleash the power and potential of people and organizations for the common good. So if we are going to do that, we've really got to believe in that. I'm working on getting more Chief Spiritual Officers around the country. I think it's a great title and we should get more of them.

WRIGHT

So those people for whom you pray, where do you get the names?

BLANCHARD

The people in the company tell me who needs help—whether it's a spouse who is sick, or kids who are sick, or they are worried about something. We have over five years of data about the power of prayer, which is pretty important.

This morning, my inspirational message was about an event my wife and five members of my company participated in. They walked sixty miles last weekend—twenty miles a day for three days—to raise money for breast cancer research. It was amazing. I went down and waved them all in as they came. There was a ceremony, and 7.6 million dollars was raised. There were over three thousand people walking, and many of the walkers were dressed in pink. They were cancer victors—people who had overcome cancer. There were even men walking with pictures of their wives who had died from breast cancer. I thought it was incredible.

There wasn't one mention in the major San Diego papers on Monday. I said, "Isn't that just something." We have to be an island of positive influence because all you see in the paper today is about Michael Jackson and Scott Peterson and Kobe Bryant and this kind of thing, and here you get all these thousands of people out there walking and trying to make a difference, and nobody thinks it's news. So every morning I pump people up about what life's about, about what's going on. That's what my Chief Spiritual Officer is about.

WRIGHT

I had the pleasure of reading one of your current releases, *The Leadership Pill*.

BLANCHARD

Yes.

WRIGHT

I must admit that my first thought was how short the book was. I wondered if I was going to get my money's worth, which by the way, I most certainly did. Many of your books are brief and based on a fictitious story. Most business books in the market today are hundreds of pages in length and are read almost like a textbook. Will you talk a little bit about why you write these short books and about the premise of *The Leadership Pill*?

BLANCHARD

I developed my relationship with Spencer Johnson when we wrote *The One Minute Manager*. As you know, he wrote *Who Moved My Cheese*, which was a phenomenal success. He wrote children's books, and I was a storyteller.

My favorite books were, *Jonathan Livingston Seagull* and *The Little Prince*. They are all great parables. I started writing parables because people can get into the story and learn the contents of the story. They don't bring their judgmental hats into reading. You write a regular book and they'll say, "Well, where did you get the research?" They get into that judgmental side. Our books get them emotionally involved and they learn.

The Leadership Pill is a fun story about a pharmaceutical company that thinks they have discovered the secret to leadership, and they can put the ingredients in a pill. When they announce it, the country goes crazy because everybody knows we need more effective leaders. When they release it, it outsells Viagra. The founders of the company start selling off stock and they call them Pillionaires. But along comes this guy who calls himself "the effective manager," and he challenges them to a no-pill challenge. If they identify two non-performing groups, he'll take on one and let somebody on the pill take another one, and he guarantees he will out-perform by the end of the year. They agree, but of course, they give him a drug test every week to make sure he's not sneaking pills on the side.

I wrote the book with Marc Muchnick, who is a young guy in his early thirties. We did a major study of what this interesting "Y" generation—the young people of today—want from leaders, and this is a secret blend that this effective manager in the *Leadership Pill* book uses.

When you think about it, David, it is really powerful on terms of what people want from a leader. Number one, they want integrity. A lot of people have talked about that in the past, but these young people will walk if they see people say one thing and do another. A lot of us walk to the bathroom and out into the halls to talk about it. But these people will quit. They don't want somebody to say something and not do it.

The second thing they want is a partnership relationship. They hate superior/subordinate. I mean, what awful terms those are. You know, the "head" of the department and the hired "hands"—you don't even give them a head. "What do you do? I'm in supervision. I see things a lot clearer than these stupid idiots." They want to be treated as partners. If they can get a financial partnership, great. If they can't, they really want a minimum of psychological partnership where they can bring their brains to work and make decisions.

Then finally, they want affirmation. They not only want to be caught doing things right, but they want to be affirmed for who they are. They want to be known as a person, not as a number. So those are the three ingredients that this effective manager uses. They are wonderful values if you think of them.

Rank-order values for any organization is number one, integrity. In our company, we call it ethics. It is our number one value.

The number two value is partnership. In our company, we call it relationships.

Number three is affirmation, which means being affirmed as a human being. I think that ties into relationships, too. They are wonderful values that can drive behavior in a great way.

WRIGHT

I believe most people in today's business culture would agree that success in business is everything to do with successful leadership. In *The Leadership Pill*, you present a simple but profound premise, that leadership is not something you do *to* people, it's something you do *with* them. At face value, that seems incredibly obvious, but you must have found in your research and observations that leaders in today's culture do not get this. Would you speak to that issue?

BLANCHARD

Yes, and I think what often happens in this is the human ego, you know. There are too many leaders out there who are self-serving. They're not serving leaders. They think the sheep are there for the benefit of the shepherd. All the power, money, fame, and recognition moves up the hierarchy, and they forget that the real action in business is not up the hierarchy—it's in the one-to-one, moment-to-moment interactions that your front line people have with your customers. It's how the phone is answered. It's how problems are dealt with and those kinds of things. If you don't think that you're doing leadership with them, rather you're doing it to them, after a while they won't take care of your customers.

I was at a store recently (not Nordstrom's, where I normally would go) and I thought of something I had to share with my wife, Margie. I asked the guy behind the counter in Men's Wear, "Can I use your phone?"

"No!" he replied.

"You're kidding me," I said, surprised. "I can always use the phone at Nordstrom's."

"Look, buddy," he said, "they won't let *me* use the phone here. Why should I let you use the phone?"

That is an example of leadership that's done to them not with them. People want a partnership. People want to be involved in a way that really makes a difference.

WRIGHT

Dr. Blanchard, the time has flown by and there are so many more questions I'd like to ask you. In closing, would you mind sharing with our readers some thoughts on success? If you were mentoring a small group of men and women, and one of their central goals was to become successful, what kind of advice would you give them?

BLANCHARD

Well, I would first of all say, "What are you focused on?" I think if you are focused on success as being, as I said earlier, accumulation of money, recognition, power, or status, I think you've got the wrong target. I think what you need to really be focused on is how can you be generous in the use of your time and your talent and your treasure and touch. How can you serve people rather than be served? How can you develop caring, loving relationships with people?

My sense is that if you will focus on those things, success in the traditional sense will come to you. I think you become an adult when you realize that you are here to give rather than to get. You're here to serve not to be served. I would just say to people, "Life is such a very special occasion. Don't miss it by aiming at a target that bypasses other people, because we're really here to serve each other." So that's what I would share with people.

WRIGHT

Well, what an enlightening conversation, Dr. Blanchard. I really want you to know how much I appreciate all this time you've taken with me for this interview. I know that our readers will learn from this, and I really appreciate your being with us today.

BLANCHARD

Well, thank you so much, David. I really enjoyed my time with you. You've asked some great questions that made me think, but I hope are helpful to other people because as I say, life is a special occasion.

WRIGHT

Today we have been talking with Dr. Ken Blanchard. He is the author of the phenomenal best selling book, *The One Minute Manager*. Also, the fact that he's the Chief Spiritual Officer of his company should give us all cause to think about how we are leading our companies and leading our families and leading anything, whether it is in church or civic organizations. I know I will.

Thank you so much, Dr. Blanchard, for being with us today.

BLANCHARD

Good to be with you, David.

About the Author

Few people have created more of a positive impact on the day-to-day management of people and companies than Dr. Kenneth Blanchard, who is known around the world simply as "Ken."

When Ken speaks, he speaks from the heart with warmth and humor. His unique gift is to speak to an audience and communicate with each individual as if they were alone and talking one-on-one. He is a polished storyteller with a knack for making the seemingly complex easy to understand.

Ken has been a guest on a number of national television programs, including *Good Morning America and The Today Show*, and has been featured in *Time, People, U.S. News & World Report*, and a host of other popular publications.

He earned his bachelor's degree in Government and Philosophy from Cornell University, his master's degree in Sociology and Counseling from Colgate University, and his PhD in Educational Administration and Leadership from Cornell University.

Dr. Ken Blanchard

The Ken Blanchard Companies
125 State Place
Escondido, California 92029
800-728-6000
Fax: 760-489-8407
www.blanchardtraining.com

Chapter Eleven

WORK SMART – NOT HARD

THE GUIDE TO GETTING IT DONE!

JENNIFER STEPHENS

DAVID WRIGHT (WRIGHT)

Today we're talking with Jennifer M. Stephens. Jennifer is a passionate leader who believes anyone can do anything if he or she is truly committed to being the best person he or she can be. She is an author, professional speaker, corporate business and ethics consultant, college professor, executive mentor and coach, and retired Army Major. Throughout the past twenty-two years, Jennifer has traveled the world mastering her business and leadership skills creating a successful environment in every organization she touches. She has run multimillion dollar exercises and has worked in many countries throughout the world. Her leadership skills have won her national awards and she continues to work with emerging leaders to ensure success as new entrepreneurs.

In addition to her corporate success, Jennifer is vigilant in child advocacy issues and speaks nationally to support the cause. Jennifer has been featured on *The Montel Williams Show* after writing her book, *Escape from the Dungeon: Jennifer's Survival Story*. She uses her story to inspire people to use personal trauma as a catalyst for success instead of a crutch for failure.

WRIGHT

Through her motivational speeches and training sessions, Jennifer creates an environment where there is a passion to succeed and create the most successful results within in any organization.

Jennifer Stephens welcome to *Roadmap to Success*.

JENNIFER STEPHENS (STEPHENS)

Thank you.

WRIGHT

So how would you define the concept of working smart versus working hard?

STEPHENS

Ultimately, David, every successful leader should believe in this philosophy. If you ask these leaders, they might phrase it a little different, but working hard and working smart are two very different things.

You can work hard all of your life and not be efficient or effective. Further, you can work smart and never work hard a day in your life. The goal is to have the most amount of effect with the least amount of effort using every ounce of energy to further your current goals, whatever they may be.

Some think they cannot get ahead without working hard every day of their life when in truth the smarter you are, the less you have to work and the more you can gain, both professionally and personally.

There are all sorts of strategies to follow when working smart, and hopefully those are some of the things we are going to cover today. The bottom line is that when it comes down how to succeed, it is simple—set priorities, apply a directed focus, and have a plan.

I live by the five P's: Prior Planning Prevents Poor Performance. This is my philosophy—my mantra—for every task that I am presented. With the right mental planning and preparation in your objectives, the better the execution in tasks and projects you will have. Ultimately it is the managing of those priorities that is one of the most important aspects to working smarter versus working harder. The better you plan out a project, the more seamless the execution becomes.

For example, for one client, we were setting up a marketing plan for a local trade show. We walked through the entire process quite a bit; we looked at the situation as if we were the customer. What do you want to see at a trade show? What drives a person to the booth so you can give your pitch? How do you make yourself stand out from the same type of business to your left and right?

So for weeks we talked about it, we asked average people on the street, we looked at where the crowds were at the trade shows that were going on. Why are certain ones getting the business? Then we took those elements we discovered and tweaked them, made them our own, and owned the ideas as though they were the best ideas in the world.

Something as simple as standing next to the table versus behind the table can make you appear to be more approachable. It can draw a potential customer to the table. Have materials that potential customers can take with them—something memorable, different, and useful. Taking the time to prepare for what the customer would want can make the difference between managing a crowd at your table, and fighting to get one person there. Do not wait for customers—go and get them!

WRIGHT

Will you give our readers perhaps a set of steps to follow in order to work smarter on any project?

STEPHENS

Absolutely. What is nice is that you can take any task and break it down to manageable pieces. Any project, any task, any goal can be broken down to reasonable tasks that you can execute.

For example, let's say you have a national project you have to accomplish, and it is a project that you have very little knowledge about. You could be a logistics expert who has to write a business plan for a new startup company you are orchestrating. All you may have at your disposal is the specific or general tasks given to you by the business owner or partner and you have to set up the plan. You are the manager and developer of the plan, now what do you do?

You start by outlying the tasks. Preferably short, simple tasks are developed through a mind map process and this is where you are brainstorming the context of the project. This is your road map, your road map to success as the title of this book indicates.

As you develop a solution for each task that is noted during the brainstorming process, you will come up with more questions and more tasks. The key to success is taking those new tasks and questions and developing them further and putting them in that all-important order of prioritization. This prioritization can be based simply on the intent of the boss. What does the boss need done first to make some forward progression in the development of the business plan?

Then each day there is the road map—the prioritized list you keep your focus on—on the project. Throughout this focus you create a framework of execution, which is how to complete everything in a systematic way—the way you think about the project, the way you lay out the execution of the project; it is very systematic in nature.

You can look at every successful businessperson or leader and he or she has a system—a way to process information. Leaders plan out projects and they execute a plan. Much like a filmmaker—when a director is shooting a movie, he or she doesn't shoot it in the order in which you see it, scenes that may be out of sequential order are filmed because of availability of locations and logistics. The project is put together in the editing process after the filming is completed. The thought process can create a situation of working smarter.

For example, have you ever been in a situation where you feel that you are spinning your wheels and doing a lot of work but really not accomplishing much. There is a simple solution—you have to refocus and work smarter, not harder. Using processes and creating a road map for completing the task will help you complete projects using a more efficient, systematic approach. One of the worst things a person can do is spend hours and hours reworking something that may never reach a 100 percent satisfaction.

Ultimately, a good manager would avoid reworking every task. Reworking causes a great waste of time and resources. You want to use your energy to get more of the project done versus perfecting a certain piece of it. I liken it to the analogy that I would rather spend an hour and get a 90 percent solution than three hours and get a 95 percent solution. It is that desire for perfection that can be the greatest enemy sometimes because, as you are trying to perfect every single piece and not worrying about having a few rough edges is kind of the premise of working smarter not harder.

Much like those steps that are described above, there are steps in any individual project you must accomplish. Anything you need to accomplish simply involves just having a solid road map to success. Here it is how to prioritize events or tasks for the day. Throughout the years I have found success in tackling projects by prioritizing what must be done today, then tomorrow, and then next week.

One mistake that is often made is working on a little bit of everything, giving the feeling of moving a whole lot without getting a lot of distance out of your efforts. Instead, focus energy and work on the more urgent tasks first. This allows you to accomplish some very visible results, thus creating motivation to move on to the next task that is biting you in the ankles tomorrow. Establishing this priority list every day is not a necessity, it is a *must do!* Every day there should be a to-do list of what to accomplish. When you go to work, have that to-do list of things that have to get done in the order that they need to be done. If they do not get done, then they are put off to do the next day. The key is to find what works for you. Do you respond to longer lists or shorter lists? Do you respond more to details or general descriptions of your priorities? Every person is different and finding the certain point of decisive motivation is key to your individual success.

Find out the tool that responds to your own personality. For some it could be a notebook or an electronic organizer. For me, it is "the notebook" that goes with me where ever I go; it is as important as my BlackBerry. It is small enough to fit in my bag but large enough to accommodate my thoughts in an orderly and clear fashion. This notebook is four by six inches and is my personal road map to success. It is a tool I have used for more than twenty years. With this tool I am able to "visualize" the completion of tasks, I can "see" the success and the progress in everything I want to do, and I have my road map right in front of me. So the questions to ask yourself are:

- How do you build your own road map?
- Is it visual?
- Is it in your mind's eye?
- What is the tool that will work for you?

When you are motivated and you accomplish your task, you get into "the success zone." This is the place where you are mentally and physically motivated to keep checking things off the list and plow through the times that are the toughest. However, you must know your own limits.

Sometimes you can give yourself goals that are a bit too lofty, and you do not want to set yourself up for failure. It is human nature to set the bar of success low. Instead, set that bar just a *little* bit higher than you think you can achieve. For example: if you have a sales goal of $150,000 in a year of a product, shoot for $170,000 to make you work just a bit harder than you originally pictured yourself doing.

Business is very psychological in nature—there are days when you will be able to accomplish a lot more than other days, simply based on your mood. Oftentimes it's that first step to any project that is the toughest. It is the project that stares at you until you begin it; but once you do, you're then in the process—you are on the map to success.

Understanding the fundamentals of motivation and why people do what they do can help you in getting your objectives accomplished. If one of your team members is motivated by praise, all of the money in the world will not motivate him or her. If the person is motivated by money, then all of the "atta boys" you hand out will be meaningless. Understanding what will get the team to do what you need them to do and make them think it is their idea is the biggest talent and leadership skill you can acquire.

I challenge you to examine your individual work days. Do you really use every minute wisely, or are you spending a lot of time spinning your wheels and not getting a lot done? How can you take your own individual day and use every minute wisely? Work smarter because time is your most valuable asset. If you master the management of your time, you can really develop that road map to success.

WRIGHT

So what is the real meaning of not reinventing the wheel?

STEPHENS

Not reinventing the wheel is the premise of working smart not hard—do not waste your valuable time creating new processes or a new way of doing things. You have to look at how you can improve on the things that are already done. How can you use that most valuable asset, your time, and create a better situation? If you want a new project to tackle at work and somebody has done something like it before, you have to go look at what does right look like and then you make it better—make it yours.

For example, let's say you take charge of a new organization or project that you have not had experience in. The last thing you want to do is go into a new job and change everything as you are walking in the door. You will overwhelm the organization and most likely, you will tend to strike down the motivation of every employee there. You have to spend those first thirty days in any new job just watching. Watch everything—how do the employees interact with each other, how are orders processed, how are the daily tasks accomplished, are the right people doing the right tasks at the right time?

After the initial thirty days, you can start adjusting (I call it tweaking things). Instead of reinventing the wheel, you examine all of the tasks and determine which tasks need the greatest attention and the greatest amount of detail right away. Sometimes changing one thing can have a great effect on the overall process. As a successful leader, you must decide what things can have the least amount of change but the greatest amount of payoff for you and for the employees and the organization overall.

WRIGHT

So how do you improve an existing process?

STEPHENS

In my experience of managing organizational change and behavior, and according to my study of this phenomenon for a couple of decades now, I have come to find that there are basic steps and phases, regardless of what the job is. People are people and basic business is basic business. Whatever the job, organization, project, or person, there are four basic phases to any process:

> ➤ The first phase is to observe, examine, and evaluate the current process.

> ➤ The second phase is to examine what is working and what is not working with the existing process.

> ➤ The third phase is to make small changes in the process that can create a higher level of efficiency that may not have been there before.

> ➤ The final phase is the most important. It is the follow-up—how well are the changes you made working for you? After the final phase, you restart with the next objective.

Phase 1

Phase 4   Phase 2

Phase 3

For example, let's take a random process you want to improve such as getting all of your employees to show up at a sales meeting, especially the ones who are top performers. Sometimes, when folks are at the top producing level, they believe they no longer have to come to weekly meetings—there is nothing in it for them.

> ➤ Phase 1: Define the problem—the lack of participation in the weekly meeting—so you have to fix that, which is the answer. This could grow to be an organizational problem if it's not addressed.

> ➤ Phase 2: Determine what is going right and wrong with the situation. When the weekly meetings are important to the employees, you get a higher turnout. When there is no reason to have a vested interest in the meeting, there is lower attendance, so you need to solve that process. You want to get those top performers there at the meetings so 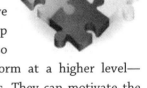 they continually motivate and perform at a higher level—they're inspired by their own success. They can motivate the lower performing employees.

> ➤ Phase 3: Implement a change in the process. As a leader, I employ the KISS method—Keep It Simple Stupid. The more changes you make, the more complex the solution. You don't want to do that because the more complex the solution, the less effective it will be. In this case, the road map is simple—small changes, large effects.
> When you come up with a solution, you have to consider it from the point of view of the problem. In this case, what would

motivate the high performer to come to the weekly meetings? Once you look at the manager and the leaders of the organization, you have to decide what you have available to you to inspire a higher turnout. As a leader, you could make it a rule for them to attend, but you want them to be there because they want to, not because you demand it.

One solution could be that each week during the month, a top performer has to present a nugget for success and highlight his or her success. Each top performer would sign up for one of those four weeks. So every month, you have one of four top performers highlighting his or her success and what that person did to achieve it. This way, the top performers succeed at the meetings and because they sign up for the weekly meeting themselves, it is their choice to be there, you are not forcing them. It's human nature to highlight personal success, so by highlighting their success, top performers are motivating themselves and they're motivating their fellow employees.

> Phase 4: Ultimately, you as the manager watch how this process goes for a few months. This is the follow-up part, the important part. This is where you continue to tweak the process until you have regular attendance, and even then you have to adjust and constantly change the way you do things to create a higher level of enthusiasm. Complacency is the enemy here; complacency creates a level of contempt and no one wants to work around that type of negativity. Keeping things in a constant state of change and keeping the business moving forward makes that road map to success in constant motion.

WRIGHT

So do you have to be smart to work smart?

STEPHENS

Absolutely not! You do not have to *be* intellectually smart to work smart; however, you *are business smart* if you work smart. A person does not need the collegiate intelligence as much as the practical intelligence to succeed in business and leadership. Some of the smartest people in the world dropped out of school. There are some folks like myself who cannot get enough of school, but a degree is only a piece of paper until you learn to use it well. A person needs to know what to do with the degree in order to be a smart worker and a great manager. It is not the degree that makes a person smart, it is how a person uses it, it is how a person uses the information that he or she has learned over the years to become a *smart* worker versus a *hard* worker.

Some of the smartest workers in the world are people who never attended college. In everyday life, they are doing great and wonderful things. Take your own situation and create your own road map to success that fits both you and your lifestyle. There are many opportunities to educate yourself on life, work, and, of course, school.

WRIGHT

So how do you gather the right information to make your project successful?

STEPHENS

It all depends on what the project is. You do not have to be the smartest person in the room to make a project successful, but you do need to know where to go and get the information. Knowing where to go and who to go after is three-quarters of the battle of succeeding in any organization or in any project.

When I took command of an organization that I knew nothing about, I had no fear whatsoever because I know that I have to find the technically smart people. I found the people I could trust—those who knew everything about the organization. If I didn't trust them, I could not use them because I could not trust that they had the good of the organization on their mind and their interests were purely self-serving. You can have all the technical expertise in the world but if you cannot communicate your vision to your organization, you will have no success whatsoever.

As the leader, it is okay not to possess every piece of information you need to succeed, but you need to know where to get it and how to create the element in your organization. The leader is only as strong as the shoulders of the employees he or she is standing on. By giving the power to the people around you, you are giving them a vested interest in the organizational success. Empowering people will also give them a vested interest in your development of the process, in changing the way you do things, making things more efficient, and working smart not hard.

Be open to soaking up those experiences around you and learning about the organization as it is, and how you want it to be. The toughest part is when you have a leader who thinks his or her thought process is the only way to go. Adjusting your thought process to the current organization is the way to be successful as well as knowing who to go to, where to go, and how to use all the information you gather.

WRIGHT

So how do you get that element of expertise in your area of choice?

STEPHENS

Through education, experience, and knowing the right place to pick up important information. Much as I described, it is not what you know, but knowing where to get the information you don't have. It is the art of knowing where to go for specific pieces of information. Expertise does not come in the form of a college degree—it comes from the application of your experiences and what you learned in school. I have known about people who think they are smart because they attended college for four to eight years.

I have been going to college for more than twenty years for a reason—there is still more to learn; every degree has taught me something new. I will never stop going to school, simply because I have not met anyone who has cornered the market on knowing it all. Regardless of the job, the project, or the organization, there is always going to be a nugget of information you can pick up to make yourself smarter, to make yourself smarter about the organization, and smarter about how to lead. If you are faced with a new challenge at work, research it, know it, and focus on that project until you have mastered the road map to success for it.

The best leaders in the world have had failures, but those terrible experiences gave them expertise on how to handle problems, people, projects, how to plan, and how to work smart and avoid working hard. It is easy to be a good leader and manager when things are going well. The true test of the leader and manager is how he or she handles chaos.

Instead of expending all of your energy running in place and wearing out fast, work smarter, and you can work well past traditional retirement age. If you work hard all your life, you are going to get tired. Use that energy in the most efficient way possible by using your road map to success—the one you have built throughout the years by working smarter. You can do that through focus.

WRIGHT

Focus, focus, focus, that seems to be a mantra for you. So how do you create a successful situation with focus?

STEPHENS

Your mantra defines your inner core; having that ability to constantly focus well will allow you to mentally tackle the toughest of tasks. Having razor-sharp focus is what will create a level of gratifying behavior that will cause you to want to accomplish the tough projects because you'll just know you can.

One of the best examples that comes to mind is a conversation I had with one of my leaders. I told my boss that I needed very little guidance and that I could take his intent and act on it with incredible focus. I would tell him that I was a fast-moving train and the only way he was going to stop me is if he threw something big on the tracks. He was very grateful that all I needed as a focused manager was the *intent* of his focus. I translated his intent to my focus, which translated into the organizational focus.

Now, what boss doesn't love to hear that you want to succeed under his or her tutelage? I would seek out those projects that no one else could seem to handle and work them intently. I would focus on the tasks and create a road map that would make the completion look easy, simply through focused effort. I would say that the absolute best (and my most favorite) position in the world is taking control of a company or an organization that is down on its last legs and seems doomed to failure from all outward perception. The great news is that you have nowhere to go but up.

A focused leader can take the poorest performing organization and through working smart and not hard and utilizing energy wisely, he or she can make the organization a top performing one within twelve months. Yes, it does take time for sure, but nothing can stop an organization where you motivate the employees to vest themselves in the success of the project. That type of motivation and focus in an organization is contagious. When an organization has successful employees, or horizontal level of managers, operating on high levels of focus, it creates a mentality with the entire organization that makes it work more efficiently. Once employees and leaders in a company have that focus, they must to learn to keep it, even the most motivated person can lose his or her focus on occasion, and only a good leader and manager can keep the focus with innate leadership skills, inner abilities, and all the employee talents that can pay off in tangible results.

When you procrastinate, when you think about failure, or allow someone to control your thought process you become defeated. But when you take that project one task at a time, it creates focus. When you think of the success you are having every day, it creates focus and enthusiasm to move to the next day. When you are in control of your motivation, your focus, and your purpose, you are an unstoppable force and nothing can bring you down. That is an acquired talent and it comes with success, failures, and experience. Failures in life determine what kind of person you are. It isn't the action that makes the person—it's the reaction that a person has when something does not go quite right. What happens if you lose that focus for the day? Do you allow yourself to lose it for the whole entire week? No, you pick yourself up, you dust yourself off, and restart the day with more enthusiasm.

Every person loves to see a success story and when you are in charge of a company, an organization, a project, or teams and when your subordinates see you rise above these small issues that can bring people down, you create a stronger, more powerful team. You are creating the road map to success, not just driving down the road. Do not let anyone disturb your focus or question why you work so diligently to create this level of success.

WRIGHT

So how do you think people should pick their particular focus?

STEPHENS

The simplest answer is *passion*. You can only focus on something that you are personally passionate about. You must have passion for business, for success, and for leading others. Passion develops the type of business leader you are. Donald Trump has a particular focus, Warren Buffet has a focus, Steve Jobs has a focus. The questions to ask of yourself are: What is the focus you are going to be bringing out in an organization? What are you going to bring out in your subordinates, or even a project? The more passionate you are about a subject, the better the project will be. The more passion you have in the vision, the more successful the result will be.

- Focus creates passion.
- Passion creates success.

Passion is what will get you up in the morning. It will allow you to tackle the tasks that seem insurmountable one day and a memory the next. The most successful folks will tell you that they could not picture the entire process in the beginning, they tackled the pieces. They succeeded at the pieces with a great deal of passion and focus and created the success of the entire organization or the entire project.

You do not want to struggle to make your business a success. You want the success in your business to drive you and to drive those around you to do more, become more creative, and perform at a higher level of success. Struggles will debilitate you if you let them, but your passion will drive you and build every success. It will inspire you to create a road map for success that you never want to divert from.

WRIGHT

In your biography I said that in addition to your corporate success you are passionate about selfless service and giving back to the community. How do you use all this information as you go about being vigilant in giving back and bring it to the business world?

STEPHENS

People all have individual stories of why they are who they are. I am a child abuse prevention advocate because I come from a tough upbringing; it has made me the person I am today. Every leader out there, who has enjoyed some form of success, will tell you that there is a reason why he or she is so passionate and focused on his or her particular craft.

For every emerging business leader, entrepreneur, or manager will have a reason for working in the capacity he or she is. As the coach in this scenario, it is important to understand why people do what they do so that you can properly motivate them. Sometimes all a new leader needs is a cheerleader. New leaders need someone to say that they can do this, that they can get up and make a difference today, they can create a greater world, and they can create that business they have always wanted. If people have had a rough past as they grew up, they can tell that next person in that position that he or she can grow up and be a resounding difference in life as a way of paying it forward. I use that incredible stored passion for life, and I use that incredible talent for focus I have in succeeding. I try to get folks to see that very thing in their own lives. My ultimate goal is to show people how they can be successful and create a better world in business and in life.

WRIGHT

Well, what a great conversation Jennifer. I really appreciate the time you've taken to these questions for me. It's been very interesting. I've learned a lot and I'm sure our readers will as well.

STEPHENS

I really hope so. This is a passionate subject for me and I'm really glad to be a part of the process here.

WRIGHT

Today we have been talking with Jennifer Stephens. Jennifer is a passionate leader, an author, a professional speaker, a corporate ethics consultant, a college professor, an executive mentor, a coach, and a retired Army officer. Throughout the past twenty years, she has traveled the world mastering her business and leadership skills, creating a successful environment in every organization she touches.

Jennifer, thank you so much for being with us today on *Roadmap to Success*.

STEPHENS

I appreciate it, David. Thank you.

About the Author

Jennifer has lived a truly extraordinary life. She is the second oldest of sixteen children. As a child, she endured the horrors of child abuse, which included physical torture, mental cruelty, and near starvation. Upon Jennifer's escape in 1987, her family was identified as one of the most severe child abuse cases in Wisconsin's history. At age seventeen, Jennifer's teachers risked their careers to notify the authorities and saved her life from certain death. After her escape, her lifelong quest was for excellence and higher education. To achieve this she enlisted in the U.S. Army and became an officer to hone her leadership skills. Jennifer has spent her entire life striving to succeed in spite of the foundation that was laid for her.

After incredible success, currently Jennifer is retired from two decades of service as an Army officer. She is now a college professor, speaker, and author. She is finishing her PhD in Organizational Behavior and Leadership at Northcentral University.

Jennifer has a bachelor's degree in International Business and Finance from the University of Louisville, Kentucky, a master's degree in Business Administration and Global Management from the University of Phoenix, Arizona, and an Executive Juris Doctorate from Concord School of Law.

Jennifer Stephens
Vision for Tomorrow, LLC
P.O. Box 510451
New Berlin, WI 53151
262-786-1885
Jennifer@jenniferstephens.org
www.jenniferstephens.org

Chapter Twelve

BECOMING RELATIONSHIP RICH

CHERYL BREUKELMAN

DAVID WRIGHT (WRIGHT)

Today I'm talking with Cheryl Breukelman. Cheryl is the founding partner of Epiphany Coaches, a professional coaching agency, and thought leader. The Epiphany team is evolving the leadership landscape through their coaching work around the world. She and the team passionately believe that relationships and collaboration are the biggest leadership opportunity today.

Cheryl gained her twenty years of business experience through her decade at Microsoft and her work coaching hundreds of leaders and teams globally for the last ten years. She and the team regularly coach, write, and speak on the value of relationships and collaboration in various business and coaching forums.

Cheryl, welcome to *Roadmap to Success*.

CHERYL BREUKELMAN (BREUKELMAN)

Thank you, David. It's great to be here.

WRIGHT

Would you tell our readers what is happening today that is having the biggest effect on leaders?

BREUKELMAN

Yes, what's big is the evolution of connectedness or, in other words, the rise of collaboration and transparency as a core skill for business success. This evolution is already having the biggest affect on leaders today and will continue to play an even larger role in defining our leadership and success.

Here's what I mean. Let's start to understand this evolution of connectedness in terms of cloud computing. Cloud computing is a new business imperative. It's about broad access, sharing, and collaboration. Think about the effect of Facebook and Twitter and Google. These new services have changed how we work and moreover how we communicate and interact with one another.

Now, transfer that same notion of cloud services to a newly created cloud culture—a culture of connectedness that thrives on more openness, collaboration, and transparency and demands it from our leaders and organizations. These relationship skills of openness and collaboration and transparency are newly important and, at the same time, this is not an area that we have typically been taught or trained in, outside of the kindergarten classroom. In fact, in some cases, this evolution flies in the face of historical management practices like "not getting personal at work" or "not letting your guard down." Those days are over. We can look at our newest generation to join the workforce. These people grab a device to get connected as soon as they wake up, proof of the evolution of connectedness. This is an amazing opportunity for leaders today.

WRIGHT

So what have you learned from coaching thousands of leaders?

BREUKELMAN

The biggest thing we have learned is that leaders are eager to embrace cloud culture and enhance their relationship skills, but the truth is that they are often conflicted by competing information like "have all the answers" and are not adopting new relationship skills or behaviors in their day-to-day lives yet, or in their working lives anyway.

The typical leader we encounter is struggling with a lack of collaboration and support from others and feels siloed. They admittedly have poor relationship skills and haven't made this a priority. They don't feel connected to the people around them or trust others. They don't show up fully as who they are or show vulnerability due to the need to stay professional. These smart, hard-working people are also leading in high stress situations with fast-changing and uncertain environments where they are expected to always be on call. This is the typical profile of the leaders we first meet. They recognize the need for more collaboration and relationship skills but the truth is they're not really behaving that way, and they're not really sure how to move forward.

So when they arrive to coaching to set up their leadership coaching goals and share their challenges, their hopes, and their fears, it really comes down to relationships. Now, they might not say the word "relationship," David. Instead, they would use words like "help me manage up," "help me be more visible in the room," "I want to have more presence," "I want more impact with particular people or projects," or "help me engage and inspire my team." All of these come back to requests to help them grow their relationship skills to navigate their way through this ever-increasing world of connectedness in order to be successful.

Relationship skills have many applications including: change management or strategy development or career progress or virtual teams or customer relationships.

applications of relationship skills

Knowing how to build strong relationships in a complex work environment affects everything leaders do, and turns out to be the focus for most of the coaching that we do with them.

WRIGHT

So how can we address today's leadership challenges?

BREUKELMAN

There is a massive opportunity to develop our relationship skills and to redefine work relationships to better serve us. It's about becoming relationship intelligent and doing business from a relationship perspective.

Consider all of the key relationships that we have in the workplace. We

complex relationship systems

have key relationships with our peers, our manager, our own team, our vendors, our customers, and so on. We have a multitude of relationships that affect how we do work, how quickly we do it, and how well we do it. What an opportunity!

Historically, we have focused on tasks to drive results, on getting things done. We have been rewarded for getting the numbers, moving quickly and looking strong. Relationships were more of a nice-to-have versus a dominant strategy for success. What we know and what we see here at Epiphany is that great results are achieved when strong relationships enable us to work better together to achieve success.

The top minds are writing about the power of relationship, too. In Covey's, *Speed of Trust,* he shares that organizations with high trust are three times more productive. Wow, that evidence directly ties productivity to relationship skills. *Harvard Business Review* shared that deep social bonds were the major predictor of team success. Deloitte recently wrote that trust and transparency were going to be leading factors in voluntary turnover.

Relationship skills are the new technology for success. Where can you use a boost?

WRIGHT

Back when I was in college, we only talked about IQ. Then, a few years ago, we heard about emotional intelligence. What does it mean to have strong relationship skills or to be relationship intelligent?

BREUKELMAN

Thanks for asking, David. As you know, we are passionate and committed about helping leaders grow their relationship skills to achieve greater success. Over the last two years, we have created a relationship model that identifies five key elements of relationship. From that model, we also built out a diagnostic coaching tool in partnership with Dr. Nancy Salay and created a series of exercises that guide and grow our clients' relationship skills.

I'm reminded of a story from a negotiations course I attended years ago. I learned the story of the orange from the book, *Getting to Yes* by Fisher, et al. Maybe you know it, too. This story demonstrates well the value of relationship.

In the story, two people need an orange. Unfortunately, there is only one orange. What to do? How do you decide who will get the orange? How do you make a pitch to convince the other person that you deserve the orange more? Or that your purpose for the orange is more important? Do you bargain a future orange or two in order to obtain this one now? Do you take the orange when she isn't looking? How do you feel in this predicament? How do you show up with her? What would you do?

Here's the rub. The truth is that the first person needed the juice of the orange while the second person needed only the peel of the orange to make a cake that called for orange rind. One orange would have satisfied both people. And only strong relationship skills would reveal this truth. A good conversation of asking questions, exploring the other person's perspective, working from shared goals of each having the orange, being courageous enough to tell the truth, being open, and willing to ask for help from the other person to solve the challenge would have provided a positive outcome for everyone.

Now, let me share the Epiphany Coaches Relationship Model with you.

The first element of relationship is conversation. Conversation explores how to lead and transform conversations to ultimately have greater impact and influence. A great conversation includes a high level of awareness of one another, communication skills (listening, questioning, speaking), clear intention, and sheer engagement. Imagine if we applied that level of engagement and purpose inside the workplace to our conversations. We gain such insight and understanding and ultimately impact and influence when we have great conversations. We can apply core concepts and see our conversations become more powerful.

The second element of relationship is called safe haven, which involves being intentional and designing our relationships. The point here is to be purposeful and directive in our key relationships. Sharing expectations, needs, commitments, and preferences allows us to build and navigate our relationships well. We build trust and safety as we honor the relationship over time. Team alliances, working agreements, and relationship plans are the crux of safe haven. Again, look to your personal life as example. Did you get married before you found out if you and your spouse wanted the same things out of life like having children, travelling, or a career? Apply the same purpose to your workplace relationships and watch your relationships flourish.

The third element called generosity focuses on being generous with time, talent, and resources in order to develop others and apply resources where the business requires them, losing our self-interest for the collective good and bringing adaptability and positivity to the workplace. Through generosity, we influence organizational capacity and agility because we can scale and assist in the most applicable areas. Did you know that Googlers can generously reward one another through $175 peer spot bonuses?

The fourth element is candor. Candor involves bringing courage and honesty to the table to have the tough conversations, especially when it may be unpopular feedback or provoke conflict. I think we can all think back to instances where no one was willing to risk their neck to speak the truth and as a result the real issue went ignored and unaddressed. In other cases, we are shy or unskilled in engaging in healthy conflict when, in fact, we need healthy conflict to drive strong solutions and innovation. We need candor so that we can address the real business issues with clarity and speed.

The fifth element of relationship is transparency. Transparency includes openness, authenticity, and owning our fallibility. This means being able to admit when we are wrong, when we don't know the answer, or when we need help. While it may be counterintuitive, the truth is that revealing our humanity actually connects us more closely to people and creates more employee retention and customer loyalty. It's a huge untapped advantage.

So by developing the five elements of relationship—conversation, safe haven, generosity, candor, and transparency—we increase our opportunities and results.

WRIGHT

How does your approach provide a road map for success?

BREUKELMAN

Overall, at an organizational level, these relationship skills affect core business outcomes. They can influence the speed, productivity, innovation, and loyalty within an organization.

Says one manager, from SAS, ranked number one in Fortune's 100 Best Companies to Work For, "People stay at SAS in large part because they are happy, but to dig a little deeper, I would argue that people don't leave SAS because they feel regarded—seen, attended to, and cared for. I have stayed for that reason, and love what I do for that reason."

Uniquely, from a leadership perspective, these relationship skills map directly to leadership competencies including: impact and influence, executive presence, strategic thinking, organizational capability, and collaboration. And likely there are even more links there than I've mentioned.

In fact, each element of relationship has its own unique benefits. Through great conversations, we gain insight and understanding that allows us to have higher impact and influence. When we design our relationships, we build trust and safety to operate together at higher levels. When we are generous with our time, talents, and resources, we increase the organization's capability and agility because we are focused on developing others and putting resources and energy in the right places instead of holding on to personal interests. Candor brings clarity and speed because we can get to the root of the real issue and find solutions more quickly and easily. Transparency builds stronger connections with our own staff, suppliers, and customers that result in loyalty and retention.

As you can see, each element of relationship develops a unique skill with benefits to leadership and business outcomes.

Epiphany Coaches Relationship Model

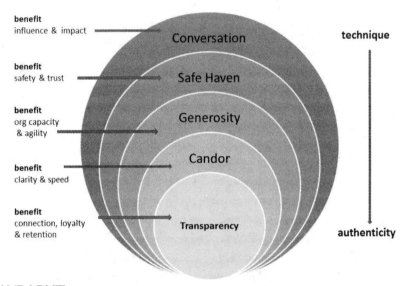

WRIGHT

So what is your vision for the future?

BREUKELMAN

The Epiphany vision is for a future where people-focused organizations and communities are the norm, where we embrace our humanity to realize our best. Spreadsheets, scorecards, and project tasks will always be critical for strong management but they fall short of inspiring full potential. Leaders in companies who focus on their people first, and leaders who make time and space for people to be authentic and build stronger relationships will be more successful.

Imagine coming to work and enjoying the ease of fully being yourself.

Imagine knowing exactly what other people expect from you.

Imagine feeling safe to say almost anything.
Imagine being able to do what's right.
Imagine being able to admit when you don't know what to do.
Imagine helping others to be their best.
Imagine feeling courageous.
Imagine feeling strong.
Imagine feeling valued.
Imagine feeling excited.

So, David, I send a challenge to leaders right now to ask yourself:

- How can you build strong relationships in and around your organization?
- How can you lead by example today?

WRIGHT

I remember a wise man told me one day that if I were walking down a country road and saw a turtle sitting on top of the fence post, I could bet he didn't get up there by himself. So, as you look back on your business life or personal life, who are the people who helped you get where you are?

BREUKELMAN

It started with my parents. They taught me to believe in myself and that I can be what I want to be and create what I want to create. An early example comes from when I was eleven years old. I moved up from T-ball to join a softball team with many older girls on the team. I remember anticipating the year playing outfield because I was the youngest.

I shared my disappointment at the dinner table one night. My dad asked me what position I wanted to play on this team. I said, "The pitcher." And he asked me, "Then what do you have to do to be the pitcher?" I spent time pitching every day for the next two months, working with one of my best friends, Cathy Lees, perfecting our pitch and catch. It worked. We enjoyed a fun and fulfilling three seasons as pitcher and catcher . . . and we even won a few games! I have witnessed many times in my life how it is possible to shape and create the world we live in. This gives me the confidence and optimism to know that leadership through relationship is possible and powerful.

In my professional life, when I worked at Microsoft, my biggest influence was the then President of Microsoft Canada, Frank Clegg. He lived and breathed candor and transparency. He held regular updates with the team, sharing the good news and the bad news, asking us to find the solutions we needed. I didn't see weakness when he shared that he didn't know how to fix these things but that he was sure we did. Instead, his honesty and disclosure created a strong connection with the entire team and inspired us to create solutions. I saw the benefits of being a transparent leader and the effect that it had on the business, watching the business grow dramatically year after year through his leadership.

We need only to look at our most admired public leaders to understand how important relationship is to leadership. Who do we fall in love with? Mother Teresa. Gandhi. Nelson Mandela. Princess Diana. Relationship is powerful and fulfilling.

Today, the circle of amazing people in my life supports me. Great relationships make everything better. I enjoy an incredible life with my amazing husband, Dan, who shows unwavering support and love in countless ways, including playing guinea pig for my many experiments and ideas. My kids, Charlie and Ella, are incredible human beings who also hold my heart and inspire me to love fully and model the values of relationship that mean so much to me. My brother, Jason, has been a constant in my life since we were very little and encourages me all along the way.

My Epiphany circle includes my dear old friend and business partner, Simon Geoghegan, who shares and inspires relationship in everything and everyone he knows. This very interview, this topic, this model, is only possible through the great work and collaboration with my team. My voice is truly the voice of Epiphany. The larger Epiphany team—our suppliers and past and current clients—all value collaboration and relationship and we create success together. Great relationships enable great success.

WRIGHT

I appreciate you taking all this time with me this morning to answer all these questions, it's been delightful. I've learned a lot, the five elements. I'm going to read them after I get back to my office and see if I can improve my leadership skills.

BREUKELMAN

I love it.

WRIGHT

Today I have been talking with Cheryl Breukelman. Cheryl is the founding partner of Epiphany Coaches, a professional coaching company. She and the Epiphany team are witnessing that relationships and collaboration are the biggest leadership opportunities in the world today.

Cheryl, thank you so much for being with us today on *Roadmap to Success*.

BREUKELMAN

Thank you so much, David. It's a pleasure.

About the Author

Cheryl is the founding partner of Epiphany Coaches, a professional coaching agency, and thought leader. The Epiphany team is evolving the leadership landscape through their coaching work around the world. She and the team passionately believe that relationships and collaboration are the biggest leadership opportunity today. Cheryl gained her twenty years of business experience through her decade at Microsoft and her work coaching hundreds of leaders and teams globally for the last ten years. Cheryl and the team regularly coach, write, and speak on the value of relationships and collaboration in various business and coaching forums.

Cheryl Breukelman

Epiphany Coaches Inc.
19 Bold St., Hamilton
ON Canada L8P 1T3
905-572-6224 office
905-572-3937 cell
cheryl@epiphanycoaches.com
www.epiphanycoaches.com

Chapter Thirteen

ENGAGE THEIR HEARTS TO GROW YOUR PROFITS

CHRISTY ERBECK

DAVID WRIGHT (WRIGHT)

Today we're talking with Christy Erbeck. Christy founded Metamorphic Consulting Inc. in 2005 to inspire positive change in people's lives and workplaces following a nearly two decade Fortune 1000 career. She served in three critical strategic posts with Flint Ink, the largest privately held ink manufacturer in the world. She also served as director of sales and marketing for a division of the international freight and logistics giant, Con-Way Transportation Services.

Metamorphic Consulting is committed to inspiring positive and lasting change in people and companies through consulting, workshops, coaching, and continuous education. By applying innovative and holistic concepts, models, and ideas, Metamorphic Consulting helps clients create an engaged and motivated workforce, thereby increasing their competitive advantage and brand equity.

Christy has a master's degree in Industrial and Organizational Psychology from The Chicago School of Professional Psychology, a BA from National Louis University, and is a graduate of multiple sales training programs. She is a member of the International Coach Federation (ICF) and the Society for Industrial & Organizational Psychologists (SIOP).

WRIGHT

Christy, welcome to *Roadmap to Success*.

CHRISTY ERBECK (ERBECK)

Thank you, David.

WRIGHT

So what is brand equity and what does it have to do with my employees?

ERBECK

At Metamorphic Consulting, we believe that brand equity is simply the amount of money someone would pay for your business beyond its book value or tangible assets. It's the dollar value that goes along with intangible assets, such as your company name and reputation, its logo and marketplace identity, and the good will that has been created through your efforts over time. Of course, it's also the value encompassed within your employees' knowledge, skills, and talents that can be difficult to measure and encapsulate.

WRIGHT

So it's everything other than the net worth?

ERBECK

Correct. Brand equity is particularly valuable when employees have specialized information with customers or technical knowledge. Most importantly, employees influence a company's brand equity when it comes to the relationships they "own" with vendors, suppliers, customers, and the general marketplace. These are all assets that don't show on a company's balance sheet.

WRIGHT

Why should I care about whether or not my employees are happy?

ERBECK

Well, David, the adage that says "a happy employee is a productive employee" is incredibly true. The challenge becomes how can we, as business owners or business leaders, help our employees be happy and productive by finding meaning within their work, their work relationships, and relating to what the company does. When they do, there is a depth and contentedness that empowers employees to go beyond just doing their job—it becomes purposeful work. A happy employee engaged in purposeful work is productive, which leads to a more profitable organization.

WRIGHT

I've heard about engaged employees or employee engagement, but what does that really mean?

ERBECK

For those of us at Metamorphic Consulting, it means capturing the whole person—heart, mind, and soul—and creating a space for full expression of an employee's dreams to manifest and flourish. The result is that the business flourishes. Employee engagement actually begins with the business leader. It's important for the leader to be fully engaged in purposeful work to model the desired employee behavior. It starts at the top and permeates throughout the organization. If you, as the business owner or leader, are not living your fullest expression then how can you expect your employees to?

WRIGHT

The term engaged employee is fascinating. How can I identify employee engagement—how do I know it's actually happening in my company and with my employees?

ERBECK

We know what's happening in our life by the actions surrounding us, right? The same applies here—observing behavior identifies the belief system permeating the culture. Some leaders are naturally more comfortable in the field and they're good at managing by walking around, yet as we go higher in organizations, that freedom to walk around and really grasp what is going on wanes.

We encourage our clients to get out of their office and walk the aisles, visit the cubicles, the research labs, or the manufacturing facilities to see the behavior that is actually happening, whether it's listening to your receptionist or seeing what goes on in the lunch room. What is the behavior that you see happening? If the company has core values listed, such as teamwork or honesty, are the employees living those values? How are those values showing up within the organization, behaviorally? To what extent is collaboration alive and well? Finally, is there genuine respect displayed toward all employees, regardless of rank?

WRIGHT

So what difference will it make if my employees are engaged and how can I track that back to my balance sheet?

ERBECK

We are frequently asked this question, and in response we ask our clients to replace the word "employees" with the word "customers." When posed that way, it is usually an "a-ha" moment for our clients and the question makes more sense. If customers are not engaged, then your balance sheet will be negatively affected, of course. Similarly, if your employees are not engaged, that, too, will affect your balance sheet. It may not be as blatantly visible as quickly, but it will show up eventually.

If employees are not engaged, then companies will experience a slow decline, apathy among staff (i.e., the, "There's nothing I can do about it, so why bother?" syndrome), and decreased profitability. It is also more difficult to attract and retain top talent, which influences a business's competitive edge and growth potential.

As leaders, we have to realize that we are privileged to have grown our dream beyond ourselves. Now it is our job to serve those employees so we can continue growing. We have a business, it's real, it's alive, it's an organism unto itself, and has the potential to do amazing things. Leaders have to get out of the way and get over ourselves. We have to "put our self on the shelf" as my friend Al Ritter states, and serve our employees so they can serve others.

WRIGHT

Christy, how do you know so much about employee engagement?

ERBECK

That's a great question, David. Serving others has always been a passion. Before starting Metamorphic Consulting, I noticed people who had really cool ideas and unique talents, but who were being emotionally destroyed within the corporate environment. Then they'd leave and that idea and the hundreds of other ideas they had would leave with them.

Over time, I was fortunate enough to come into a position of influence and began to educate the people around me about various ideas employees had, giving those employees a place to come and share their ideas in a way that allowed the leader to really see that great ideas could come from anyone. I witnessed a change, both for the individual and for the organization, when people were recognized and their ideas were validated and implemented. Humans crave attention, not in a bad way, but in the simple desire of wanting and needing to be heard, seen, and understood. We crave to be deeply understood by others to validate our existence, our thoughts, and our ideas. It's one reason why Stephen Covey's principle to "First seek to understand and then be understood" resonates so deeply. We all want that.

My interest and passion for helping companies see and hear their employees grew as Metamorphic Consulting evolved. As a result, we created The Metamorphic Experience, a leadership development program that puts these ideas into practice, ideally institutionalizing employee engagement at all levels. It's been a privilege to be in positions of influence with executives, helping them understand the value of employee engagement so that there is a balance between the emotional and intellectual aspects of business operations.

WRIGHT

When did you make the connection between brand equity and employee engagement?

ERBECK

It all came together while working for a large private global manufacturer implementing a change in their corporate strategy. The first connection was that employees who trusted and were in sync with their immediate supervisors and division presidents made the transition much easier than those who didn't, which had a positive effect on sales and earnings. The second connection occurred when the company took its focus off the strategy, and sales and earnings dropped and employee morale plummeted. This reinforced Metamorphic Consulting's belief that until a behavior is institutionalized, a strategy is vulnerable. We also noted the direct correlation between the relationship of an employee with his or her supervisor and a company's performance.

WRIGHT

So how do you influence a paradigm shift in leaders' minds relative to defining brand equity?

ERBECK

You don't. There will be no paradigm shift until a leader's heart is influenced. Then there is a chance. Once that shift is made, there is less chance of a backslide, which is great news for companies. At the point of heart engagement, we can work with that leader and help that person refine, adjust, embrace, and empower his or her organization to redefine brand equity, how it is measured, and how it shows up within the organization.

It's similar to the buying process that occurs in a purchase decision. The buying process occurs because an emotional decision is made first and then the person uses intellectual reasoning to justify that purchase decision, so nothing meaningful, nothing permanent occurs until it occurs in the heart.

WRIGHT

How can companies create a culture of engaged employees?

ERBECK

Our methodology takes a holistic approach to creating a culture of engaged employees, marrying the linear process with the abstract and organic, creative process that generates innovative thinking and development.

The first step is to define what "engaged" looks like within that particular organization. Each company is unique, so while you may be able to borrow ideas from other organizations, the best source for defining "engaged" is internally by leveraging employees' ideas.

Then everyone in the organization has to start living it, and being accountable to it. Our consultants help them do that by analyzing their systems and their processes—what procedures need to be created to support it? What's currently in place that goes against that definition and culture? Everything has to be evaluated, from compensation to review processes. Also important is taking into consideration, for example, how compensation is managed and handled against the behaviors they want to reward. So when there is a compensation or development plan that is contrary to the culture they want to create, it has to be changed so that the process, system, or procedure supports the change needed.

The next step is to measure it. Six Sigma's philosophy tells us that "what gets measured gets done" and that is absolutely true in the case of creating a culture of employee engagement. The leaders have to set the example and their personal standards have to be modeling and deploying that behavior as consistently as they would expect any other employee to do so.

WRIGHT

Isn't it awfully expensive to create a culture like the one you're talking about?

ERBECK

Isn't it too expensive not to? If you think about it, years ago companies could expect employees to stay twenty, twenty-five, thirty years, and that no longer happens. The average tenure for CEOs is about eighteen months and for employees it's really not much better—I believe three to five years is the average tenure for employees today.

WRIGHT

CEOs stay eighteen months?

ERBECK

There is a lot of data out there right now showing that CEOs don't last much longer than eighteen months due to shareholder and market pressures. The importance of driving brand equity and employee engagement with everybody from the janitor to the sales person to that executive suite is critical. Everyone from the top down has to be engaged in order for that change to occur, and for the sales and earnings to really take hold and increase. That doesn't happen overnight, and unfortunately Wall Street hasn't understood that or hasn't cared. There is some indication that this attitude may be changing, but it is in limited markets and industries. In the end, it makes it very challenging for publicly held organizations to implement these types of strategies, which is why we see high turnover with CEOs.

If we can go back to the "it's too expensive" argument, let's talk about the cost of attaining a new employee. For example, let's say you want to hire a receptionist and your annual budget for that position is $30,000. We have to also consider the ancillary costs associated with that talent acquisition—training, development, benefits—as well as the ramp-up time for that person to actually be efficient and productive in your work environment. You can expect to add about 30 to 50 percent on top of the hard salary costs of any employee. That $30,000 investment is really costing about $39,000 to $45,000.

So don't you want to receive the most benefit for that investment? Of course you do. By creating an environment that engages employees, not only will you recoup that $39,000 to $45,000 investment, you potentially can double it through productivity, idea generation, and customer retention. Additionally, think about the competitive advantage you create through employee retention and the cost savings if you beat those industry tenure averages so that your employees turn every six to ten years or longer? Now, you've not only reduced your costs, but you've also improved your competitive advantage through your employee knowledge base.

WRIGHT

Many people might think this is insipid and fluff and that it really doesn't add value to a business, so how do you respond when you hear a company's leader say that?

ERBECK

David, personally, it used to really frustrate me. Today, our perspective is one of empathy—for the employees and customers as well as for that company's leader. Our consultants see it as an opportunity to ask questions, to better understand their perspective, and then to look for opportunities to plant seeds that would allow that person to consider a different perspective. We also see it as a business that is in trouble, maybe not today or tomorrow, but shortly down the road that business is in for a rude awakening if that is their hard and fast perspective.

WRIGHT

So why should business leaders care about retaining employees and isn't that too costly nowadays?

ERBECK

I think retaining employees is critical, and I want to clarify that we don't want you to retain somebody just to retain somebody. It's about retaining the right people in the right jobs doing the right things and for the right reasons, to paraphrase Jim Collins's theory in *Good to Great*. Just as it costs ten times as much to acquire a new customer as to keep an existing one, it can be that costly to acquire a new employee. Further, if we look at why people leave their jobs, the number one reason is a poor relationship with their direct supervisor.

If we're working to engage all of our employees and utilize them in the best manner possible, then we're minimizing the cost of losing those employees, and losing everything they know when they walk out the door, about our customers, about our business, about our competitors.

WRIGHT

If I were reading this book, how could I get my CFO to understand the importance of brand equity and employee engagement whether through hard or soft dollars?

ERBECK

CFOs love their numbers. That's where they live and that's what they're paid to do and to know. So we go to them with the information in terms that they can understand—acquisition costs, turnover costs, lost customer costs or opportunity costs, and training costs. Then we include them in a conversation about measuring, implementing, and integrating a process for measuring behavior that's tied to sales, profitability, or other cost savings.

Metamorphic Consulting takes a business process improvement (BPI) approach toward our client engagements. We take what is good and what is working within that system and improve upon it. In doing so, we align compensation to the new strategy or culture. Even though it may be a sensitive subject, we have to understand that people are motivated by what they are paid to do. To that end, we want to make sure there are financial incentives to support the company's direction.

The other piece to remember is that CFOs are also employees, so careful thought must be put into how to engage their heart as well, while still giving them what they need to manage the financial health of the company. Simply put, it does come down to measure, measure, measure.

WRIGHT

What an interesting conversation, especially since I own a company; I've been taking copious notes here. The idea of increasing a company's value beyond its tangible assets is really a fascinating subject and I think you've covered it well here today. I really appreciate all the time you've taken with me to answer these questions. As I said, I've learned a lot and I'm sure our readers will.

ERBECK

It's been my pleasure and privilege, David, and I appreciate the opportunity.

WRIGHT

Today we've been talking with Christy Erbeck. Christy founded Metamorphic Consulting in 2005. Metamorphic Consulting is committed to inspiring positive and lasting change in people and companies through consulting, workshops, coaching, and continuous education. By applying innovative and holistic concepts, models, and ideas, Metamorphic Consulting helps clients create an engaged and motivated workforce, thereby increasing their competitive advantage and brand equity.

WRIGHT

Christy, thank you so much for being with us today on *Roadmap to Success*.

ERBECK

Thank you, David.

About the Author

Christy Erbeck founded Metamorphic Consulting, Inc. in 2005 to inspire positive change in people's lives and workplaces following a nearly two-decade Fortune 1000 career. She served in three critical strategic posts with Flint Ink, the largest privately held ink manufacturer in the world, and was director of sales and marketing for a division of international freight and logistics giant, Con-Way Transportation Services.

Metamorphic Consulting is committed to inspiring positive and lasting change in people and companies through consulting, workshops, coaching, and continuous education. By applying innovative and holistic concepts, models, and ideas, Metamorphic Consulting helps clients create an engaged and motivated workforce, thereby increasing their competitive advantage and brand equity. Christy has a master's degree in Industrial and Organizational Psychology from The Chicago School of Professional Psychology, a BA from National Louis University, and is a graduate of multiple sales training programs. She is a member of the International Coach Federation (ICF) and the Society for Industrial & Organizational Psychologists (SIOP).

She and her husband, Bruce, own Flat Squirrel Scooters, and have two college-age daughters. They live in Illinois' northwest suburbs with their yellow Lab, Harley. Her hobbies include yoga, reading, writing, and scooter and motorcycle riding, music, and other creative arts.

Christy Erbeck

Metamorphic Consulting, Inc.
421 N. Randall Road
Lake in the Hills, IL 60156
224-558-7004
christy@metamorphicconsulting.com
www.metamorphicconsulting.com
www.linkedin.com/in/christyerbeck

Chapter Fourteen

BLIND SPOTS

HELEN TURNBULL, PHD

DAVID WRIGHT (WRIGHT)

Today I'm talking with Helen Turnbull, PhD and CEO of Human Facets. Dr. Turnbull is a global inclusion and diversity consultant. Her client experience includes Texas Instruments, JPMorgan Chase, Hewlett Packard, Citigroup, Baker-Hughes Oilfields, Miller Coors, and Southern Company. More recently, she has been working in Australia with a number of major clients on Unconscious Bias and how it influences their leadership decisions." Dr. Turnbull has assisted international clients to win prestigious diversity awards; she has two online assessment tools, Cognizant on Unconscious Bias, and the Inclusion Skills Measurement Profile. She has won the Distinguished Research Award for coauthoring a journal article titled "Diversity and Inclusion: Developing an Instrument for Identifying Diversity Skills Deficiencies," published in *The Academy of Strategic Management Journal* (January 2010). She has a second article published (Volume 15, No. 1, p. 11) in the *Journal of Organizational Culture, Communications, and Conflict.*

She is currently a member of the Academy of Management (AOM), The American Psychological Association (APA), the Organizational Development Network (ODN), The Society for Phenomenology and the Human Sciences (SPHS), The National Speakers Association, and the Global Speakers Network.

Dr. Turnbull, welcome to *ROADMAP to Success.*

HELEN TURNBULL (TURNBULL)

Thank you very much, David, I'm happy to be here.

WRIGHT

If you don't mind, I'd like to start this interview a little differently. I'd like to read what you have written and then ask you some questions about it. You write: "In the twenty-first century, a key component of any road map to success must include consideration of diversity and inclusion challenges faced by each individual. Our social identity group memberships frame our experience of our world and form a lens through which we judge others and ourselves. Understanding the complexity of our own differences, our affect on others, and our response to differences are critical leverage points on the road to personal and professional success."

So having read that, what does understanding diversity have to do with personal and professional success?

TURNBULL

Our diversity has a lot to do with our personal and professional success at multiple complex levels. We are members of numerous social identity groups simultaneously. I am a woman, Scottish, and a Baby Boomer. I have different perspectives and knowledge about my life based on each of these frames of reference. I form not only values and beliefs but attitudes and feelings about myself and others based on the life stories I have gathered.

Socrates said "The unexamined life is not worth living," and for all of us, part of the work we have to do is look at ourselves and be constantly examining our own views, beliefs, and attitudes. Where did these views come from? Where did I get my messages? What unconscious biases am I carrying? Do I have a positive or negative predisposition based on these multiple frames of reference? If I believe that being a woman and a Baby Boomer limits my work experiences, then I am likely to help create that reality. If, on the other hand, I believe that not only can I accomplish anything I put my mind to, but that being a Baby Boomer brings wisdom and experience, then I have increased my chances of continued success.

Being Scottish, I may tell myself that having a Scottish accent in America is advantageous, and it will positively influence how I feel about myself and how I interact with others. If, on the other hand, I tell myself that my new boss is English and she does not like Scottish people then I may well negatively influence the outcome.

Values are formed very early in life and many of our beliefs about ourselves and judgments about others are being driven from messages that have dropped into our unconscious and formed shortcuts or heuristics and blind spots.

You predispose yourself toward success or failure based on your attitude. The stories you tell yourself will strongly influence the outcome. If you believe someone does not like you, then you are much more likely to draw negative energy to yourself to confirm that belief each time you interact with that person. It is equally true that if you believe your social identity group (e.g. being a woman), is also a disadvantage, then that will hamper your success prospects.

WRIGHT

So what does it mean to "do your own work on diversity and inclusion"?

TURNBULL

Similar to what I just said, what it does mean is to be self-reflective—it is important to know yourself. I have been working with major corporations all over the world on Diversity and Inclusion since 1985 and I speak to a lot of people, particularly women, people of color, and gay or lesbian employees who have internalized negative messages from the dominant culture. This phenomenon is known as "internalized oppression." The flip side of the same coin is "assimilation." Many people are caught in the psychological traps created by both of these negative processes—internalized oppression and assimilation.

In her book, *The Loudest Duck*, Laura Lismore refers to the assimilation process as the Elephant and the Mouse syndrome. The elephant is so large and imposing that he does not need to care what others think, but the mouse on the other hand needs to know everything about the elephant, including every move it makes in order to avoid being trampled.

When you try too hard to fit in to another group, you lose touch with a piece of who you really are. You lose touch with your own identity because you've assimilated so much and are trying so hard to fit in and be accepted that it drains some of your energy. Recent research in the field of neuroscience using Functional MRIs revealed that the experience of feeling excluded activates the same part of the brain (the dorsal portion of the anterior cingulate cortex) as it would for the experience of physical pain

(Eisenberger, UCLA, 2009). In other words, the pain we feel from social exclusion is affecting us in the same way as physical pain.

Doing your own work on diversity starts with understanding your own behaviors before judging others. You will be much more open-minded to the stories from other cultures, whether it's race, gender, religion, age, sexual orientation, etc. if you understand that you're standing on solid ground around your own identity.

WRIGHT

In reading some of the things you have written, I came across the "diversity paradox." What is that?

TURNBULL

The diversity paradox is interesting. I'm sure you've heard people say, "All I need to do is treat people with respect and treat them as human beings." Equally popular is the statement, "I always hire the best person for the job, regardless of diversity; I don't care if they are purple with yellow hair as long as they can do the job." The misnomer in this belief is that there is no such thing as a meritocracy. Meritocracy is a myth; there is no such thing as a level playing field and no one ever treats everyone alike.

I had a professor who told me, "There is no such thing as the innocent eye." If our views of a level playing field matched our heart monitors we would not be breathing. We need variance. We are all subjective and have a predisposition to hire in our own image, showing a natural tendency toward affinity bias.

The diversity paradox presents three different ways of looking at people. The first line of the paradox states that *"we are all alike,"* We have a common universal human experience, we all get up in the morning, we all get dressed, we all have to eat, we all have to sleep, we all have to feed our families, etc., so therefore there is a universality in the human experience.

The second line of the paradox states that *"we are like no other human being."* Each one of us is unique, with our own DNA, our own genetic structure, our own life experience, our own history, our own stories, and our own personality. When you hold both of these lines of the paradox in your hands simultaneously, you have "we are all alike" and "we are all uniquely different." How can both be true? And yet, they are.

The third line of the paradox, and this is where I believe the diversity work resides, is that *"we are like some people more than others."* This speaks directly to our social identity group membership. As a woman, I have things in common with other women and I can make some assumptions that as women we have had similar experiences in life, knowing what it's like to go through life as a woman. If you're a person of color you can make the assumption that another person of color, particularly if he or she is from your own group, will have had some experiences that are similar, even if you have never spoken to that person.

The diversity paradox therefore means that in order to truly embrace the challenges of embedding inclusion in organizations or in society, we need to understand that all three things are alive and functioning simultaneously—yes it is true that we're all human, it is also true that we're all different, and yet at the same time, the third truism is that some of us are more similar than others. I have things in common with some people and a life experience with some people that others don't share or necessarily understand.

There are two other levels of complexity in the diversity paradox. The first one is the falsely held belief that we treat people as individuals and do not notice their group membership, and indeed, do not care about it. This is very far from the truth. If you do not notice color you are most likely at risk for running red lights. We all notice differences, but when people say they do not notice differences it is because they have conditioned themselves to cognitively deny what they are seeing. The belief that we treat everyone as individuals and their group identity does not matter is an illusion. My questions to people who tell me they don't care about other people's race, gender, or sexual orientation (as long as they can do the job) are: "What if they care? What if it matters to them?".

Messages from the group membership frame of reference provide another layer of complexity. They often unconsciously shape the experiences people are having. For example, as a woman, if you tell yourself you are being held back by the "Old Boys Club" then you probably will be and even if you are not aware of that message, it can still be operating in the background. The collective group experience can also contribute to whether people have a tendency toward a success or failure mentality. The stories you tell yourself about the abilities of your social identity group(s) influences how you view yourself and your own abilities.

WRIGHT

Will you provide examples of when incompetence around diversity and inclusion has impeded success?

TURNBULL

Incompetence always impedes success, but from a diversity and inclusion perspective it has a particularly insidious role to play. Going back to the diversity paradox, if the story that you've told yourself is that life doesn't treat you well because your societal group isn't treated well, then that will impede your chances of succeeding.

For example, there is a glass ceiling for women and it is true that women don't have the same opportunities as men—sexism does exist and is still alive and not well. At a collective and systemic level, we must continue to address these injustices; however, each individual woman has a choice about how she approaches these in-built inequities. Some women have taken a perspective that says, "I know there are obstacles. I'm not going to worry about them; I'm going to strive ahead anyway."

Other women take more of a victim role, believing they are not going to get ahead because men are the dominant culture, men are the leaders, and men call the shots. It also needs to be said that even if a woman makes a choice to "ignore" the injustices, the injustices still exist and she is most likely still experiencing them. As with everything in life, there is complexity—very few things are one-dimensional. There are variables involved in the decisions that each person makes. We do not consciously decide to take a position in life merely based on our social identity group membership. For example, a woman who decides that she is not getting a "fair go" and sexism is at the root of the problem, probably also has other factors involved in her story.

The collective consciousness of the group and the unconscious beliefs that the group carries about itself are manifest through the individual members. If you are carrying the negativity from these messages, they can impede your success. Let me reiterate that this is not to say that sexism does not exist and that it does not have a real effect on women, it clearly does, but it is a delicate balancing act that women have to walk. We must not let the glass ceiling and sexism drag us down and at the same time we must strive forward while remembering to reach out and help other women.

WRIGHT

I was interested to read some of your notes about the myriad of examples. For example, the latest Dr. Laura problem, the police officer and the Harvard professor.

TURNBULL

You don't have to go very far these days, other than to switch on the news, to see that there are myriads of examples of when people step in their own way.

The police officer incident with the Harvard professor is a reminder that racial tension is just under the surface. I think it's a misnomer for people to believe we elected a black president and ergo, that proves that we're not racist anymore. I think that it doesn't prove anything other than the country elected a Black president, and the issue of racism doesn't go away just because President Obama is Black.

In actual fact, I would argue that what's begun to happen is that racism has moved closer to the surface and people are becoming more irrational. Accusing President Obama of not being an American is an example of this irrationality.

WRIGHT

Can you provide examples of when competence, diversity, and inclusion have made a major contribution to becoming successful?

TURNBULL

I have a number of clients—a lot of the Fortune 500 companies—who have done an excellent job of including diversity and inclusion in their organization and to really promote it in a way that actually builds an inclusive environment. These companies are really doing good work on their Diversity and Inclusion policies and practices. A number of clients I am working with, particularly in Australia, are very leading edge in their approach to Diversity and Inclusion and are addressing the issue of Unconscious Bias with their leadership teams, particularly through the use of my online assessment tool, Cognizant.

There is a difference between *diversity* and *inclusion*. Diversity means differences and inclusion is about the environment you create. I tell my clients, "Just because you've got them [diverse employees] does not mean you get it [what you need to do to create an inclusive environment]." You can look around your organization and you can see diverse employees, but if you're not doing something to help people understand what needs to happen to build inclusion, understanding, and awareness, to remove unconscious bias and work on blind-spots, you're going to have a revolving door of women and people of color leaving your organization, and LGBT employees staying in the closet.

So I think that the competence around diversity and inclusion is where these top companies have figured out that it's not just about hiring diverse people, it's about the environment you create so that people can bring their best and most authentic selves to the table.

WRIGHT

Are there particular diversity challenges that need to be addressed in order to be successful in the business world?

TURNBULL

Yes, I think that there are a lot of diversity challenges that still need to be addressed. We have learned in the last decade or so how to be politically correct. All that does is take the issues and push them under the table. Then they start to manifest in what I call "leakage," where our attitudes and beliefs are really driving our behaviors, even when we try to mask them. If you haven't looked at your own unconscious biases and blind spots, then the attitude you have toward people of difference is still there and it will leak out in small ways. Sexism, racism, or homophobia may not be overt, but it will still be there and it will be there in subtle ways and people who are affected by it will feel it. So there are multiple challenges to working on our own diversity and inclusion perspective. I think there is also the issue of conscious and unconscious bias. Most people recognize when they consciously dislike individuals or groups, but there is also a myriad of unconscious ways that they can, without really paying attention, be treating others in an inferior manner. For example, your tone of voice can be patronizing or condescending without you being aware of the derogatory effect.

WRIGHT

What is "internalized oppression" and why does it matter?

TURNBULL

Internalized oppression is a phenomenon that occurs when people in minority cultures—anyone who is not dominant in society—take on the messages of the dominant culture and turn them on themselves and each other.

Internalized oppression is the result of taking on the negative messages about our own group that we consciously and unconsciously receive from members of the dominant culture and then turning these negative behaviours on ourselves and each other (e.g., women believing they are bad drivers because men tell us we are).

Internalized oppression is also inextricably linked to the desire to assimilate into the dominant culture in order to fit in and be accepted. It can manifest as assimilation behaviors (e.g., women becoming more aggressive in order to be accepted by men), and ethnic minorities or LGBT distancing themselves from their own social identity group in order to not be seen as surrounding themselves with too many people like them (Turnbull, 2005).

Willie Lynch, a slave owner from the West Indies, told the American slave owners, "I'll teach you how to control your slaves for three hundred years. Just set them against each other, (i.e., put the light colored slaves in the houses, put the dark colored slaves in the fields) and constantly set them against each other and if you do that successfully, you can step back and watch them fight against each other.

Internalized oppression therefore means that women, people of color, and the LGBT community internalize the negativity that was perpetrated by the dominant culture. For example, if women are told that they are not good at math, then that message bleeds into the psyche of women and they buy that belief. Of course, on any standard deviation curve there will be women who are brilliant at math and women who fail miserably. Women are consistently told they are not good drivers and recent studies have shown that stereotype threat (reminding people of the negative beliefs about them) is realized when women are reminded they do not drive as well as men.

Another insidious aspect of internalized oppression is how it turns people against their own group. For example, the illusion that women all get along is just that—an illusion. Other women are not always our best friends or supporters, in fact, in order to succeed in the corporate world it is imperative that women align themselves with successful men and this is often accomplished by distancing themselves from other women.

The insidious nature of internalized oppression is that I may sabotage myself and other people from my social identity group. This goes back to the question, "How can you be personally successful when you are carrying the burden of that kind of negativity?"

WRIGHT

When you consider race, ethnicity, gender, sexual orientation, religion, generational difference, can you describe the challenges for each diverse group as they show up for them professionally? How might they impede their own success?

TURNBULL

If you look at race for example, the challenge for people of color is that they have to walk a delicate road between being true to their own culture and keeping the dominant culture "comfortable." The more they assimilate into the style and mores of the dominant culture, the more they are "accepted." So either they do that on a semi-permanent basis, that's who they are and that's how they've learned to be and it's not something they question about themselves, or they're leaving a lot of their identity in the parking lot in the morning when they walk into work and not able to be fully themselves all day because they're walking on eggshells.

As a coping mechanism, people become skilled at the art of assimilation, but it really is an energy drain. Think how much more productive we could be if we were free to bring our more authentic selves to work. This happens for women, people of color, members of the LGBT community, etc. It also, in fairness, happens for white men, particularly when they are not an easy fit for the "bloky culture." There are many men who do not easily fit the mold and find themselves having to adjust their style or pretend to "go along" in order to be accepted. There are also "degrees of difference" that make it easier to be accepted by the dominant culture(s). In other words, while we all have to play the game and figure out how to fit in, the degrees of difference also make a difference. If you are a Hindu Indian female in cultural dress, have English as a second language, and speak with an accent, then you are six degrees of difference away from the Western "norm" and are more likely to have difficulties trying to "fit in." An Indian male born in a Western culture who speaks English as a first language, has an accent congruent with that country, and dresses in a Western business suit has an easier time being viewed as a "good fit," as he is only one degree of difference removed from the "norm" and will more easily be accepted as "the model minority."

There is a huge energetic difference between compliance and commitment. When I'm in compliance mode, I'm holding something back even though I'm not conscious of it. The assimilation process mirrors compliance and for all of these groups, it is much more intense than we realize.

Corporations need to work on imbedding inclusion so that people can feel free to be more fully themselves and let go of the need to copy others. We put the words "diversity" and "inclusion" in the same sentence, but in reality "diversity" is about demographics and managing the numbers and "inclusion" is where the real work is. If they want to truly value differences and avoid the perpetual revolving door and leakage from their talent pipeline, corporations need to figure out how to create a more inclusive environment and to widen their peripheral vision so that leadership potential can be viewed through more than just a Western lens.

Women are very aware that if we are too feminine we are accused of being soft and ineffective and using our sexuality in the workplace. However, if we move to the other end of the continuum and become aggressive and/or too assertive, speak up, argue back, and state our position strongly then they assign the "B" word to us and I don't mean "beautiful."

So how do you walk on that line to know how you can be fully yourself as a strong woman? Another complexity in this scenario is that it is not just men who assign the "B" word, it is other women. That is what I mean about turning the internalized oppression in on ourselves and each other. Women are often the first to criticize other women, which of course leaves men shaking their heads and saying "Well, if they cannot get along with each other, what chance do we have?" A 2009 UK survey of 2000 women in full time and part time positions showed that 63 percent preferred male bosses. A 2008 study from the University of Toronto revealed that women working under a sole female supervisor reported more physical and emotional distress when working for a woman.

WRIGHT

Will you describe the challenges for each diverse group as they show up for them personally? How might they get in their own way?

TURNBULL

We are all capable of getting in our own way on a myriad of issues, but when you focus on our social identity group membership, such as being a woman, a person of color, or a gay or lesbian person, then what we are talking about again is the concept of internalized oppression. Suzanne Lipsky (1987) describes internalized oppression as hurts and mistreatments that are not healed and therefore continue to be restimulated, causing individuals to turn the distress in on themselves. San Juanita Garza (2000) said, "White people are not the only people acting out of Whiteness. I have known Hispanic and African Americans who act more White than some of the White people I know" (p. 61).

On the subject of sexual orientation, for example, the challenge for people who are gay and lesbian is that they have to make a constant decision whether to come out or stay in the closet and if they come out, who do they come out to? If they have been in the closet and laughed along with the homophobic jokes that their colleagues are making, then that is collusion in the oppression and is yet another example of internalized oppression. Participating in the negative behaviors of the dominant culture toward your own group shuts down a part of your authentic self.

WRIGHT

If you were given the sexual orientation example, when would participating in the internalized oppression not be your fault?

TURNBULL

There is a difference between the idea of doing your own work, which means being cognizant of who you are and how you portray yourself and asking yourself: What do I need to do to learn and grow. How am I affecting other people, and what do I need to do to become more successful? Internalized oppression is insidious, it's complex, and it's systemic. It goes back to the paradox of diversity—it's not just about you individually, it's about you as part of a system and the system is already sick because the system is set up to be oppressive. Derrick Bell, the author of *Faces at the Bottom of the Well*, eloquently sets out the scenario that there will always be a group at the bottom.

Most people are well-intentioned and are not saying to themselves, "I think I'll go to work and oppress somebody today." So I don't know if any of this can be assigned as blame so much as it's built into an already oppressive system and we all have to own a piece of it and be aware of its existence—whether or not we are members of a dominant culture or subculture, or, as Laura Lismore said, "whether you are an elephant or a mouse." As long as oppression exists, the flip side of the coin will always be internalized oppression and assimilation.

WRIGHT

I was interested in some things I had read. You were talking about micro-inequities, micro-aggressions, micro-invalidations, and diversity tipping points. It was interesting to me, but I didn't completely understand what you were talking about.

TURNBULL

I have spoken to the systemic issues such as assimilation, political correctness, and internalized oppression, but the micro-inequities is another aspect of the Diversity and Inclusion challenge. In fact, there are two excellent books written by an Asian American, Derald Wing Sue, *Microaggressions and Marginality* and *Microaggressions in Everyday Life.* Sue has done an outstanding job of pointing out the insidious nature of all the little things that happen to people—the microinequities. It can be something as simple as my asking you to do something for me and then double-checking your work and do it again. If you see me do that often enough, you pretty much know that I do not trust you. You then start asking yourself why and that is where the doubt about social identity membership creeps in. Is it because she does not like me? Is it because I am a man of color? Is it because I am gay, etc. Women experience microinequities when they're in meetings and they say something and nobody listens to them and two minutes later a man says the same thing and it's declared to be a great idea. That is another excellent and well-recognized example of a micro-inequity.

People also say things such as "when I see you I don't see color," "America is a melting pot—there is only one race and it's the human race." These are the examples of color blindness. They're said with good intention but the effect of them on a person of color is like water dripping on a stone because you know that the person who is saying them doesn't understand, doesn't know your story, and hasn't done their own (diversity) work.

WRIGHT

I was interested in a statement you had made and, if you will, I'll quote you and you can tell me what you mean: "stop sitting on a rusty nail and get out of your own way."

TURNBULL

Yes, I sometimes say to people if you don't like the situation, how long are you going to sit there? There is no point in sitting on a rusty nail and complaining about the pain. Only you can choose to get up; the sooner you do, the sooner things can change for the better.

Wayne Dyer is often quoted as saying, "If you change the way you look at things, the things you look at change." So in order to get off that rusty nail, we have to change the way we look at things. If you're miserable doing what you're doing or being who you are, then decide to think differently. If you don't like your co-workers, then how about going in to work tomorrow and deciding that you are going to spend the day smiling at them and wait to see if that changes anything.

It goes back to having personal power—if you're going to become successful regardless of your diversity, you absolutely have to do self-examination and ask yourself, "Do I choose to be a victim or do I choose to be a victor?"

WRIGHT

Well, what an interesting conversation, Dr. Turnbull. I really have enjoyed it. I appreciate all the time you've spent with me talking about diversity and inclusion. It's extremely helpful; I have learned a lot and I'm sure our readers will.

TURNBULL

Thank you, David; I appreciate it.

WRIGHT

I have been talking with Helen Turnbull, PhD. Dr. Turnbull is a global inclusion and diversity consultant. Her client lists reads like a Who's Who in American businesses and she has helped many of them win prestigious diversity awards. She has two online assessment tools, "Cognizant on Unconscious Bias" and the "Inclusion Skills Measurement Profile." She has won the distinguished research award for co-authoring an article, "Diversity Inclusion: Developing an Instrument for the Identification of Skills Deficiency" She has been published in *The Academy of Strategic Management Journal* and the *Journal of Organizational Culture, Communications, and Conflict.*

Dr. Turnbull, thank you so much for being with us today on *ROADMAP to Success.*

References:

Bell Derrick (1992) *Faces at the bottom of the Well,* Basic Books

Dyer Wayne (2004) *The Power of Intention,* Hay House.

Garza San Juanita (2000) *Dismantling White Privilege: Pedagogy, Politics and Whiteness.Counterpoints: Studies in the Post-Modern Theories of Education,* volume 73

http://www.eric.ed.gov/ERICWebPortal/search/detailmini.jsp?_nfpb=true&_&ERICExtSearch_SearchValue_0=ED456010&ERICExtSearch_SearchType_0=no&accno=ED456010

Liswood Laura (2010) *The Loudest Duck,* John Wiley & Sons, Hoboken, NJ.

Lipsky Suzanne (1987) *Internalized Racism,* Rational Island Publishers, Seattle Washington.

Sue Wing Derald (2010) *Micro-Aggressions in Everyday life,* John Wiley & Sons, Hoboken, NJ.

Sue Wing Derald (2010) *Micro-Aggressions and Marginality,* John Wiley & Sons, Hoboken, NJ.

Turnbull Helen PhD (2005) *The experiences of internalized oppression by female diversity workers of different social identity groups,* University of Michigan.

"63% of women prefer male bosses"
http://www.forbes.com/2010/04/23/management-issues-workplace-forbes-woman-views-worst-bosses.html

Functional MRI study on social exclusion

Naomi Eisenberger and Matthew Lieberman with KD Williams, "Does Rejection Hurt? an fMRI study of Social Exclusion" *Science* vol 30, no 5643 October 2003, 290-292: Covers the Cyberball experiment.

Naomi Eisenberger and Matthew Lieberman, "The Pains and Pleasures of Social Life," *Science*, vol. 323, no. 5916, February 2009, 890–891: Explication of social pain and social pleasure, and the impact of fairness, status, and autonomy on brain response.

ABOUT THE AUTHOR

Dr. Helen Turnbull has thirty years of experience assisting businesses in enhancing organizational capabilities. As a practiced Organizational Development consultant, Dr. Turnbull assists clients in developing a full range of organizational development consulting services including strategic planning, diversity and multicultural change management, training, leadership development, executive coaching, team-building, and merging of organizational cultures. She is a global inclusion and diversity specialist. Her dissertation research was on internalized oppression across cultures and she has a deep knowledge and understanding of organizational culture and what it takes to create an inclusive environment.

Dr. Turnbull's extensive experience includes working with Blue Chip clients such as Texas Instruments, Raytheon, JPMorgan Chase & Co., Lehman Brothers, Motorola, Hewlett Packard, AT & T, Lucent Technologies, IBM, Citigroup Europe, Commonwealth Bank of Australia, National Australia Bank, and Ernst & Young, Australia. Dr. Turnbull made major contributions in assisting Texas Instruments to win the Catalyst Award and the Malcolm Baldridge Award, and was instrumental in helping both JP Morgan Chase and Citigroup Europe win the prestigious Opportunity Now Award and Business in the Community Awards. She has also developed leading-edge online assessment tools that provide clients with behavioral metrics for individuals and organizations, including "Cognizant," an unconscious bias assessment tool, and "ISM Profile," the Inclusion Skills Measurement Profile, which is a 360-degree online skills identification assessment for Diversity and Inclusion.

In addition to her doctorate in Human and Organizational Systems, Helen has two master's degrees—one in Industrial Psychology and Mental Health Counseling and a second in Human and Organizational systems. She received her undergraduate degree in Sociology and Psychology and is a current or past member of a number of significant professional organizations such as the Academy of Management, American Psychological Association, and the American Sociological Association. In 2009 she won the "Distinguished Research Award" for her article, "Diversity & Inclusion: Developing an Instrument for the identification of Skills deficiencies" published in the *Academy of Strategic Management Journal*. In 2010 she had an article published in the *Organizational Culture & Conflict Journal*. In 2009 she won the faculty nomination to speak at the "Last Lecture series" at Nova Southeastern University. She is also the author of an allegorical tale, *Village of Illusions,* and an upcoming nonfiction book, *Looking through the Liking Glass.* She is a member of the National Speakers Association and the Global Speakers Network and she is an accomplished keynote speaker.

Helen Turnbull PhD, CEO

Human Facets
954-370-6343
drhelenturnbull@humanfacets.com
www.humanfacets.com

Chapter Fifteen

RESISTANCE TO CHANGE— "INSANITY"

KEITH NABE

DAVID WRIGHT (WRIGHT)

Today, I'm speaking with Keith Nabe. Keith brings more than thirty years of experience in Management Consulting to Businesses and Corporations worldwide in more than one hundred industries. Keith is a results-oriented, continuous improvement professional in Change Management who has successfully effected bottom line profitability by reducing operational costs while improving processes, quality assurance, on-time deliverables, and management operating systems. Keith is a professional speaker, former radio and television broadcaster, and a certified training facilitator and presenter in Change Management, Sales, Reorganizational Change, and Process Improvement. Keith has been an active community supporter within the Chamber of Commerce and is a member of the International Speakers Network.

Keith, welcome to *Roadmap to Success*.

When did you begin your consulting business?

KEITH NABE (NABE)

I began my consulting career in 1978 with a humble beginning working in coal mines and manufacturing operations in the United States. In those days, it did not require more than a bachelor's degree and some willingness to really get dirty and dive into the operational dysfunctions of companies. One of the first noticeable road blocks that was huge then and remains huge today was behavioral resistance to change at all levels of the management food chain.

Today, more than thirty-four years later, businesses worldwide remain very resistant to change. This is *"insanity!"*

Of course you know the definition of *insanity*, right?

Businesses still continue to do the things they have always done and expect different results.

Most still want to do things their way. Now more than ever they reject experienced, professional help from the scores of professional consultants, not because of their costs, but because CEOs and management teams think they can do the operational changes themselves. *Big mistake!*

Resistance to Change may be active or passive, overt or covert, individual or organized, aggressive or timid, and on occasions totally justified.

Sadly, most significant change fails to meet the expectations and targets of the proposers. The failure is given the catchall name "resistance," yet resistance can be principled and creative as well as from vested interest. Top management is frequently unreasonable in their expectations and time scale, forgetting the process it went through or is about to go through when it decided to make the change.

WRIGHT

So, how do you effectively change this change process?

NABE

An effective change manager will prepare an organization for change in the early stages of project definition and stakeholder review by taking managers at all levels through a similar sales process and responding to their apparent resistance: *The Creative Conflict.* This process is likely to improve the project definition and buy-in. It will also ensure that it is clear the moment resistance becomes vested interest.

But, it is unrealistic to expect an independent change manager to tackle vested interest resistance. The change director, normally the CEO, can use his or her intervention as a signal to the organization. Such interventions should be few but telling.

Too often, an independent change manager is a cross between a foil and a lightning conductor—foil ensuring that positive energy is deflected to the right place, the lightening conductor removing negative energy from the organization.

What execs *really* don't understand is that it's the process *management* piece that is more important than the process improvement piece. They think that "Okay, we've allocated all these resources to this process improvement project and now that it's completed, we can pat ourselves on the back, say we've joined the twenty-first century, and stop allocating resources." In actuality, without continuous process *management* they've wasted their time and resources. The PI piece is just the beginning. They fail to realize that they must continually manage the process, tweak it, make changes, adjust metrics, and ensure the pertinent players are the right ones and are buying in instead of reverting to old ways and habits.

After many years of working in various organizations, we would add that change and resistance are promoted or dismissed on the simple premise of whether or not it's good for *me*—WIIFM (what is in it for me). Enlightened self-interest is the prime motivator for so much of human activity, whether it's in a multi-national corporation, a municipal council, or any other field of human activity.

It's irrational to behave in a way that is harmful to the whole, but yet so many people actively do it, why? The only reasonable response is because this is going to hurt me. The executive won't get it if their continued survival depends on them not getting it!

WRIGHT

Will you explain to our readers what kinds of change do people resist?

NABE

Of course, people don't only resist the kind of change that is not "what's good for me." People often resist change that *is* good for them. For example, if they feel they don't have the skills or capabilities, or even if they are not quite sure. My friend's son totally resisted a certain college course, knowing that it was essential and in his best interest, but was (as we eventually came to discuss) worried that he did not have the skills (it was statistics, so I should have known). After ensuring that he received the right support, he actually enjoyed the course and did well. So, the reality is that resistance is a normal part of any change, even when it's a valuable change. In that sense, resistance needs to be used as a necessary and constructive part of the change process. Open and constructive resistance should even be encouraged, otherwise you can get subtle sabotage or malicious compliance.

When organizations are ranked by external metrics such as FTSE, dividend rates, cost reductions, market share, league tables, and so on, then the organization becomes more internally focused on achieving these (publicly desirable?) outcomes. This, in turn, gets translated into internal behaviors to do what gets counted.

WRIGHT

What's the next logical step?

NABE

The next logical step is then for the executive to focus on this "what gets counted" to the exclusion of almost all else. In your own experience, what are the two most common justifications for proceeding with or cancelling projects/change programs? I think that, like many, you will find the answer is, "What will this make me or save me" in financial terms, thus, there is no accountability to performance indicators that make the financials what they are. Resistance to Change—"insanity."

Now, with that mindset and those questions uppermost, if you were the leading manager for a change program and you require whole swathes of change to the organization including changing and scrapping the process involved in the collection of those metrics mentioned above, how would your colleagues and executives (non-sponsors) feel?

What we are driving at here, in essence, is the personal drive of the leadership. If an individual seeks recognition and reward for doing a good job "he or she may like and even be an architect of some of the metrics in use." In this case, the change, no matter how good for the organization, becomes hostage to the personal desires, mindset, influence, and control of the said individual.

Even when shown the improvements to the system without all of this, the personality of the leader becomes paramount in determining whether the organization stops doing the things that hinder performance. I suggest that this is because the leader might be thinking, "All the other companies use those metrics, if we don't use them, publicize them, etc., I may not be able to get promoted, the company may not be able to raise finance, we (I) may look bad to the other companies in the rankings, etc." Sound familiar? This is where we were going with our comment about "it's good or bad for me." We think that this is a little explored and quite possibly under-acknowledged phenomenon.

A final point here that we have used in explaining organizational control structures is to say that an executive board is like a rubber circle with a number of directors around the rim. At any point in time, there will be more powerful forces pulling the circle into an ellipse thus directing the organization down X path. However, while they may have some support, they will also have some neutral and some actively working against the direction they are taking the organization. Over time, with shifting patterns in the business and the world, the ellipse changes shape to favor a new direction again with supporters neutral and opposed. Because this happens over relatively short spaces of time, then any given change can be stalled by simply waiting for the time at which this happens. Oh, and no sustainability to make sure the change sticks.

WRIGHT

In your experience, what are the largest obstacles to change?

NABE

In our years as a contract consultant, the two biggest obstacles to change that we have encountered are the fear of change itself and lack of communication. Employees who actually do the work affected by any change, fear they will lose control of their own destiny or, worse yet, lose their job. The other obstacle, lack of communications, is often the single largest contributor to failed change, projects, and many other initiatives. Effective and ongoing communications has to be regular and at every level of the organization. An exec who cannot clearly communicate the benefits of change does nothing but create chaos.

We have seen this time and time again. We should add here that management also believes that they alone are people who can best determine how certain external requirements can be met. We are thinking here of things like external inspections, compliance with regulatory authorities, and so on. This then imposes solutions on the workforce to do something that adds little or no value to the task at hand. Again, insanity.

Change can never be just about people and culture alone, and to think that this is all a change manager needs to overcome is surely a recipe for the change not to be successful.

WRIGHT

How is it possible for change to succeed?

NABE

Change needs to embrace people and the culture of the organization working with these two factors hand-in-hand. Simple communication, meetings with staff involving all the stakeholders from the start, and understanding their own fears and resistance to the change is wholly important.

Change is inevitable, as is the resistance to the change being planned. If managers do not consider that resistance will present itself, then this will cause problems. But working with resistance can also have a positive effect on the change.

Therefore change managers must understand all the factors and draw a map to chart the people, organization, resistance, planning, and implementation of the change. They must have an understanding of the issues before they become problems, and they must create the will, desire, and culture for change before even thinking of implementing the process of change.

WRIGHT

What are the most important factors before implementing change?

NABE

Getting the team on board and creating the right culture for change from the onset is the most important factor, understanding their team, the resistance, cultural beliefs and fears, and make the process of change more likely to succeed.

We have worked with many senior management teams at a significant number of Fortune 500 companies. While there are a number of good, decent people in these positions, we find that a significant number are self-indulgent and totally, morally bankrupt. Again, more than thirty-four years of resistance to change is insanity.

It's truly shocking to witness an august elder statesman banging on the boardroom table demanding significantly higher compensation in one meeting and then in another meeting, propose curtailing increases and benefits for the rank and file. The really sad part of this is that they have no sense of the hypocrisy and simply cannot make the connection.

We have had to participate in "town hall" meetings and weekend retreats with senior managers who have been almost in tears delivering tough messages or decisions affecting the work force. Then go out for dinner later and they ask for feedback on their "performance" followed by some cynical comment about "hoodwinking" as a required skill. You got it—"insanity."

Well, we suppose it's part of the natural selection process that causes the "wolves" to raise to the top, but if you wanted to point out "what's wrong with corporate America today," this is it—resistance to change—"insanity."

Those driving the changes should remember one simple rule—the workforce makes the changes, not the management. So, despite strategizing and planning the changes at a senior level, unless the workforce understands and commits to their involvement, nothing much will happen.

Okay, let's add something here. Change cannot be an initiative, it cannot have a team responsible for it, it has to be the culture, and it has to be part of everyone's job. We do this by understanding that business is dynamic, as is the world, and thus our markets and customer requirements. So what we need to do is process cultural shifts to create a customer-centric (internal or external) organization. As process owners realize their customer requirements are changing, they happily and eventually easily adapt change to adhere to the needs of their customers.

WRIGHT

So, when does resistance start to diminish?

NABE

We normally see the resistance to this from the top start to diminish once senior management starts to see their lives and jobs getting more clearly defined and in general easier as with the rest of the organization, giving people control of their work. Once they see what is in it for them, and not just the owners/shareholders, the senior team begets less resistance. This is not always easy. It needs to be communicated well to all levels and the trust has to be built so that it is good for everyone.

Executives still don't get it? This is a very general statement and we might modify it because not all executives "get it." Many executives have risen through the ranks and in many cases avoided or side-stepped the necessary hard issues that they could have used as lessons in learning how to identify and deal with resistance to change. They hit executive roles and are under-prepared to deal with resistance and how to avoid it. They take the whole ship down with them. Some don't even understand how they themselves react to and resist change. They don't know themselves or their people and the root causes for resistance behavioral loops.

Conversely, there are executives, usually the "new" leaders or consultants, who are "hired guns" brought in, who have their ways of dealing with resistance. They are readily expendable. Usually the person who brought them in was aware of the need to make change but didn't have the experience. You get what you reward in these instances and it is not only financial reward! Usually those who know how to overcome resistance are not always seen as corporate promotable to executive role material and sadly become consultants! But they make a lot of money so it's not really "sadly"!

Agency Theory tells us that managers will act in their own best interests, and executive management is more prone to these effects (in our opinion) than lower levels of management in any given organization. This has been true for thirty-four years without change, thus a paradigm to insanity.

WRIGHT

How does one develop change leaders?

NABE

There are a lot of articles on developing change leaders or change champions whose sole purpose is to find a way to communicate to employees how any given change project will be beneficial to not just the company, but to them as individuals; every one of them talks about success only if there is top down buy-in.

Just like others in the organization, proposed change has to be presented to top management in a way that will rationalize the benefits to each of them as individuals. We think that part of the resistance (or why they do not understand it) is because there is a skew between their risk/reward metrics and the risk/reward associated with the ongoing need for business to innovate.

If top executives are rewarded on short-term performance metrics, and they are presented with a change model that may create a short-term negative effect but may yield increased gain long-term, they may be less apt to embrace that change. Without some sort of economic signaling from the marketplace creating a real drive for change, we think that most top executives will opt for the status quo because they believe it is in their best interests. Thus, our current economic dilemma in 2011 and going into 2012

Let's deal with management's resistance to change. In many ways, as a group, they are a tougher nut to crack. Top management is often blinded to needed change by either arrogance or complacency. As for middle management, the potential loss of political power, along with complacency, fear, uncertainty, and doubt contribute to middle management change resistance. Finally, managers aren't typically prepared for dealing with change on a day-to-day basis. After all, most managers learn that control is one of the basic functions of management, whereas control is largely counterintuitive to the notion of change. Thus, managers must unlearn the need to suppress change and instead learn skills for anticipating and managing change simultaneously, and in unison with managing their core business.

WRIGHT

How do many company leaders view change consultants?

NABE

We are sure that many company leaders see business process consultants as masters of impractical theory who seek to imbed themselves in the lucrative trade of resident expert without imparting their knowledge or providing the leadership to implement the self-organizing teams needed to effectively transform their organizations. I've also seen top executives passionate about process and thwarted at every turn by a complacent and bureaucratic culture intent on pounding down the nail that sticks up. But, yes, many executives see their role as approvers of finances rather than leaders responsible for change. Perhaps intuitively knowing their lack of involvement will doom the project, they decline.

The empowered organization is one in which individuals have knowledge, skills, desire, and opportunity. Failures are great learning tools but they must be kept to a minimum.

Change is inevitable, right? It always is! And we think resistance to change appears to linger and linger. But, should it linger as it has for all these many years? We think not!

Sentiment around the world appears to take many different avenues of thought. For more than thirty-four years, some of what we constantly have heard bantered about included confusion on who was resistant to change and what was precipitating the resistance.

WRIGHT

What specifically about change do people resist?

NABE

Resistance to change is largely a misunderstanding or a misreading of the evidence. People do not resist change in general. Life is change, and everyone does a million things a day that represent a change. What people resist is control and making some change because someone else wants them to.

When people talk about change in the organization behavior sense, they are referring to some innate psychological reluctance to change. That, clearly, is not true. More generally, of course, we all do (thank goodness) resist change that fails rational tests of value—putting oneself in harm's way for no purpose, for example. It's important to denote the realm in which any of these words are being used.

Most companies have one or two clear goals such as growth or improved service. The problem is that this focus on one or two goals creates problems somewhere down the road. If the goal is to grow, that's great but at what cost? You need to limit goals but they still need to focus the organization on running the whole business well, not just one aspect.

We could (generally) argue the case that most people do not resist change, rather they resist being changed. It's mostly about how the change is designed and deployed. Many surveys clearly show that top leaders are disconnected from what is going on "in the trenches," so to speak. Senior leaders are not trained in how to lead change in their organizations. This critical aspect of managing change seems a little like a "no-brainer" in many ways. They feel that the change they are championing is proceeding very well, while the "troops" feel (and more likely know) that it is not going well at all—their perspectives of success are very different.

The systems that are implemented as a result of the change are important. We know from neuro-science that when we are trying to change habits (behaviors and mindsets) it is the new routines that will have the long-term effect.

WRIGHT

What more than anything else will insure continuation of implemented changes?

NABE

If we don't get the buy-in of leaders up front, then the continuous improvement system that is put in place is at risk of not being continued. Without the commitment and focus of senior leaders to ensure that sustainability is applied, it is highly likely it will not succeed. Like getting fit, it's a challenge to keep going because it might feel difficult at first, but by persevering we get the benefit. Sounds so easy doesn't it?

Remember, resistance to change is insanity.

What about incentives to change? The fundamental problem with change is the transition. It is not easy for humans in general to change their ways. Add to that the general fear of change and it is clear that anybody has to have an incentive to make the change happen.

This aspect—incentive—is most often ignored or rather assumed to be evident and/or the same as for those who decide to initiate the change. The problem is that it is almost never the case. Some persons in the organization will welcome the change, but for other reasons than the initiators. Other persons will only see extra work for no extra benefit at all (i.e., no incentive). There will always be a few nay-sayers and there will always be a few "there's work to be done, so let's get it done" persons. We can do nothing much to either group, but there are many people who will do something for recognition and rewards and change is about changing the ways of the many. This is where incentive comes in.

WRIGHT

What kind of incentives are we talking about?

NABE

We have two types of incentives: sticks and carrots. Using sticks in a change situation has the unfortunate side effect that people often leave or otherwise obstruct, compromising the transition. That leaves the carrot.

Transitions are most often planned in quite some detail. It would therefore not take much to identify the effect on the persons involved. If the persons affected were rewarded, probably moneywise, according to their contribution then I'd be surprised if the transitions were not accomplished much faster than is currently seen.

The contribution rewards really should be variable, not only time-based, but result-based and should be sizeable enough to entice persons to actively contribute (i.e., comparable to a pro rata salary). A $30 reward for three days' work, in addition to normal work, don't forget, is not going to get anybody moving.

So, let top management look at their ROI, extend it by, say 20 percent, and use that extra cost as incentive bonuses. My guess is that the ROI will stay the same, company cohesion will go up, employee turnover will drop, and productivity will rise significantly. Or will It?

When we think of resistance to change in an organization, we think about it in terms of what the benefits are—why that system exists in the first place—and we think that "corporate antibodies" often get a bad rap. For example, foreign objects in the body are not welcome and are handily disposed of by antibodies because it is safer for the entire organism; the antibodies have purpose and a job.

But sometimes our immune systems can be a little too aggressive and attack more often than we would like. We think that sometimes it isn't the people that are resistant to change, it is the system that is reinforcing this resistance. And sometimes change is dangerous even if necessary, like heart surgery. At least in the body, it seems like the ways to get around the resistance is by either suppressing the immune system or by fooling the immune system to think that the change belongs in the organism, and also by making sure the intrusion is as sanitary and safe as possible. We think it is important to remember that if there is resistance, it is probably because it is considered a foreign object and may not belong.

On the other side, we worked for a small, progressive company where change was embraced instead of resisted. We pretty much improved everything and quickly found that change needs to be supported by the system. Getting there involved key system and paradigm shifts that allowed the changes to be safe, incorporated if useful, and quickly shunted if they weren't. And you have to wait for feedback that a change is successful or not before changing it, but, we think that might be if you swing the pendulum too far to the other side!

WRIGHT

I have always heard that fear is the major impediment to change. Do you agree?

NABE

Anxiety is certainly a result of change being implemented in any organization. Preparation and training about what change is going to be implemented must be clearly communicated and shown to prevent anxiety. Simply not dealing with individual, group, and organizational anxiety during these times of economic insecurity and fear about the future is not good. It's always there, but in today's climate the "worry" levels and lack of leadership/engagement/communications perhaps makes it ten times worse. High anxiety and high resistance to change correlate quite significantly. Working at the rubbing edge of technology, process, and people change, it's still the latter that matters!

Buzz is not something you want to sustain. Keeping people connected and purposeful is.

Establishing and sustaining positive new behaviors is one part of the problem and many of our comments here have addressed that well. Another part is that when we speak of systemic rather than local change, it has to do with laying the foundation for continuing adaptive responses to changing conditions over time. Change is not a one-time thing. In our work, we pay attention to how to "keep the system whole" so that everyone can see enough of the big picture to make wise decisions in their daily work. People need to see how what they are doing affects achieving the end state that we want. Then, they need to be able to act on that information, making sure that processes and organizational structures support adaptive responses is important. In the end, people need to focus on outcomes and create a culture of accountability that leads to achieving those outcomes. Without sustainability we will still have, Resistance to change.

WRIGHT

Any last thoughts on resistance to change?

NABE

In summary, resistance to change remains an insane and lingering kind of cancer among so many organizations worldwide. We remain amazed that after thirty-four years it continues to be a significant obstacle to continuous improvement. We still are concerned that management and organizations as a whole continue to ignore the need to change and keep up with our fast-changing needs to remain competitive in this wild ride we call Economic Challenge 2012

It all depends on what that "change" is. If the change is going to affect individuals personally, it is natural that people are going to be resistant to that change. Sometimes, when new ways of doing things are introduced, people are slow to change. While change is inevitable, it is not easy to bring change into an organization. Top-down change enforcement always works the best.

How do you make a horse drink? Well, maybe the horse is not thirsty or maybe the horse doesn't want to drink from this particular well you are leading the horse to. Or, maybe the horse has other wells to drink from. Or, the horse is, simply put, so stubborn!

So, what do you do to make the horse drink? Well, you can do many things. You can get rid of this horse and get another horse, which is more amiable to your command. Or you can dry all the other wells that the horse can drink from so that there is only this one that the horse has to drink from when it gets thirsty. Or, you make "fire" in the surroundings of the horse so that the horse begins to perspire, eventually gets thirsty, and you can hope that the horse might drink. Or try to find out what the horse likes. For example, if the horse wants to sing, you sing with the horse, if the horse wants to dance, you dance with the horse. But the bottom line is making the horse drink from this well you are pointing to. Do you think the horse will drink? Or will the horse continue to drink from this well you are leading to? There is no guarantee, is there?

A couple of final questions for thought.

First, Mr. or Mrs. Operations Manager: Did you get what you paid for today from each of your direct reports?

Second, what did each of your direct reports accomplish in the past two hours? Did you get what you paid for?

Third, at the end of the day, are you confident that you can tell your CEO, backed up with actual real data, that you met or exceeded your key performance indicators, by direct report? Did the CEO get what he or she paid for?

Finally, what consequences might you face for not accomplishing your Key Performance Indicators today, tomorrow, end of the week, or end of the month?

About the Author

Keith Nabe brings more than thirty years of experience in management consulting to businesses and corporations worldwide in more than one hundred industries. Keith is a results-oriented, continuous improvement professional in change management. He has successfully effected bottom line profitability by reducing operational costs while improving processes, quality assurance, on-time deliverables, and sustainable management operating systems. Keith is a professional speaker, former radio and television broadcaster, and a certified training facilitator and presenter in change management, sales, reorganizational change and process improvement. Keith has been an active community supporter within the Chamber of Commerce and is a Member of the International Speakers Network.

Keith E Nabe

Accelerated Relief, LLC
311 Seattle Slew Ct.
Crestview, Florida 32539
850-685-3719
www.linkedin.com/in/knabe09

CULTIVATING HIGH PERFORMANCE

MICHELLE L. BONAHOOM

DAVID WRIGHT (WRIGHT)

Today I'm talking with Michelle L. Bonahoom. Michelle is passionate about making a significant impact in the lives of leaders, their organizations, and communities. She spent the first ten years of her career applying these principles within her own organization, resulting in 80 percent less turnover and 98 percent increasing customer referrals resulting in more than a 200 percent increase in productivity within eighteen months. Since then, Michelle has helped leaders effectively develop, communicate, and execute their strategies through the intentional alignment of their strategies in organizational cultures. This work has resulted in significant returns and transformed lives. She is an active advocate of excellence in organizational health, strategic execution, and talent management and she serves on several boards, professional associations, and community organizations.

Michelle welcome to *Roadmap to Success*.

MICHELLE BONAHOOM (BONAHOOM)

Thank you.

WRIGHT

What is the key to building to a sustainable organization?

BONAHOOM

A sustainable organization is one that is thinking of creating long-term value.

There are four keys to building a sustainable organization. First, a sustainable organization continually assesses where they are so that they can make effective decisions. Second, they leverage their core competencies to overcome whatever key challenges they have and they can do that through establishing an effective strategy. Third, they create a line of sight between their strategy and their people. For example, the people who work for the organization know exactly what activities they need to focus on to be able to make a difference, not only in their own minds, but also in the organizational goals. Last, they measure and continuously improve those results by making fact-based decisions and linking all of the decisions to the organizational strategies.

WRIGHT

So what are the critical elements required to build a sustainable organization?

BONAHOOM

There are seven key indicators of a healthy organization, or what we also call a "high-performing sustainable organization."

1. Heart-to-Heart Alignment of Mission, Values, and Vision
2. Clear, Consistent, and Balanced Strategic Processes
3. Customer-Focused Culture & Engagement
4. Strength-Based Leadership
5. A Highly Engaged Workforce
6. Effective Customer-Oriented Processes
7. Continuous Performance Measurement, Improvement, and Alignment

The first indicator is having a heart-to-heart alignment of mission, vision, and values. This means that all employees understand the organization's mission, vision, and values and align their behaviors to support them. This is accomplished with the second indicator, a clear and consistent strategy, along with a process to be able to execute that strategy.

Then the third indicator of a healthy, sustainable organization is that there is a client-focused culture. The organization is constantly thinking about its engagement with the client. The fourth indicator is what we call a strength-based foundation and strength-based leadership. This foundation builds a platform throughout the organization that allows the organization to draw on the strengths of not only the individual, but also the strengths of the key processes and key stakeholders within the organization. Finally, the final three indicators: an engaged workforce, customer-oriented processes, and continuous improvement result from the foundation that is built in the first four, resulting in an organization that is always looking to breakthrough to new levels of greatness.

WRIGHT

Would you elaborate on your concept of a "strength-based foundation" just a little bit?

BONAHOOM

The strength-based foundation is a platform that allows for that heart-to-heart alignment I talked about previously. There are six key principles that we focus on when we're building a strength-based foundation. The first is building authentic relationships—being authentic and having an environment that offers the ability for others to be authentic. This allows the second principle to be in place, which is individual uniqueness. That is just understanding and appreciating others' uniqueness and, at the same time, leveraging those differences to make sure that everybody is working within their strengths. When that is applied on top of continuous improvement (the third principle) and a failing forward mentality (fourth principle), the organization is able to empower its people to make mistakes, to learn from their mistakes, and to continually strive to be better. This allows them to be listening to the needs of their stakeholders and their clients.

That is done through the last two principles that bring in a level of accountability for each individual to take responsibility for their own actions. Through servant leadership, the management and the leaders of the organization empower and listen to all people within it to reach for success. This foundation allows an organization to be flexible and agile, and to be able to respond to the needs of the clients. This creates sustainability.

WRIGHT

Why is this important to the success of an organization?

BONAHOOM

The environment is changing and so organizations can't remain status quo. So it's important to build that necessary foundation before you start developing your strategy as an organization because if that foundation isn't in place, then the wrong behaviors will be rewarded. It's important to reward the right behaviors to be able to achieve that alignment between the individuals of the organization and the strategy.

WRIGHT

So why is it important to consider culture when defining and executing organizational strategy?

BONAHOOM

The number one reason that strategy execution fails within organizations is because of a lack of strategy and cultural alignment. Many leaders don't think about the fact that, depending on their specific types of strategy, they need to align certain types of cultures to best support those strategies. Cultures are very organic but there are certain characteristics of cultures that lend well to different types of strategies. Because effectively aligned culture is the best differentiating factor in an organization and it can't be copied, that's the one factor leaders can focus on to make sure they make a sustainable difference.

WRIGHT

So what are the different types of cultures and strategies that align with each other?

BONAHOOM

There are four typical types of cultures. The first is a competence culture. A competence culture is one that is mission- and goal-oriented with a focus on goal achievement, competition, profitability, and market share. This culture supports a lock-in type strategy, which means that the organization wants to be able to gain market share, complementing products and services, and strategic platforms that service a large percentage of the customer's needs.

The second type of culture is a cultivation culture. A cultivation culture is adaptable, innovative, and draws on the creativity of those leaders within it to create new markets, customers, and opportunities. With this type of culture, the product leadership strategy tends to be a good fit because you are known by your customers as producing innovative and high quality products/services not typically available to competitors.

The third type of culture is a collaborative culture. This culture is one where everybody within the organization needs to be able to work together effectively. It focuses on a high level of involvement from everyone within the organization. There can't be any silos within the organization and it involves a great deal of commitment, communication, and development. This culture works well with a strategy called complete customer solutions, which requires the organization to be able to deliver a myriad of solutions to its customers, whether it be during a lifetime or through a bundle of products and services. With this strategy, an organization becomes a partner with its customers and provides solutions that best meet their overall needs.

Then the final culture is that of a control culture. This culture needs to be very efficient; it needs to be very controlled and very consistent. This culture works well with what we call a low total cost strategy. With a low cost strategy, an organization focuses on becoming the lowest cost provider of a product/service to its customers. As a result, it needs to be very efficient, and its operations need to be very streamlined.

WRIGHT

So are you saying that this is either/or? Can these four be within one organization?

BONAHOOM

That's a great question. High-performing organizations have the ability to go back and forth between all culture types. In fact, they have characteristics of all four of those cultures and they have been very intentional about building them into their customer focus, internal system and processes, people, information, and leadership. When they have successfully accomplished this, they are able to adapt to changing market conditions. However, it takes time to build this type of a culture. Therefore, it is important to focus on leveraging and building upon your organization's strengths as you intentionally develop the areas of culture that are lacking within your organization.

WRIGHT

So you have developed a Strategic Ambassador System© that helps leaders effectively deploy strategy throughout an organization. Would you share with our readers the key elements of this system?

BONAHOOM

We have developed a proven system to get all people within the organization thinking about and working on the strategy together. As a result of this system, organizations are able to dramatically improve their performance results and cultural alignment.

There are four key phases of this system. The first is an assessment phase where people within the organization are working together to assess where the organization is and then determine where they need to go as an organization. This allows them to establish a clear strategy based on that gap. What is effective about using this system, along with involvement from people throughout the entire organization, is that it builds the necessary buy-in to create sustainable change. It also allows us to get outside of some of the biases that may occur if you had formed a team of only senior leaders to determine what the strategy of the organization needs to be.

The next element of this system is the alignment phase. During this phase there is a cross-organizational team formed to determine the key measures, targets, and initiatives that are necessary to carry out the strategic plan. They come up with an actual plan and a road map for the organization to meet its objectives. Then, in the application phase, they also work together to make sure those initiatives are effectively being carried out and they are aligned to their budgets, the processes, and to the reward system within the organization. Then that cycle just continues into a reassess phase where leaders in the organization continuously reassess how they are doing on their strategy, if they are meeting their objectives, and if they still have the right strategy as things change.

The single greatest element of this system is how we leverage the strengths of each person within the organization to work together to deploy the strategy at all levels. This also becomes a significant leadership development opportunity for succession planning. Finally, it positively affects employee engagement, which leads to greater customer loyalty and satisfaction. The end result is a higher performing organization that is on its way to sustainability!

WRIGHT

So how will this system help leaders to more effectively meet their organizational objectives?

BONAHOOM

This system gets everyone pulling together, causes leaders in the organization to be intentional about their thinking, and determines the key things that they need to do to differentiate themselves from their competitors. It allows the leaders to involve everybody in translating and aligning that strategy in operational terms so that everyone knows how and why their daily activities affect the success of the organization.

It also creates a balanced and objective team because people from all parts of the organization contribute their unique strengths, skills, and abilities. It makes strategy everybody's job and everybody starts to take ownership in the performance of the organization and making the organization win.

Finally, it provides a clear level of accountability throughout the organization because everybody is involved. There are clear expectations laid out about how each person's role directly affects the strategy of the organization. Because of this, the success of the company becomes everyone's job!

WRIGHT

You have developed a Strength-Based High Performance Work System© that helps leaders hire, develop, and retain the right people, in the right roles, for the right reasons. Would you describe for our readers how this system helps leaders build high-performing and sustainable organizations?

BONAHOOM

This system takes a look at the critical roles needed to support the strategy rather than just keeping people in the roles and trying to fit the strategy within those roles. The key strategic jobs are benchmarked in a way that we can make sure people are in the right roles and they have very clear guidance on how to develop themselves within those roles. Once the right person is in the role, they are then intentionally developed and rewarded based on their role, their strengths, and their individual motivational needs. This creates that heart-to-heart alignment we discussed earlier, which is one of the critical elements of a high-performing and sustainable organization.

A critical part of this system is our AssureFit© talent hiring process. This process not only helps you find the right candidate, it also ensures that your selection is effectively introduced and integrated into your organization, understands your organizational goals, and develops a formal plan for individual performance and development. Finally, the process helps to build buy-in throughout the organization as the new-hire is successfully integrated into his or her new role.

When you have the right people, in the right roles, for the right reasons, overall employee engagement, satisfaction, and commitment increases dramatically. Studies show that more than 63 percent of all employees are disengaged at work, which results in costly turnover and significantly reduced productivity. Engaged employees are more than four times more productive than non-engaged employees. Therefore, a small increase in organizational engagement can have a large affect on the bottom-line. This system focuses on leveraging the strengths of the employees, lines them up with the strategy and direction of the company, and provides them with a sense of meaning and fulfillment in their work. This meaning and fulfillment is one of the top influencers of high engagement in a high-performing organization.

WRIGHT

What are the results of effectively aligning strategy and culture within and organization?

BONAHOOM

There are many results; the greatest result is higher performance. Higher performance means that organizations are going to have clearer direction. They're going to be able to make better fact-based decisions because they're basing their daily activities on a clear strategy that has been developed from the voice of all of the stakeholders. They're also going to have greater accountability, which is going to create more clarity and creativity throughout the organization. People take more responsibility and they're actually rewarded based on the results of the organization, so that drives higher performance.

Two of the greatest things I have seen happen as a result of aligning an organization's strategy with an appropriate culture is first a greater focus. People know what they need to do so the frustration level goes down within the organization. Second, there is improved efficiency, and less stress. This results almost immediately in a greater level of engagement, both for the customers and the employees.

WRIGHT

Would you describe some case studies of how this approach to strategic management has been effective in the past?

BONAHOOM

Yes! We have been working with an organization for several years. The leaders have determined that their differentiating advantage is to be able to partner with customers to provide a diverse line of products that competitors cannot produce. This has required them to build strong relationships with their customers as well as to continue to develop new and innovative product offerings. They determined that they needed a complete clients' solutions strategy, with a secondary emphasis on becoming a product leader. However, when we assessed their culture we saw that they really had a controlled culture. It had many silos with a very hierarchical leadership structure. Therefore, it was very difficult for leaders within the organization as a whole to be able to make decisions and to be able to meet the needs of the clients without a great deal of delay and red tape. This prevented them from being able to break into that strategic direction they believed would bring the organization success into the future.

So what we needed to do was start to transform that culture and align it to the characteristics that were needed for a complete customer solutions/product leadership type of strategy. We worked over the course of about 18 months to integrate the Strategic Ambassador System into the organization and to educate and train the leaders around the strength-based principles. Then, we worked with their leadership team to learn how to model and live out those principles daily. Because of engaging the entire organization in the process, we immediately noticed increased engagement, but with the organization we also started to notice that customers and suppliers were seeing a difference as well. We had several reports that customers and suppliers were asking questions about what was different with the organization. That had actually noticed the improvement throughout! Immediately, there were many intangible results, but over the course of a very short period of time there were very tangible results as well.

In fact, there was one example of a job that was not going to meet its deadline, which was very common for this organization in the past. This job was with a new client. When the customer was first told that they weren't going to meet the deadline, they expressed a great deal of frustration and indicated that they shouldn't have given this organization a chance at the job. In the past, the employees of the organization would have started finger pointing and finding someone to blame for the error. However, because we had integrated a new sense of accountability and a new sense of ownership and leadership through the focus on building a more collaborative culture through integrating the Strategic Ambassador Process© and Strength-Based High Performance Work System throughout their entire organization, we had aligned people to roles that they could really excel in. As a result, the entire organization came together without leadership having to drive the solution.

Non-management teams met to put together a plan for everybody to come out and work on the shop floor and get the job done. They presented the plan to the senior leadership team, received approval, and deployed the plan through the direction of this same non-management team. The job ended up shipping on time, which saved the company $1.3 million on that particular job. However, they also ended up getting about $3 million in additional revenues from that customer later in the year. This is a $40 million-a-year company, so it was a pretty significant effect.

At the same time employee engagement went up dramatically from people being able to work together and not having to get approval on every decision. They had the framework in place to be able to do that and to make the right decisions. It was a huge success that engaged the organization to continue to find ways to build more of a collaborative culture to support their strategy. As a result of that they have seen quite a few other tangible and non-tangible results.

WRIGHT

I'm interested in the strength-based part of what you are talking about. How do you assess the strengths of your organization's employees? Is it by assessment or experience? How does that happen?

BONAHOOM

We use proven assessments to be able to assess the key behaviors and communication styles of the employees. We also take a look at what people value, what motivates them, what gets them excited each day. Then we look at the actual hard and soft skills of the employees. This is drawn from understanding how they see the world, themselves, and what they appreciate from each.

Finally, we take a look at their strengths to see how we can maximize their potential. We use a layered approach to our assessment process so that we can understand the core of each individual person. This allows us to know exactly how to maximize the talent within each person, how to motivate him or her, and how to develop the skills necessary to be effective in each individual's role. We have also built the results of these assessments into the entire hiring and development process, so that individuals fit like a glove to his or her role. Each employee develops an Individual Performance Plan and a Professional Development plan that focuses on the alignment of his or her individual role to the organizational objectives.

New-hires also are able to develop their strengths to offset their weaknesses through the several leadership development tools that we have linked to their individual job benchmarks. This fully integrated process allows employees to take ownership for their own development and engagement within the organization. It also helps managers objectively and effectively coach employees to reach their true potential. This leads to higher levels of engagement and improved productivity throughout the entire organization.

WRIGHT

So how does this affect leaders and the organization into the future?

BONAHOOM

Organizations continuously have to work at a faster pace as we move into the future. They need to make sure that leaders are making the right decisions. By ensuring that they are being intentional about valuing the individuality of their people and aligning that individuality to the needs of the organization and its strategy, they're going to be able to make faster decisions, better decisions, and their organizations are going to be able to be more adaptable and agile to those necessary changes. At the same time, they're going to be able to understand and leverage the key competencies they have as an organization in order to better differentiate themselves against their competitors. Or, if they don't have the right competencies, they will to know who they need to intentionally hire and develop to have the right competencies into the future. It takes a lot of the guess-work out of leadership, allowing leaders to focus on leading the organization toward becoming a high-performing and sustainable organization.

WRIGHT

Well, what a great conversation, Michelle. I really appreciate all this time you've taken to answer these questions. I have certainly learned a lot; I have been taking copious notes. What you are talking about seems that it would fit in my organization and I really do appreciate you giving us all this information. I'm really sure our readers will get a lot out of it.

BONAHOOM

Thank you. I am passionate about helping leaders to be more effective in their organizations! Our mission is to radically transform the lives of leaders, organizations, and communities. We believe that the way to do that is through the effective alignment of an organization's culture and its strategy! This allows everyone to play a significant role in leaving a sustainable legacy.

WRIGHT

Today I have been talking with Michelle Bonahoom. Michelle is passionate about making a significant effect in the lives of leaders and their organizations. She has helped leaders effectively develop, communicate, and execute their strategies throughout the intentional alignment of their strategies of their organizational cultures for years.

Michelle, thank you so much for being with us on *Roadmap to Success*.

BONAHOOM

Thank you.

About the Author

Michelle Bonahoom is passionate about making a significant effect in the lives of leaders! She spent the first ten years of her career applying the principles and strength-based paradigm within her own organization, resulting in an 80 percent reduction in turnover, 98 percent increase in customer referrals and more than 200 percent increase in productivity within eighteen months. Since then, Michelle has applied her years of experience to helping organizations maximize overall effectiveness through identifying their unique character and aligning it to the unique strengths of their employees, strategic objectives, and daily activities. She is an active advocate for excellence in organizational performance and strategy, cultural performance, positive psychology, and talent management strategies through:

- Serving as a Chairman Club Member of Target Training International,
- Participating as an active member of the Minnesota Council for Quality,
- Speaking and partnering with several CEO Roundtable groups,
- Speaking with executives around the country about making a significant difference in the lives of their leaders through effectively aligning their organizational strategy with an effective culture.

Michelle is a certified Kaplan-Norton Balanced Scorecard Graduate, Certified Professional Leadership Coach and Trainer, Certified Professional Behavioral Analyst, Certified Professional Values Analyst, Certified EQ Mentor, Certified TriMetrix Talent Management System Analyst, and Certified Organizational DNA Analyst, as well as a life-long learner and leader. In her free time, she enjoys helping young leaders and families understand their unique identity and intentionally discover and walk out their callings and destinies.

Michelle Bonahoom

VisionOne Advocates
12400 Portland Avenue South, Suite 130
Burnsville, MN 55337
952-426-1521
mbonahoom@visiononecoach.com
www.visiononecoach.com

Chapter Seventeen

CHARTING YOUR ROADMAP TO FINANCIAL SECURITY

WILMA G. ANDERSON, RFC

DAVID WRIGHT (WRIGHT)

Today I'm talking with Wilma G. Anderson, RFC. Wilma is CEO of Senior Care Associates Inc., located in Littleton, Colorado. This firm was established in 1987 to respond to the changing financial needs of individuals who are planning for financial success and retirement. In addition to her services as a Financial Advisor, Wilma's specialties are long-term care protection, critical illness coverage, VA planning, and retirement distribution strategies for clients who are fifty-five or older. She has more than thirty years of experience working with physicians, hospital management, CPAs, financial planners, and insurance companies. She is a Registered Financial Consultant. In 2007 she was given the CATO Award for Excellence in Financial Journalism. Throughout all the insurance and financial industries, she is known as the LTC Coach, the Critical Illness Coach, and the Veteran Benefit Coach, too. She has authored sales systems for financial professionals, written consumer booklets about financial choices, and appears regularly as a columnist for *The Register*. She has published more than two hundred articles for the financial community and her articles have appeared in magazines such as *Business Week, Senior Market Advisor, Agent Sales Journal* and *Advisor Today.*

WRIGHT

Wilma Anderson, welcome to *ROADMAP to Success!*

WILMA G. ANDERSON (ANDERSON)

Thank you very much!

WRIGHT

So what is the very first step to designing my road map?

ANDERSON

The very first thing you should do with an advisor is to evaluate your risk tolerance factors. With your advisor, answer several simple questions he or she will ask such as: What type of investments would work best for you so that you can sleep at night? If you like to invest in the stock market, that's certainly one type of risk. Would you feel okay with your account value perhaps going up and down every month? Or, do you want more guaranteed types of incomes and investments? Would a blend of the two scenarios be better? A good financial advisor will start right there as their first step of working with you.

WRIGHT

Do you think I really need a financial advisor, even if I want to do this myself?

ANDERSON

A lot of people ask me that very same question. You need a financial advisor to help you through the really rough times of the stock market, and to also give you a lot of information about the choices you may have. There is a lot of information on the Internet of course, but a good financial advisor will either work with you individually on a consulting basis for a fee, or he or she might suggest that the advisor manage your investment account for you. You have different choices and you can pretty well design how you'd like to work with a financial advisor when you meet someone who can be of assistance to you.

WRIGHT

So how do I prevent my investment accounts from any future losses if I don't want to take much risk—should I stay in the stock market?

ANDERSON

Staying in the stock market means, at least for the next couple of years, that it might be like a roller coaster. There will be days that it's really up, and days that it's really down. If you need to look at your account several times a day and are apprehensive about losses, then buying stocks and bonds and mutual funds might not be the best solution for you. There are investment choices that allow you to earn interest on your account based on the growth of indexes like the S&P 500, or the Dow Jones. The companies credit interest to your account each year, based on the growth of the index you selected over a twelve-month period. If the index doesn't have any growth, then you don't lose any money but you wouldn't be earning any additional interest that year, or just a very minimum amount.

So, what it all gets back to is how much risk do you want to take with your invested dollars? Do you want to sleep at night? You have your greatest potential of growth in the stock market, but you also have your greatest potential of loss. Somewhere in between (based on what your risk tolerance is) would be the solution that you'd want to have for your investment accounts. There are ways to prevent losses in your account, but it will mean that you'll have to earn a little bit less interest each year.

WRIGHT

So is life insurance really that important?

ANDERSON

Life insurance means different things to individuals and families, depending on their age. For example, when we're in our twenties and thirties and raising our families, we buy life insurance to protect us should one of the spouses in the family die. The life insurance policy will give the remaining spouse money to live on for quite a long time or pay for the kids' college educations. The funds can be used in any number of ways if one of the spouses is no longer there.

When you are in your forties and fifties and sixties, life insurance can be used almost like a Roth IRA for the Rothschild's, meaning you can put cash into the life insurance plan and the funds will sit there and grow over the years. When you get to be sixty-five or better, you can withdraw funds from that life insurance policy with absolutely no cost, it's tax-free retirement income. So, in the forties, fifties, and sixties, when we're working, this is a great way to create tax-free retirement income for later on.

When we're older than in our mid sixties and seventies and even into our eighties, the reason we would buy life insurance is to pay future estate taxes. I don't usually find individuals who purchase life insurance for any other reasons when they're over sixty. It is a great way to be able to pass as much of your estate tax-free to your beneficiaries as you would like to.

WRIGHT

So how do I prepare for the cost of educating my children later on?

ANDERSON

There are all sorts of programs that are available right now. You can buy life insurance as one of the planning tools. I usually recommend whole life insurance for that and then borrow from the life insurance policy accumulated cash benefit when the children are getting ready to go to college. You should start that type of plan when your children are very young. There are also 529 plans that are available. These types of plans will let you put money into a plan and the balance continues to grow. When your child is ready to go to college, the money will be available there to help pay for his or her education.

There are lots of incentives with either one of those plans. These are usually the two best ways to plan to pay for college and have the money be there, available for you when you need it, and to be secure. You can also invest in stocks and mutual funds, but again you have the potential of risk of loss if those stocks don't do well. When your child is ready to go to college, the money you need might not be there. Your financial advisor can give you some good advice and some good choices.

WRIGHT

I've heard about Critical Illness protection. What exactly does that do and how does it protect my family?

ANDERSON

Critical Illness protection is a fairly new product in the United States. In all other parts of the world, Critical Illness protection is something that every family purchases, but here in the United States we're just starting to see great policies be available.

What these policies do is pay you a lump sum of money if you were to have a heart attack, cancer, a stroke, or some other major illness that you would require some rehabilitation. It's tax-free money and you can use the money for anything you want. You can use it to fund your family's living expenses while you recuperate or you can use it to fund your business expenses too.

All that's required to get a monetary benefit is to have what they call a Qualifying Event, like a heart attack, cancer, or a stroke. It's really one of the best protections you can select. You purchase this protection so that when you're ill, you don't have to worry about money being available to you for your family's needs or to fund your business expenses. Policyholders fully expect to go back to work after they have recuperated. It's an excellent type of coverage for business owners. Or, if you own a business and have a partner, you can protect the revenue your partner would be generating if he or she were to get ill. That's why these types of policies are a great way to protect your business, and it's also a great way to protect your partner's family, too.

WRIGHT

Long-term care insurance is something I don't even want to think about. Are there other ways to get this coverage?

ANDERSON

Yes, there sure are! Back in the eighties, traditional Long-Term Care insurance was the only option we had. You could apply for what they called "A Stand-Alone' policy and you paid your annual premiums forever until your health changed and then your LTC policy paid out for your long-term care expenses. But, if you never used your policy and died, it was just premiums that you had paid for a long time without getting anything back. Now we can get life insurance that has what they call a "living benefit rider" where you can use 50 to 80 percent of your life insurance policy's death benefit to help pay for your cost of care. It's a terrific rider for people to add to their new life insurance policies, if possible. You can also purchase an annuity that has a long-term care benefit. This makes a lot of sense because money is there to use for long-term care if you need it. If you never need care, the balance in the annuity goes to your beneficiaries.

So, depending on what you would like for long-term care coverage, there are different vehicles available. When you have an annuity that offers an additional sum to use for long-term care expenses, you have one of the best situations possible. Money to pay for care and a death benefit will go to your beneficiary.

Life insurance can have almost the same benefits! With a life policy, if you didn't have to use the rider for long-term care expenses, then 100 percent of your death benefit goes to your family tax-free. If you *do* have to use the long-term care benefit rider, then whatever is left as the remaining death benefit gets paid out to your family tax-free, too. Most of my clients these days are looking at either life insurance with a daily benefit rider to pay for care, or they're looking at an annuity. It makes sense to look at all three options and see what fits best for you and your budget.

WRIGHT

I'm getting close to retirement. What do I do with my company 401k?

ANDERSON

When you retire, most companies allow you to do what they call a Rollover of your retirement account. You can transfer the balance of your account into a self-directed IRA, which makes great sense. It's not a taxable event to do that, and then you can decide how you would like to invest that money. But remember, no matter what investment you select, make *sure* that it fits your risk tolerance profile! Whatever decision you decide to make, you want to plan for your money hopefully lasting as long as you do.

WRIGHT

I'm a war-time Veteran. Is there any program that will help me pay for my care costs in my old age that I don't know about?

ANDERSON

There is a very special program that was created in 1951 for Veterans that allows them to receive a monthly tax-free income to help pay for the cost of home care, assisted living, or nursing home expenses. It's called the Special Aid & Attendance Pension for War-time Veterans and their Spouses. You can apply for this benefit if you are a war-time Veteran who is sixty-five or older, your health has changed, and you are using and paying for home care services, living in an assisted living facility, or residing in a nursing home. The benefit is also available for spouses if they are married to a Veteran, and for their surviving spouses, too, when they need care. This benefit comes directly from the Veterans Administration and the benefit can be up to approximately $1,950 a month tax-free. If you are a surviving spouse of a war-time Veteran, the benefit is approximately $1,047 per month and that money is tax-free. So, when you are thinking about how to plan for paying for long-term care expenses in the future, if you are a war-time Veteran, this benefit is available and can be part of your planning strategy. Even better, there's *no cost!* It's free from the VA; you just have to go through the application process.

WRIGHT

So what questions should I ask if I'm looking for a new financial advisor to make sure that he or she is listening to me?

ANDERSON

First, when meeting with financial advisors, ask about their background, what type of investing they do for clients, and how long they've been in the business. Next, ask them for referrals. They should be able to give you the names of three to five individuals they have been working with for a while. You will need to call those people and find out what type of services they have received. Then, be sure to ask what their fees are. Do they charge to consult with you? Do they charge for their services as they are providing them to you? Or, is their fee a percentage (1 to 3 percent) of the assets that they are managing for you each year, whether the stock market goes up or down? If you are the type of investor who purchases stock and holds on to it and who doesn't plan to trade very much, will they charge you a commission/transaction fee when you trade those stocks? Or, do they charge you a fee based on the value of your assets? There are lots of financial products that don't have any fees or a service charge. Does your new financial advisor sell those, too?

You must ask these questions and find out what the financial advisor's own investment philosophy is. Does he or she like to take risks with his or her own accounts? If you don't like risk, then you need to avoid a situation or financial advisor that would not be the best for you. You want to find someone who will ask you questions and who allows you to ask questions, too. At the end of that first appointment, if the advisor makes you feel comfortable, ask him or her to review your account and to make some suggestions. But, do *not* sign a contract with anyone you don't feel absolutely comfortable with! When you are ready to retire, you want to make sure that your money has the possibility of lasting as long as you will. The financial advisor you select should be someone who takes into account your risk tolerance, gives you options to select from, and who can fully explain everything they would like to do with your investing dollars. If you don't understand something he or she wants to sell to you, it isn't the time to make a decision or to buy, so be very careful.

WRIGHT

So, can I leave part of my estate to a charity so that the taxes after I die aren't so large?

ANDERSON

Absolutely! There are a number of things you can do: You can change the beneficiaries on your life insurance. For example, leave a portion of your death benefit to your church Endowment Fund, or to a favorite charity. There is no estate tax on those gifts. You can do this with annuities too, called charitable gift annuities. These are annuities that can pay you income for the rest of your life, and then whatever is left after death will go to the charity you have chosen to receive this gift. There are so many choices and you can be sure that your charity receives your gift as part of your legacy.

WRIGHT

So what can I do to prepare for my funeral so my family doesn't have to worry or dig out—no pun intended—their credit cards later on to pay for everything?

ANDERSON

There are now some new products in this area, too. Most everyone who is sixty or better has been contacted by a funeral home to make some pre-arrangements, such as paying for a funeral service or a casket, and putting your wishes together for a viewing of the body (commonly called a wake), etc. The funeral homes charge their fee, keeps those funds, and then will give you a certificate that shows your family what you have selected and paid for.

The new products are called Final Expense policies, and these are probably the best thing that I have seen in a long time. In addition to what you have paid to a funeral home, you can still set aside anywhere from seven to fifteen thousand dollars, depending on the state you live in, into a Final Expense policy. When you die, your family would call the company to inform them that you have died. The money you placed in that policy has been earning interest and is fully insured. Any additional bills from the funeral home or the florist or any additional expenses at that time are submitted to the company and are paid out within forty-eight hours. The company doesn't have to wait for a death certificate as it would for a life insurance policy. This is a significant benefit for your family since they won't have to dig out their credit cards to pay for your funeral.

Even if you want to be cremated, there are costs with cremation, costs with a service, costs for a family if they live out of town coming to your service, and all of that can be paid for with these final expense policies.

This is one of the best pieces of planning that I suggest to individuals and families. You are actually giving your family one last gift and it can make a huge difference for the family members when someone has died. There is no worry about how to pay for the funeral arrangements or questions about what Mom or Dad really wanted. This is something I recommend to each and every family.

WRIGHT

Well, this has been a fascinating conversation of financial planning. It's never been my forte. I can remember my wife walking in one day and saying we lost $30,000 in the stock market this month.

ANDERSON

That was a *big* ouch!

WRIGHT

The only thing I could say is we hadn't lost anything until we tried to sell it.

ANDERSON

Well that's true, but sometimes the papers we get each month make us worry. I think there are definite ways to make you sleep better at night.

WRIGHT

Well, this has been very interesting, especially the war-time Veteran's program. I had never heard of that.

ANDERSON

You know, not very many Veterans have heard of that program because, even though this program has been available since 1951, the VA has really not told the Veterans that it's there, except for one paragraph on the VA Web site. When you think about a Veteran who needs financial assistance to pay for their long-term care and being able to get up to almost $2,000 a month tax free for the rest of their life, it's quite a gift.

WRIGHT

That's *huge*. I really appreciate all the time you've spent with me this afternoon answering these questions. As I said, it's been really enlightening. I am positive that our readers are going to get a lot out of it.

ANDERSON

Thank you! It's been my distinct pleasure to speak with you today and if anyone has any questions they can contact me.

WRIGHT

Today I have been talking with Wilma G. Anderson. Wilma is the Chief Executive Officer of Senior Care Associates, Inc, located in Littleton, Colorado. In addition to her services as a Financial Advisor, her specialties are long-term care protection, critical illness coverage, VA planning, and retirement distribution strategies for clients who are fifty-five or better.

Wilma, thank you so much for being with us today on *ROADMAP to Success*.

ANDERSON

Thank you very much. Have a great day!

About the Author

Wilma G. Anderson specializes in long-term care, planning, pension and IRA investing, life insurance, annuities, and is a fixed money manager for her clients. Wilma is known throughout the financial industry as The Long-Term Care Coach and additionally, has worked with Veterans for more than twenty years, helping them to access the Aid & Attendance pension from the VA.

Working closely with families, Wilma will help them to be as tax-efficient as possible with their financial resources, show them how to invest carefully, and help to consider the avenues which are available for wealth transfer to their families, churches, and charities.

She has authored several books for the financial community, has written consumer booklets about investing, and is a speaker for national meetings and workshops concerning the importance of making informed choices regarding insurance, investments, and retirement plans.

Wilma G. Anderson, RFC (Anderson)

President
Senior Care Associates, Inc.
P.O. Box 631940
Littleton, CO 80163
720-344-0312
WilmaAnderson@q.com
www.WilmaAnderson.com

Chapter Eighteen

DREAM BIG AND WRITE IT DOWN

LISA ASBELL

DAVID WRIGHT (WRIGHT)

Today I'm talking with Lisa Asbell. Lisa is a true entrepreneur and woman of reinvention. Lisa enjoys teaching while entertaining and making her audience laugh. She is also a registered nurse, wife, mom, and professional speaker. Lisa has a passion for the stage whether it's motivational speaking, comedy, or acting. Lisa is a member of the prestigious National Speakers Association. She has spent the better part of her career helping people reach goals and inspiring them to reach within themselves to find their mission in life and turn that mission into money. Lisa is a serial entrepreneur, she has successfully started multiple businesses with less than a hundred dollars and turned them into $100,000-a-year businesses on a part-time basis. She has coached hundreds of people and has also helped them launch successful businesses based on their mission in life.

In the past ten years, she has coached and entertained thousands of people in the medical, dental, sales, and insurance professions. She has spoken in more than forty states in five hundred cities across the United States to audiences as large as fifteen thousand.

Lisa, welcome to *ROADMAP to Success*.

LISA ASBELL (ASBELL)

Thank you, David, I appreciate being invited to be a part of such a great project.

WRIGHT

So how do you define success?

ASBELL

I think there are a lot of different ways to look at success, but I guess the most important way for me is that when you wake up in the morning you can look yourself in the mirror and feel good about what you do, who you are, and what you are going to do that day. Success means that for this day you are giving all of yourself to whatever your current mission is in your current stage of life. If you are the best Mom you can be and you are giving it all you have that day, then you, in my book, are a success!

WRIGHT

What do you think are the two most important attributes to attaining success?

ASBELL

Belief in yourself will always be the most important attribute to attaining true success. Even the most basic things like learning to cook does take some form of belief in yourself and your abilities. I think people have more belief in themselves than they realize because they do little things every day that require guts, grit, and belief, but they often think themselves incapable of "big" things. I like to think of myself as a Belief Coach!

The second most important attribute in attaining success is having the ability to dream big and put those dreams down on paper. I tell everyone I coach, "I can't work with you if you can't dream big and then write it down." If you are not writing your dreams and goals down, how in the world can you know where you are going?

I feel like God put us all here for a special reason and that each one is designed to accomplish some mission in life. It could be a very simple thing or it could be something on a much bigger scale. My advice is to start small but start—write something down today!

WRIGHT

You say that belief is important. Does a person who has little success do that?

ASBELL

I do think that people have the ability to believe in themselves. If you look at success and you don't consider it in terms of money, but in terms of waking up every morning and being able to say, "I am happy where I am. I'm doing what I was put here to do," to me, that is the definition of success. I really believe in order to do that you need an internal belief in yourself. There are a lot of people who probably aren't happy doing what they are doing but they don't have the internal belief in themselves that they can accomplish more. I don't think they can be successful if they don't have that belief. I think that if they are not attaining the goal they have set for themselves, lack of belief is probably why. There is a difference in being content versus being satisfied. I have learned to be content with every stage in my life but I can't be satisfied because I'm always looking ahead to even bigger and better things. That's belief! I know I can and I will.

WRIGHT

Having the ability to dream is important. Along with dreaming and making a plan comes writing it down in the form of goals. I've talked about goals with several people; some people say set them high, some people say be realistic. I've heard all kinds of different things about goals. How do you start writing goals?

ASBELL

That is such a good question, David, because it's not whether the goals are "high" or "realistic," it's that you took the time to think enough about your life and what you want to accomplish that you wrote something down.

Now, here's a great way to start. Take a blank piece of paper and start dreaming about where you see yourself five years from today. Who? What? When? Where? Is the scenery on your way to your "office" the beach, the mountains, or the city? Who are you? A CEO, a television personality (that's me, by the way).

I was coaching somebody recently and I asked, "What does your life look like five years from now? What is your zip code? What kind of car would you walk out of your house and get into? What does your lawn look like? What are you going to be wearing? Where are you driving to? Are you headed somewhere that you can't wait to get to? If that's the case, then you are dreaming in the right direction."

I think that it's being very realistic to think I want to get into a BMW or Mercedes and I'd like to be at the beach or I'd like to be in New York City or I want to be on a ranch. I think the fact that you can dream and actually visualize and write something down means that you are dreaming in the right direction.

Statistics say that only about 3 percent of people actually write their dreams and goals down, and you know what? Those are the wealthiest people in America. That statistic alone makes me want to go write more, dream more, and plan more.

One of the things I've been doing for years is making a "dream board." Dream boards are great way to visualize; putting dreams on paper in a fun activity. Here's how you do it: Collect magazines of all types; gather markers, tape, and glue. Use poster board and start flipping through those magazines and cutting out things that you would like to have during the coming year and glue them to your poster board. That becomes your "dream board." Mine is in my home office, I look at it every day. It can be a simple thing like a new set of Bose headphones because you travel all the time. That was actually mine a few years ago. Yep, you guessed it—I got a pair of Bose headphones. I love to see what happens at the end of the year. As I'm making my new dream board for the next year, I look at the dream board I've been looking at it all year and, you know what? Probably 75 to 80 percent of those things that are on that dream board, I have accomplished. It's such a great activity for New Year's Eve when hanging out with friends or family. I have been making dream boards with my children for years. For those reading this who don't know how to start dreaming or writing goals, make a dream board—do it today. It's an easy, simple, fun way to get dreaming in the right direction.

Part of the problem with success and the lack of it is people have forgotten how to dream and most people have never been taught to make it real by putting down on paper. Whether you write it down or cut a picture out, put it where you can see it every year, it will change your life; it has absolutely changed my life.

WRIGHT

When I was introducing you, I said that you helped people find out what their mission in life was. Tell me, how do people find their mission?

ASBELL

There is no short answer to that. In fact, my next book will be about exactly how to find your mission. But first we have to define the term "mission inspired." It's *simply discovering what you were put here to do and then doing it every day. It is using your God given talents and it must include serving others in some way.*

How do you find it? Start by examining your childhood. What have people always told you that you did well? What were some of the things that you did naturally without thinking? For me, it was that I naturally made people laugh. I was the class clown and I did not even have to try.

Next, think about what you do now that you love to do even if you don't get paid for it. For me, it's talking and inspiring people. I do it all the time and I don't get paid for it. It's my calling in life. It helps people and it uses my God-given talents. It's my mission.

Here is an example: Sally knows that she really likes cooking and baking. She's tired of being a secretary. She needs a plan. So first I coach her to start dreaming of her own bakery—what the building looks like and where her goodies would be sold.

That kind of dreaming and visualization will help you make it come true. You must dream it and see it before you can have it.

The second step in finding your mission (calling) is to pay attention to what others say about your gifts or natural abilities.

Here's a true story about me. Mr. Williams, my seventh grade teacher said to me almost every day, "You'd better learn this material. You'd better study in school because you'll never get paid for talking!" Guess what, Mr. Williams? I get paid a lot of money to talk! Boy, I have had some fun with that story in front of the crowds.

With all joking aside, though, that seemed very negative as a kid and then as a teenager. I had a touch of ADD and was in trouble all the time. I was always on the go, would talk to anyone and would take on any challenge. Who would ever think that ADD could be positive? I'm living proof that it can be. So all you parents out there with children diagnosed with ADD, there is hope for your child, too. This is a classic example of making lemonade out of lemons.

So let me recap. To find your true mission (calling), start with things that people told you were good at and then think about things you enjoy doing that you'd do for free or that you'd do just because you love it. For example, you love working out. You love fitness. Become a fitness trainer. Do what you love and the money will come!

The last thing I will say about finding a mission versus a career is that it has to involve something that serves others. For instance, a great basketball player may have a great career but unless he or she finds a way to serve others with those talents or money that athlete has because of his or her talent, that person is not on a mission. God Himself came to serve. He created us in His image, therefore, we are to serve! He was also on a mission!

The very essence of God is in finding your mission. He fulfilled His mission, created, and served! We're all given these creative genes and maybe it's to create a great meal, a successful company, or maybe a beautiful Web site. We all have a creative gene in us and I don't think any of us will fulfill our mission until we use our creativity to serve others! Then the magic of your mission becomes a reality.

WRIGHT

So the question is, how do people turn their mission into money?

ASBELL

As I said, David, it can take years; this is not an overnight thing. Believe it or not, learning to make money from your mission is easier than actually figuring out exactly what your mission is!

One of the keys to making money with your mission is your passion for that mission! When you know what you were put here to do, your passion will seep from your very pores. You will become the world's best salesperson! I don't care what business you try to start or grow, you have to have clients! Sell is not a four-letter word! Once you have finally figured out what your mission (life's calling) is—you will pursue it with everything you have and the money will come.

I'll give you a great example. I know that I make probably one of the best red velvet cakes in the country. If it were my mission, there is no doubt that it wouldn't take much of my talking about it before people would say, "I'd like to buy it," and then I'd go from making one a day, two a day, and they tell other people and pretty soon I can turn it into a full-blown red velvet cake business. So I think because it's something that you naturally do, it's pretty easy to turn it into money because you are your own salesperson, whether you realize it or not. We all know that nothing happens in the world until somebody makes a sale.

So if you have always loved animals and you want to save them, then start a non-profit rescue on a part time basis. Of course you are going to talk about that to other people, and soon the money will begin to pour in. It's important to remember that it's not about money and it won't happen overnight, but if you stay at it, it will happen!

So, now let's talk about specific steps to turning your mission into money! Start with a simple one page website, buy inexpensive business cards and start networking. On a side note, the tax benefits are stellar! You should always have a home-based business of some type just for the tax benefits.

You will need to find a unique business name that says who you are and what you do. For example, if I were going to sell my great red velvet cakes, I might call my company *Best Red Velvet Cakes!* Many of the places where you purchase a domain name will also publish your site and host it. If you can copy and paste or build a PowerPoint presentation, you can build a Web site.

Let's talk about marketing. Marketing is something that scares people to death. Let's say you want to start a part-time baking business. Learn to do your own marketing. You'll find that it is networking as much as it is sales. You're excited about it; you've got this great cake-baking business. So the first thing you do is tell your friends and your family. Say something like, "I'm starting a part-time baking business. You know how you love my red velvet cakes. Would you share some of my business cards with people? Maybe I could bake one and you can take it to your office and let people have a sample. I'd appreciate any help you could give me."

The next step is to write out a simple five-year business plan. You can't just go into the bank and say I need $15,000 for a business idea. It doesn't work that way these days. Of course, you could go and get a wealthy friend, or if you have somebody with connections you could find a lot of money. But there is no need to do that. You really can launch a business and make a profit with a hundred bucks.

So come up with a name, get your Web site going, and then the third step is figuring out how to market yourself. You have to think outside the box. Forget buying ads—it's costly and does not work. Word-of-mouth is the best advertising! If you want to bake cakes, then you've got to think about who buys cakes—brides buy cakes, people throwing birthday parties buy cakes. This is one of the easiest businesses to start because it's very inexpensive to bake one and take it in for tasting. If you don't get orders soon, then your cake may not be as good as you think it is! Never leave home without a business card and your calendar. *If* someone seems interested, take their name and number. Don't just settle for letting them say, "I will call you." You will starve to death if you do that! Another idea is connecting with people who are also in the industry to whom you would like to sell. Use the Internet to search for florists and photographers who specialize in weddings. Call them up and I say, "I bake fabulous cakes and I am looking for someone to network with. Can I bring you a sample of my cake?" Do your homework, though. Make sure the person is respected in the community and great at what he or she does!

When it comes to marketing, the Internet has made life so much easier for us today with social media. You can always join LinkedIn, have a Facebook page, or go on Twitter. There are a lot of different ways to put out there what you do without the traditional radio or newspaper advertising. Remember, word-of-mouth is the best advertising you can do!

WRIGHT

You have started multiple businesses with less than a $100. Would you tell our readers about that?

ASBELL

I'd love to! More than twenty years ago, I paid ten dollars to join Avon and to become an Avon representative. I decided it would be better to sell to small offices like doctor's offices or printing offices than it would be to go door-to-door. Boy, did that pay off big! I was twenty-three years old with no college education, two small children at home, and I sold $50,000 worth of Avon my first year.

I learned quickly to think outside the box! I would walk into a business and say to the receptionist, "Do you currently have an Avon representative? If she said no, I would say, "Would you be my point of contact for a 20 percent discount on everything you purchase? In no time, I was one of the most successful Avon reps in the entire state of Florida—in a small town of eight thousand! It's not your state that determines your success. It's your State of Mind that determines your success!

Again, by thinking outside of the box, I got this idea to have a fundraiser because I'm only one person and there are only so many hours in a day. I decided that I needed leverage. I approached an elementary school about doing a fundraiser. I did not know anyone at the school it was a true cold call! Yikes! But, it paid off. They loved my idea and within eight weeks, I had five hundred little kids selling Avon all over a town of eight thousand! They took up one thousand orders and I got to have one thousand business cards put into the hands of people I would have never been able to contact! I did one of the first fundraisers in Avon history!

My next business for less than $100 was in the insurance industry. I paid $99 and they showed me an insurance product that I thought everybody in America should have.

So while all the other representatives were going to homes and presenting the products, I was going to business owners and offering the service as an employee benefit, selling dozens at a time. I was the number one representative in the company and was only working fifteen to twenty hours a week making $100,000 a year. I have done that with Avon, I've done it with cakes, I've done it with insurance, and currently I'm doing it with consulting and coaching.

That's what I was saying about your path evolving—it's not that you wake up one day and said, "I know, I'm going to own a successful bakery. If you had asked me a year or two year ago what my ideal dream job would be I would have said I want to travel around the country and speak. Well, now that is what I do on a full-time basis. I fly across the country and I speak every other week, and you know what? I am really not fulfilled at all doing that. It turns out that is not my calling or mission. It was a dream and I fulfilled it. Now it's time to move on. My career path is evolving. I now want to live in New York City and pursue the entertainment industry. Now that my kids are older, I have new options that were never open for me before. It's a very exciting time in my life and I plan to write about it, talk about it and use it to encourage others.

WRIGHT

So we've been talking about success here today, what drives you, Lisa, to be successful?

ASBELL

It's certainly changed over time. A few years ago, when my kids were little, my focus was family-oriented. It was about money and putting food on the table. I grew up very poor and wanted to make sure that my kids had everything they needed and some of the things they wanted. So initially it was money. I don't mean fancy things or that kind of thing. As I started making what I call "grown-up money"—well over $100,000 a year—it became about lifestyle. You can have all the money in the world but if you have no time, you have nothing. Time became important. I wanted to be at home with my kids; so again, I reinvented myself and my career so I could have time freedom.

Now it's not necessarily about money or time. It's about my life calling and living out my "bucket list." It's about serving others since my kids are grown and out of the house. I have plenty of time and I need less money— I have a few less mouths to feed.

I've just shot a reel for my own reality television show. I'm in a situation where I have a potential manager and we are talking about shooting a talk show pilot. So I think that will evolve, too.

So what will Lisa Asbell be doing ten years from now? I'm not quite sure because I think it's always evolving. That is a message I'd like to share with people—it's okay to change your mind. As we grow, we realize we have strengths we didn't know we had.

Since my children have left the nest, my ideas have shifted. I don't just want to live in the same house with the white picket fence. Now I realize I can live anywhere—I can choose my zip code. So I think we change and evolve over time. My mission has evolved over time, my motivation has evolved over time, and my message has evolved over time.

WRIGHT

So how does one balance it all—family, career, faith?

ASBELL

Boy, that's a million dollar question in itself. I think that women may have an advantage here because we are good at compartmentalizing and that is the key to balance. I have the ability to focus on the project at hand and in five minutes totally shift to another project and give it my all. Many people do not have that ability. Again, making dreams boards and having a coach will really help a person stay on task to achieve balance.

For family balance, one of the greatest gifts I have given my children in the last ten years is that I left a job as a nurse where people told me what time I had to be there and how long I had to stay. It allowed me to create and basically live life on my own terms so the balance wasn't as hard because I made my own schedule. There are choices for people, if they can get past the fear, to make some serious changes.

For a career, there are some hard choices. I am one of those people who believes you can have it all but probably not at the same time. Put your children first and then your career second. As they get older it shifts. That's where I am now and I love my life!

For most us, I think we start finding ourselves at about age forty. We have to dig deeper than we have ever had to before in order to deal with teenagers, college expenses, finances, and aging parents. We are able to accomplish more than we ever imagined and that, in turn, opens a floodgate of emotions, brain activity, ideas, and dreams. All of a sudden, at forty years of age, which can be the hardest time of our lives, we've got belief in ourselves. Our eyes and hearts open to the possibilities that in our twenties and thirties we would have never believed to be possible. Young people have youth on their side, but we have wisdom and experience. I will take wisdom and experience any day!

WRIGHT

So what makes you different from all the other speakers, trainers, and coaches out there?

ASBELL

I talked a lot about how what people say about you is a clue. When people say certain things about you, you can believe it. One of the things that makes me different is I'm real. Everything I coach people on and through, I have done it. It's real stuff that comes from me. It's not a lot of New Age mumbo-jumbo. It's not things that just sound good. It's the truth, it's who I am. All I can tell you is that the best compliment is, "You are so real."

I have the gift of communication. I have a natural gift to love and inspire people to greatness. I was born with it. I never think myself higher or more valuable than others, just further along in the journey of life. I want to share with people. I hold nothing back.

I am real and approachable. I have spoken in front of sixteen thousand people and those people have stood in line for two hours to get my autograph. Do you know how humbling that is for me—a girl from a trailer in South Georgia? I don't have all these letters after my name and I didn't go to Harvard and I wasn't born with a silver spoon in my mouth. We didn't even have beds when we were born—we slept in dresser drawers. Literally, we didn't have cribs. So I certainly wasn't born with anything. But thank God I was born with inspiration and I'm not afraid of perspiration. I really have started companies with less than a hundred bucks and made multiple six figures on a part-time basis. I don't think many people have done that and most certainly are not willing to coach others on how to do it!

It's such a weird thing that you can take kids from nothing and give them a little bit of belief, then teach them how dream, then write those dreams down, and their life is forever changed. I give God the credit and glory for my drive, passion, vision, and desire to help others. Without the gifts God has given me, I'd have no ability to change my life or the lives of others.

WRIGHT

What a great conversation, Lisa. I really appreciate all the time you've taken with me today to answer these questions. I think that you have given some really great information to our readers. I know I've learned a lot and I'm sure that they will.

ASBELL

Thank you, David. I appreciate the opportunity to spend some time with you today as well.

WRIGHT

Today I have been talking with Lisa Asbell. She has enjoyed teaching and for the better part of her career she has been helping people reach their goals to find their mission in life and actually turn that mission into money. She has coached thousands of people in the medical and dental fields as well as sales and insurance professionals. I think she knows what she is talking about, at least I am listening.

Lisa, thank you so much for being with us today on *ROADMAP to Success*.

ASBELL

Thank you, David. I appreciate it.

About the Author

Lisa Asbell is true Southern lady who is a great entertainer, speaker, comedian, and author. Lisa has spoken and entertained audiences in more than forty states and more than five hundred cities. She is a Registered Nurse turned business professional. Lisa is a life, belief, and business coach and is currently pursuing a career in the entertainment industry. Lisa would love to help you find your mission in life and turn it into money!

Lisa Asbell
St. Petersburg Florida
New York, NY
727-502-7427
www.lisaasbell.com
lisa@lisaasbell.com
www.facebook.com/lisaspeaks
www.twitter.com/lisaasbell